# CONSTRUCTING CHILDREN'S PHYSICAL EDUCATION EXPERIENCES

# CONSTRUCTING CHILDREN'S PHYSICAL EDUCATION EXPERIENCES

*understanding the content for teaching*

**PAMELA C. ALLISON**
Bowling Green State University

**KATE R. BARRETT**
Professor Emerita
The University of North Carolina
at Greensboro

*Allyn and Bacon*
Boston   London   Toronto   Sydney   Tokyo   Singapore

| | |
|---|---|
| Publisher: | Joseph E. Burns |
| Marketing Manager: | Richard Muhr |
| Senior Editorial-Production Administrator: | Susan Brown |
| Editorial-Production Service: | Colophon |
| Composition Buyer: | Linda Cox |
| Manufacturing Buyer: | David Repetto |
| Cover Administrator: | Linda Knowles |
| Text Design: | The Davis Group, Inc./Glenna Collett |
| Electronic Composition: | Monotype Composition Company, Inc. |

Copyright © 2000
A Pearson Education Company
Needham Heights, MA 02494

www.abacon.com

**Catalog-in-Publication Data is on file at the Library of Congress.**

ISBN: 0-205-17509-0

Printed in the United States of America

10  9  8  7  6  5  4  3  2  1     RRD–H     03  02  01  00  99

# Contents

*Preface*    xi

SECTION *1*

## CONNECTING WHAT YOU TEACH TO WHY YOU TEACH IT    1

CHAPTER **1**   *Constructing Meaning in Children's Education*    3

**The Constructivist Approach to Teaching**    5
   Goals for Constructivist Teaching    5
   Describing the Constructivist Classroom    8
   What the Approach is NOT    12
   Describing Constructivist Teaching and Teachers    12
   The Individual Constructivist Teacher    14
**Reflection—A Key in Constructivist Teaching**    16
**Developing Your Own Approach to Teaching**    17
**Constructing Meaning for Movement Experiences**    18
   Constructing Meaning for Movement Experiences in Physical
   Education    19
Chapter Summary    20
References and Reading List    20

CHAPTER **2**   *Constructing Meaning in Children's Physical Education*    23

**Constructivist Goals for Physical Education**    25
   Statement of Goals for Children's Physical Education    26
   The Physically Educated Person    29
**Describing the Constructivist Physical Education Setting**    29
**Framing a Developmental Perspective within Constructivist Teaching**    36

Creating Developmentally Appropriate Experiences in Physical
Education 37

Developmental Sequences 38

Interplay of Person-Environment-Task 39

Developmental Task Analysis 41

Chapter Summary 43

References and Reading List 43

CHAPTER **3** *A Conceptual View of Movement* 45

**The Movement Framework** 47

The Body Category of Movement Description 47

The Space Category of Movement Description 48

The Effort Category of Movement Description 48

The Relationships Category of Movement Description 48

**The Movement Framework Expanded** 49

The Body Category Expanded 50

The Space Category Expanded 59

The Effort Category Expanded 62

The Relationships Category Expanded 64

Chapter Summary 71

References and Reading List 73

# SECTION *2*

## THE CONTENT OF PHYSICAL EDUCATION 75

CHAPTER **4** *Teaching Educational Games* 81

The Problematic Issue of Competition 82

Game Playing throughout Life 83

**The Core Content for Teaching Educational Games to Children** 83

The Games Core Content Framework 84

Game Forms 84

Movement Skills 86

Basic Strategies/Tactics 92

Criteria for Assessing the Educational Value of a Game 93

**Understanding the Content from a Teaching Perspective** 93

K–5 Progression 95

Remainder of the Chapter 96

Core Content 1—Manipulative Skills as Single Skills 97

Core Content 2—Locomotor Skills as Single and Combination Skills 110

Core Content 3—Manipulative and Locomotor Skills as Combination Skills 116

Core Content 4—Basic Strategies/Tactics    123
Core Content 5—Game Forms    137
Core Content 6—Criteria for Assessing the Educational Value of a Game    143
References and Reading List    147
Instruction    148


CHAPTER **5**    *Teaching Educational Gymnastics*    153

Content Organization    153
Why Educational Gymnastics?    157
The Core Content for Teaching Educational Gymnastics to Children    158
The Gymnastics Core Content Framework    159
Locomotion and Stillness    159
Weight Bearing/Balance    160
Weight Transference    161
Using Aspects of Time, Space Awareness, Space Relationships, Body Shape, Symmetry/Asymmetry, and Aesthetic Principles    162
Working Individually, with a Partner, and in Small Groups    163
Relationship to Small Equipment and Apparatus    164
Gymnastics Sequences    164
Quality and Variety    165
Understanding the Content from a Teaching Perspective    165
K–5 Progression    167
Remainder of the Chapter    167
Core Content 1—Locomotion and Stillness as Single Skills and in Sequences    168
Core Content 2—Weight Bearing/Balancing as Single Skills and in Sequences    174
Core Content 3—Weight Transference as Single Skills and in Sequences    185
Core Content 4—Gymnastics Sequences    192
Arranging Equipment and Apparatus to Enhance Content and Children's Skill Development    206
Type and Amount    206
Equipment and Apparatus Arrangement    208
Enhancing Children's Motor Development    210
Integration of Skills and Focused Teaching 1: Five Basic Jumps    212
Integration of Skills and Focused Teaching 2: Sideways (Safety) Roll    214
Integration of Skills and Focused Teaching 3: Hand Balance/Body Curled    215
Integration of Skills and Focused Teaching 4: Shoulder Balance    216
Integration of Skills and Focused Teaching 5: Head/Hand Balance    217
Integration of Skills and Focused Teaching 6: Jump/Land/Roll Basic Sequence    219
Integration of Skills and Focused Teaching 7: Forward Roll/Shoulder Roll    222
Integration of Skills and Focused Teaching 8: Backward Roll/Shoulder Roll    223
Integration of Skills and Focused Teaching 9: Hand Balance/Body Extended    226
Integration of Skills and Focused Teaching 10: Cartwheel    227

Integration of Skills and Focused Teaching 11: Jump for Height    229
References and Reading List    230


CHAPTER **6**    *Teaching Educational Dance*    231

Unique Contributions of Educational Dance    231
The Educational Dance Teacher    233
**The Core Content for Teaching Educational Dance to Children    234**
The Dance Core Content Framework    236
Dance Elements    237
*Locomotion*    237
*Axial/Nonlocomotor Movements*    238
*Shapes*    239
Spatial Component    240
Dynamic Component    242
Rhythmic Component    243
Creative and Critical Thinking Component    244
Dance Choreography    245
Process Component    245
Structural Component    246
Partnering Component    246
Self-Expression and Communication Component    247
Creative and Critical Thinking Component    248
Framework Summary    249
**Understanding the Content from a Teaching Perspective    249**
K–5 Progression    253
Remainder of the Chapter    254
Core Content 1–Locomotion    255
Core Content 2–Rising and Sinking    260
Core Content 3–Shapes    264
Core Content 4–Dance in Another Culture    267
Core Content 5–Dance Props    272
Core Content 6–Contrasting the Dynamic Component of Dance Elements    277
Core Content 7–Dancing in a Group    282
**Unique Aspects of Teaching Dance Content    287**
Imagery in Teaching Dance    287
Accompaniment for Dance    290
Basic Understanding of Rhythm    292
References and Reading List    293
Music Resources for Dance    294
Children's Literature and Books with Dance Themes    295

## SECTION *3*

## PREPARING FOR TEACHING AND FOR BEING A TEACHER   297

CHAPTER **7**   *Planning for Student Learning*   299

The Necessity of Planning   299
Planning as a Specialized Form of Reflection   300
A Journey, Not a Destination   300
What Research Says about Planning   300
Planning as an Individualized Process   302
The Scope of Planning   303
**Factors That Influence the Planning Process**   **303**
Planning Factors Related to the Content of Children's Physical Education   304
Planning Factors Related to Teaching Physical Education   304
Planning Factors Related to Constructing Learning in Physical Education   304
Planning Factors Related to the Goals of Physical Education   305
**Linking Planning with State and National Standards**   305
**Lesson Planning**   306
Steps in Creating a Lesson Plan   307
**Using the Content Chapters to Help You Plan**   314
Conversation between Mrs. Ketching and Gail   314
Conversation between Mr. Rollings and Sandy   316
Conversation between Mr. Pressing and Chris   319
Chapter Summary   321
References and Reading List   322

CHAPTER **8**   *"Off You Go"*   323

**Constructing Learning in Physical Education Teacher Education**   325

*Index*   327

# *Preface*

Physical education teacher education is a challenging, exciting, and reward-ing enterprise. The word *enterprise* was deliberately selected as a defining term for what we do when we do teacher education because, by definition, enterprise connotes an undertaking that involves scope, complexity, and risk. That is a fairly accurate portrayal of what goes on in the teaching of teaching and the learning of teaching within a teacher education program. The chal-lenge of preparing undergraduates for their initial teaching license is an excit-ing one because the physical education class environment is a dynamic arena of possibilities for children to construct meaningful educational experiences and for beginning teachers to grow toward becoming reflective, knowledge-able, and effective teachers of children. Teacher education is also an exciting challenge because teacher educators are constantly influencing and being influenced by the ever-expanding body of knowledge related to teaching physical education and teaching it well.

Rewards in the teacher education enterprise come daily and come in many forms. There is a particular one, however, that we would like to share. An unsolicited letter from a long-time school principal arrived in the middle of the school year addressed to the chair of the Physical Education Depart-ment. One of our just-graduated majors had been hired by this principal to teach elementary school physical education. The principal felt compelled to inform the university teacher education faculty of his assessment of this new teacher. He wrote,

> "I have been so impressed with the teaching performance of _____ .
> Not only is she the best first-year physical education teacher that I have
> ever seen, she is the best first-year teacher of any kind that I have ever
> seen and I have been in education for over 25 years. Thank you for send-
> ing us such an excellently prepared teacher."

The rewards we speak of here are those that come to the children this teacher teaches because their physical education lessons are planned and taught by a highly effective and dedicated teacher. Their school experience will be richer and more meaningful because of the relationships they have had and will continue to have with this high quality teacher. That is the reward.

Our purpose in preparing this book is to support the development of beginning physical education teachers in such a way that the children they eventually teach will also have rich and meaningful experiences in physical education as a result of the effectiveness and dedication of their physical education teachers. To achieve this purpose, we have focused on presenting an approach to teaching physical education selecting two particular aspects of this approach to emphasize—philosophy and content. Philosophically, the approach we present is historically grounded in the Movement Approach to teaching physical education and is presently framed in constructivist principles of education. Within this philosophical perspective, we have chosen also to emphasize the content of physical education, or what is to be taught in physical education lessons. We draw connections between constructivist philosophical ideas and the particular view of content for physical education presented here.

Choosing two distinct emphases from among the many that are typically addressed in general purpose elementary school physical education textbooks permits an extensive, thorough, and expansive presentation of the selected emphases. The decision was made not to try to cover every singular aspect of teaching physical education so that a more in-depth consideration could be given to the philosophy and content of children's physical education; two aspects that we particularly feel need examination and dialogue.

Teaching does not occur as singular pedagogical aspects coming into play one after the other as the lesson unfolds, so writing about teaching should not occur in this manner either. Instead of the typical presentation of separate chapters on disciplinary foundations of physical education followed by chapters on activities to be taught, we have integrated biomechanical, aesthetic, and motor development information relevant to teaching physical education with the material that addresses the movement content to be taught. Such information, as part of the knowledge base of a teacher, is used in an integrated manner during teaching, and we thought that presenting it in an integrated manner here would be helpful in learning to use it when teaching. The integration of this information with movement content is a unique feature of the book.

Because of the selected emphasis on philosophy and content, we see this book as one of many textbooks to be used to support the teacher education curriculum and one to be used in a number of different classes. Individual teacher education programs develop their curriculums differently, thus, how this book may specifically support those curriculums would be an individual decision. It would be of use in those classes/educational experiences that frame teaching philosophy and that analyze and develop movement content for teaching.

The material in this book is organized into three sections. The first section emphasizes the importance of understanding that what goes on in school and what goes on in physical education needs to be grounded in a sound philosophical rationale. We argue for such a grounding to be in a constructivist theoretical perspective. We also argue for the content of physical education to be conceptualized as movement. The second section elaborates on the definition of the content of physical education as movement by focusing on three different contexts in which movement occurs in physical education—games, gymnastics, and dance. The third section focuses on two types of preparation—preparing for teaching through the process of planning and preparing for being a teacher through recognition of the need to continue to learn about teaching throughout the professional career span.

Teachers' stories are interspersed throughout the book as an organizational feature designed to enhance understanding of the information being presented. Telling stories about teaching is a great way for storytellers to reflect on their practice of teaching and to better understand what is happening in their classes. Hearing stories (or reading them) is a great way for listeners to expand their understanding of the pedagogical concepts being related through the stories. The first-person stories included here are real stories shared by the teachers in the schools that we work with in our teacher education programs. They eagerly and very effectively participate in the teacher education enterprise with us and with our students and we appreciate their efforts every day. They have graciously permitted us to share their stories in this format and we appreciate the contributions they make to enhancing the understanding of the concepts being illustrated. Pseudonyms have been used for both teacher and student names mentioned in the stories.

We believe gender-fair language is a requirement for academic authors. We also recognize that reading she/he and his/her language can be awkward. The decision was made, therefore, to alternate use of masculine and feminine pronouns and possessives throughout.

The students that we teach in the educational enterprise—both undergraduate and graduate teacher education students and the children in our physical education classes in the schools—expect the best from us in each and every encounter. In responding to that expectation, we have been challenged to teach the best that we can. We welcome the continuation of this challenge and the consequent continuation of our growth as physical education teacher educators. The outstanding colleagues with whom we have had the opportunity to interact in various professional contexts are highly valued contributors to the meaning we make of our professional experiences. We are most appreciative of those interactions and continue to seek them as rewarding professional development experiences.

There are specific people we wish to acknowledge for their contributions toward the preparation of this book. We would like to thank the following reviewers for their invaluable criticism and suggestions for improvement of the manuscript: Leon Greene, University of Kansas; Steve Grineski, Moorhead State University; James Johnson, Smith College; Mary Kirk, Northern Kentucky University; Linda McElroy, Oklahoma Baptist University; Jean Rix, Pacific University; Eileen Sullivan, Boston University; and Jane Young, University of Southern Florida. The students at Harvard Elementary School, Toledo, Ohio, under the highly capable leadership of their physical education teacher, Ms. Kay Siegel, joyfully posed for the photographs taken in the elementary school setting. Their enthusiasm and willingness to repeatedly pose is much appreciated. The physical education teacher education students at Bowling Green State University (BGSU) served as the subjects for the photographs taken in the university setting. The physical education teacher education faculty appreciates their professional efforts every day, and their specific efforts in service to this book were no exception. We thank family and friends who posed for the nonschool photographs as well. The photographs were taken by David Hampshire, Instructional Media Services, Bowling Green State University. Two colleagues at BGSU need special acknowledgment. Dr. Mary Ann Roberton, Director of the School of Human Movement, Sport, and Leisure Studies and a scholar in motor development, provided a valuable critique of Chapter 2, clarifying intended meaning and more strongly illuminating the connectedness of ideas. I am fortunate to have her influence on my professional development daily. Dr. Becky Pissanos, my physical education teacher education colleague at BGSU, has provided support and encouragement throughout the entire writing process beyond reading chapters and trying out ideas in her classes. She continually challenges me to do better teacher education simply by doing her job. We are lucky to be a part of the professionally stimulating physical education teacher education environments in which we find ourselves.

# CONSTRUCTING CHILDREN'S PHYSICAL EDUCATION EXPERIENCES

# Connecting What You Teach to Why You Teach It

this book is about WHAT to teach in elementary school physical education. What to teach is called the content of teaching. In learning to teach, the four phrases *what to teach, why you teach what you do, who is being taught,* and *how to teach* contain ideas that must be carefully addressed if preservice teachers are to have a fully developed notion of teaching for student learning in physical education. Each of these four ideas in teaching—*what, why, who, how*—is important to examine, reflect upon, articulate, and put into practice in the process of becoming a highly skilled beginning teacher.

As a field, physical education teacher education has been through a period where the greatest program emphasis was on the *how* of teaching. Teaching actions or behaviors—the how—were identified, defined, researched, taught, and practiced within teacher education curriculums. The teaching behavior of providing feedback to students on their responses to lesson tasks is used to illustrate this emphasis. We know from research that feedback is important to student learning and there is a lot to know about how to use feedback appropriately. In our teacher education programs, we considered what

forms feedback could take (e.g., verbal, nonverbal), when is the best time to give it (e.g., during the movement attempt, after the movement response), to whom to direct the feedback (e.g., individual, whole class), the amount of detail to include (e.g., general, specific), the implicit value of the feedback (e.g., positive, negative), and so on, in order to understand how to use feedback effectively in helping students learn. Other teaching behaviors were similarly considered in professional preparation programs. There are excellent literature resources currently available to beginning physical education teachers related to the *how* of teaching as a result of this period of emphasis on teaching behaviors.

What teacher educators have come to recognize more recently is that, in preparing preservice teachers, overemphasis on how to teach, especially to the demise of *what* to teach, decreases the possibility that teacher candidates will be appropriately prepared to enter their chosen profession. Teacher educators are limiting graduates' chances for success in teaching by not adequately addressing what is to be taught. If what you are teaching is educationally unsound, developmentally inappropriate, and unsafe, then how well you teach such wasteful content is irrelevant.

## outline

CHAPTER 1
*Constructing Meaning in Children's Education*

CHAPTER 2
*Constructing Meaning in Children's Physical Education*

CHAPTER 3
*A Conceptual View of Movement*

Carefully studying and reflecting on what you teach in terms of its educational value, its developmental appropriateness for children, and the safety of the environment in which it is taught is part of the *why* of teaching. In deciding what to teach, you must know why you are making such decisions. The beliefs that you hold concerning the value, appropriateness, and safety of what is to be taught will guide your content-selection decisions. These beliefs are your philosophy of physical education. Your philosophy gives you a rationale for what you choose to teach. A discussion of what to teach, therefore, must be accompanied by a discussion of why. Section One presents a sound philosophical rationale that helps make the connections between the what and why of teaching children's physical education.

In Section I, Chapter One provides a philosophical connection to the broader picture of children's education in general from a constructivist educational perspective. Since the student is at the center of this perspective, there is a focus on *who* is being taught in the schools. Chapter Two connects constructivist educational thinking specifically to physical education. Chapter Three identifies movement as the content of physical education—the *what* of teaching—and connects physical education content to constructivist educational principles.

# 1

# *Constructing Meaning in Children's Education*

*e*very day, children are coming to school eager to learn, wanting to be active, needing to feel safe, and expecting to be treated with dignity and fairness. They hope that the experiences they have in school each day will be meaningful to them in some way. As teachers in the schools, we are there to encourage the eagerness, satisfy the wants, meet the needs and expectations, and help children make meaning from their educational experiences. For children to have school be meaningful for them, teachers must reflect on and examine what is happening there. They must think and talk about what makes school meaningful for students. They must consider what is presently going on in our schools, what needs to be going on in our schools, and what changes need to be made in our schools so that children can develop in meaningful ways. Current efforts at school reform being suggested across the country are an incentive for educators to reflect on the concepts of teacher and learner and on the ways in which teaching and learning happen daily in the schools.

Giving encouragement, generating satisfaction, meeting needs and expectations, and helping children have meaningful experiences can be done in a wide variety of ways. How a particular teacher goes about creating meaningful educational experiences for children reflects that teacher's knowledge, beliefs, and values, as well as that teacher's perceptions of teaching, learning, children, schools, self, and society. For example, what the teacher *knows* affects what the teacher teaches; what the teacher *believes* affects how the teacher treats a child; what the teacher *values* affects how the teacher organizes students; and what the teacher *perceives* happening at a particular point in the lesson affects the very next teacher-student interaction. Taken together, knowledge, beliefs, values, and perceptions help to shape the teacher's approach to teaching.

When teaching approaches have been shaped, they can be named. Preservice teachers have numerous choices before them when learning about different approaches to teaching and experimenting with them. The approach to teaching that serves as the guide for how we think meaningful educational experiences are most effectively designed and carried out is named the **constructivist approach** (see Note on page 21). The shape of the constructivist approach is presented in general education terms in this chapter by contrasting it with another teaching approach—the **traditional approach.** Contrasting a newer idea against an older, more accepted idea is an excellent way to define and highlight the newer idea. It helps us see the newer idea as *not* like the older one. By contrasting the constructivist approach (the newer idea) with the traditional approach (the older idea), we are attempting to highlight the effectiveness of the constructivist approach in a more understandable way. Contrast, however, creates a potential problem. Indicating that a new idea is indeed different from an older one may lead to the assumption that the older idea was never truly a worthy one to begin with. This is not an assumption that we hold. Like many of our readers, much of our own early schooling was traditional. We were exposed to excellent models of traditional teaching. We have now come to a point in our professional growth and development where our knowledge, beliefs, values, and perceptions are much more closely aligned with constructivist notions of education than with traditional ones.

# THE CONSTRUCTIVIST APPROACH TO TEACHING

Constructivist teaching represents a change from the current traditional view of how teachers teach and learners learn. **Traditionalists** see the teacher as the *keeper of all knowledge,* the teaching process as one of *transmitting* knowledge from teacher to learner, and learners as *absorbing* what the teacher has to offer. The teacher talks; the student repeats the "teacher talk"; thus, the student learns. **Constructivists** see both teachers and students as *active* in developing knowledge and solving problems. They *work together* in the teaching–learning process to make their educational experiences understandable and meaningful. Students are not expected to repeat what the teacher says but instead are expected to explore, elaborate, and demonstrate their understanding of the subject matter being taught. The differences between the two approaches are seen in the question a teacher from each approach might pose about student learning. The traditionalist teacher would ask, "Are the students hearing my message?" The constructivist teacher would ask, "Are the students making personal meaning from the educational experiences that I plan and provide?"

## *Goals for Constructivist Teaching*

Constructivist education places the child at the center of the educational process and its broad goals are generally defined in terms of the learner. Educational experiences are then created toward achieving the following goals which are supported from a constructivist perspective:

- Children come to understand that the world in which they live is a complex, ever-changing place where diversity of perspective exists.
- Children become individuals who act responsibly in their individual, social, and cultural environments.
- Children become self confident in what they think, feel, and do.
- Children become responsible for their own learning.

Although the goals are stated separately, the interrelationships among them contribute significantly to the meaning students make from their schooling. Each goal is now elaborated.

*Children come to understand that the world in which they live is a complex, ever-changing place where diversity of perspective exists.* The world in which children are children will not be the same world in which these children are adults. What is needed to be a fully functioning member of society today will not be adequate for a fully functioning member of society tomorrow. Society is becoming increasingly complex as we attempt to deal with problems and concerns in our world; problems such as excessive patterns of human consumption of natural resources, the seemingly boundless potential of technology, development of global economies, expansion of bureaucratic structures, and decreasing levels of tolerance for those who are different from ourselves. What is known, felt, and done currently may be wrong, no longer important, or simply not enough for future times. Our job as educators is to help children prepare for change; change that will inevitably come. This job is an increasingly demanding one because the speed at which society is changing is so rapid that we, as adults, have difficulty imagining and predicting changes accurately. Yet, we are responsible for helping children prepare for them. It can seem like a daunting task.

The task will be less daunting if we have an understanding of change itself. The very nature of change requires adaptability and flexibility. Being able to take what you know, feel, and can do and adapt it to challenging, new situations signifies growth toward understanding. Having versatile ways of doing things creates a wider range of opportunities from which to choose than does having only one way to change. Consequently, versatility increases the chances for acting successfully in new situations.

Decision-making becomes an important component of adaptability when there are versatile ways of doing things. You may have two or more possible solutions to a problematic situation, but you must first choose one of them from among those available and then apply it to the situation. It is not enough simply to have successful problem solutions among the possible alternatives. A *decision* must be made to select a particular successful solution for application.

*Children become individuals who act responsibly in their individual, social, and cultural environments.* Not only is it important for children to be prepared to accommodate changes in their environments, but also it is important for children to recognize that they can generate changes in their environments. They can influence as well as be influenced. They can be the *changer* as well as the *changee*. They should not see themselves merely as reactive beings, accepting their fates as others dictate. They should see themselves as active beings, having the capabilities to create change in their surroundings. In both adapting to and in generating changes themselves, children must come to understand what it means to act responsibly within society, and then do so.

*Children become self confident in what they think, feel, and do.*     How a child experiences a situation depends in part on how she feels about herself, that is, how confident she is that she can handle a particular situation. The more confident a child feels about herself, the more likely she will be able to solve a problem, try out a new idea, have fun, feel free to make a mistake, or respond in whatever ways called for by the situation. Consequently, the educational environments created by teachers should be safe and supportive so that children are free to discover what works and what does not. A safe, supportive environment is the type of environment in which students can build confidence in their abilities to successfully handle different situations.

*Children become responsible for their own learning.*     In an ever-changing society children must be able to learn on their own. They must get to the point where they can figure out how to get answers to questions and solve problems

PHOTO 1–2
A safe and supportive environment builds confidence.

without the constant guidance of a teacher. Teachers will not always be there to guide students toward solutions, and when they are there, they won't always know the answers to questions that need answering. In addition to knowing what the answers are, students need to be made aware of the processes they must go through to answer questions.

Students also must be given opportunities to participate in educational experiences that not only empower them to generate answers to teachers' and others' questions, but also that empower them to *ask* relevant questions that are in need of answering in their worlds. The ability to frame questions is as important, or perhaps even more important, as the ability to answer them in the process of becoming responsible for one's own learning. Students will have to know what questions are important to ask. Otherwise there may not be much worth in knowing the answers that they do.

## Describing the Constructivist Classroom

The following key ideas will help you in understanding what the constructivist classroom looks like. They summarize the principles and values that are at the center of this approach to teaching. They do not describe constructivist education fully or absolutely, but they provide a framework around which you can build on your knowledge of constructivism. Each key idea is first stated and then briefly discussed.

*Learners create their own meaning for their educational experiences.* When students read a novel or study the events that led to the Gulf War or view a dance performance as part of school, they bring with them to these experiences the knowledge and skills they already possess, the values and beliefs they have already formed, and the cultural heritage that has formed around them. All of these contribute to the meaning students are trying to make out of what is going on in school. Traditionalist teachers typically do not acknowledge what students bring to the classroom or, perhaps, they see what students bring as interference in "getting their message across." The teacher tells the students *the* theme of the novel, *the* significance of prewar events, and *the* meaning of a dance performance with little attention to what other meanings students might have for these experiences. Constructivist teachers, by contrast, would encourage students to suggest themes for the novel, debate historical significance of prewar activities, and offer differing interpretations for a dance. The teacher recognizes that what students have individually experienced previously in their lives and what they presently believe and value have a powerful effect on the meanings they make from their current educational experiences.

*Student learning is the focus of constructivist teaching.*   How students come to know, to feel, and to do is a focal point in the constructivist classroom. The teacher-talk–student-listen traditional approach does not emphasize how students come to know what is being taught and does not highlight their "doing" as a focus of teaching. The focus is on what the teacher says and whether or not students hear it. How they feel about it is generally not a focus either. Thus, the teacher's style of teaching is at the center of classroom activity. The focus of the constructivist approach, with teacher, students, and content all viewed as interactive with one another, is on students' efforts at understanding what is being taught. This places the students' own attempts at learning, their "doing" in the center of what is going on in the classroom as well as emphasizing the content that is being taught.

PHOTO 1–3
Constructivist teaching focuses on students as active participants in their own learning.

*Content, organized around big general ideas, is viewed as flexible and adaptable.*
Content, or subject matter, is the what that is taught in the classroom. Each subject has a body of knowledge that defines that particular subject area of the school curriculum. For example, the content of geography defines what is known about geography and how geography is different from other subjects in the curriculum. The content of geography is very different from the body of knowledge associated with the content of math. What makes geography *geography* cannot transform geography content into math content. The bodies of knowledge, or content, of different subject areas in the constructivist curriculum are organized around big ideas that have been accepted as truth by professionals in each particular subject area or field of study. That is, the body of knowledge for a subject area is what most everyone in that area generally agrees is right or correct or true. The constructivist approach is grounded in the view that what is accepted as truth in a field is not a fixed body of knowledge. Knowledge grows and changes, therefore, content should not be seen as static or unchanging. It is dynamic and flexible. Practitioners and researchers are constantly generating new ideas and revising old ones that professionals in the field eventually come to agree on as being true. Content taught in schools, therefore, must be responsive to the growth of knowledge in the respective curriculum areas.

A dynamic view of content has implications for teaching. Static content need only be *transmitted* by the teacher and *absorbed* by the students, but dynamic content calls for exploration, innovation, discovery, inventiveness, elaboration, design, revision, excitement, venturesomeness, courage, spontaneity, versatility, adaptability, and a high tolerance for ambiguity on the part of both teacher and students. Exploration, innovation, and all the rest help students in interacting with content and learning at more meaningful levels than do transmission and absorption.

*Content should be relevant to learners.* It has already been emphasized that students do not come into the classroom as a blank page but as a page that has been written on and drawn upon by previous experiences. For learning to be relevant to students, connections need to be made between previous experiences and the present educational activity. When such connections are made, students are able to use what they have already experienced in learning about new ideas.

This does not mean, however, that learning activities are relevant only if students have had prior experiences with the focus of the present activity. Relevance for the present activity may need to be created in the classroom. While an elementary school student will be able to see the relevance of understanding the math concept of, let's say, long division, because recently she had to start dividing her lawn mowing earnings with her two new business partners/friends, she will probably need to be encouraged to see the relevance of understanding the grammatical rules for the five main interior punctuation marks. It is the job of the constructivist teacher to create relevance when needed so that student learning is facilitated.

*The constructivist classroom is seen as a community of learners.* Students in the classroom do not learn exclusively as individuals isolated from one another but as an interrelated group of learners that includes the teacher. Learning is broadened and deepened when done in the company of others. A spirit of community can emerge around the practice of sharing ideas and collaborating with others in the process of learning. In traditionalist classrooms, learning is viewed as an individual enterprise. The social context in which learning occurs is not a major consideration. Students work independently to finish assignments and accomplish learning tasks. Instead of a community of learners, the traditionalist classroom is a group of individual students.

*Diversity enhances the potential for shared student learning.* Because individual students are unique, diversity will exist within all classroom relationships— such as the interrelationships of student-to-student, student-to-teacher, teacher-to-subject matter, student-to-classroom-context, and so on. Diversity within a community of learners requires looking at learning from the different perspectives brought to the classroom by those involved. When different perspectives are used to solve problems, a larger number of successful solutions and more appropriate solutions are likely to be generated than if only one perspective is brought to bear on problems.

*Students have an important role in assessing their own learning.* Evaluation in the traditionalist approach highlights the teacher's role in this process. It is the teacher who decides what is to be evaluated (child's knowledge of spider facts), how it is to be evaluated (a ten-item written test), and what criteria indicate success (answering correctly at least six of the ten items). Assessment in the constructivist approach highlights the role that students have in determining what, how, and how much they learn. When learners assess themselves, they are directly involved in figuring out the processes that they used in learning what they did. They reflect on the ways in which they constructed meaning for the educational activities being assessed as well as on knowledge and skills that they developed, enhanced, or revised.

The constructivist teacher values the learner's current level of understanding even when it reflects partial or inadequate understanding. It is not as important to measure how far away the student is from some arbitrary standard for learning as it is to understand the student's present conceptions of what she has learned. Teachers must devise ways to tap into what students understand of their own learning.

## What the Approach is NOT

The description of the constructivist approach might have suggested the mistaken conclusion that constructivist teaching is a do-as-you-like approach. It is not. When students are given the freedom to explore and invent, outcomes are unpredictable. When teachers take the view that content is flexible, what is taught could change unexpectedly during a lesson. When diversity is valued, differing perspectives are allowed to emerge within the community of learners. What is going to happen while teaching, obviously, cannot be known in advance. Uncertainty, though, while an inevitable part of teaching, does not mean that "anything goes" in the lesson. It does not mean that planning for learning is unnecessary. It does not mean that few restrictions are imposed on the learners. It does not mean that direct instruction is ineffective and, therefore, should never be used. What it does mean is that classroom environment, lesson planning, rules, and teaching methods are defined differently in the constructivist approach than in the traditional view of education.

The description of the constructivist approach also might have suggested that constructivist teaching is an all-or-nothing approach. It is not. For example, a constructivist classroom may not in every instance support the principle of learning within the social context of a community of learners. There may be individual students or particular ideas within specific content areas that would more effectively be taught in the context of individual learning. Such a classroom would still be considered a constructivist educational environment.

## Describing Constructivist Teaching and Teachers

Constructivist teaching is highly interactive and very complex. It places greater demands on teachers (even experienced ones) than the traditional transmission–absorption approach. Constructivist teachers must work with big ideas, not just simple facts. Facts can be told to students or they can be written down and handed out with little effort or interruption to the daily scheduled plan. Big ideas cannot be packaged so neatly. They are often messy, ill-defined, and hard to grasp. And they need to be placed in a learning context, or environment, that is both relevant to learners in terms of their knowledge and previous experiences and connected to authentic "real world" contexts in which they will eventually apply their learning.

In a constructivist classroom, the teacher permits student responses to guide the flow and direction of the class. Their responses give the teacher ideas about what to do next in the lesson and what to do in the following lesson. They are the teacher's window to learners' understanding of content and the meanings they construct from their experiences. Because student responses are varied and unpredictable, taking these responses into account while teaching is a difficult thing to do.

If we accept the ideas that meaning and understanding are constructed by the learner, that content is flexible and adaptable, and that student responses are varied and unpredictable, then how does lesson planning fit into the constructivist approach to teaching? At first glance, planning would seem to be unnecessary. All that would be needed from the teacher is the ability to respond on the spot during the lesson. Responding appropriately to the constraints of the teaching situation is probably the crucial teaching skill, but it is not sufficient to ensure learner understanding. Teachers need to start with a plan of action, then be ready to revise the plan as student responses are observed.

The emphasis on responding appropriately to the constraints of a dynamic and unpredictable teaching situation highlights the importance of observing as a pedagogical skill. As a teacher, your opportunity to respond appropriately is enhanced when you demonstrate skill in observing your students' responses to the tasks that you have presented. You must first be able to see what is going on in the classroom in order to respond appropriately within the teaching situation (Allison & Pissanos, 1993–1994).

Constructivist teachers respond effectively to student attempts at learning because they understand what they are teaching extremely well. They know the bodies of knowledge for school curriculum content areas, and they also know how student understanding of content can best be promoted. They can identify a subject area's core content knowledge—the ideas and beliefs that are central to a particular field of study—aware that this knowledge is foundational to student understanding. To have core content knowledge is to have an "entry-level skill" for understanding a subject area. Core Content knowledge permits entry into the arena of subject matter understanding and forms the basis from which learners develop more refined content concepts.

Constructivist teachers seek to expand and refine students' initial attempts at learning core content. Learning tasks, situated in the same context in which the learning eventually will be applied, enhance refined understanding. Students, however, typically learn skills outside the situation in which they will most likely use those skills. What they learn in school is not usually connected to what they need to know in the real world. For example, what was successfully learned about the rules of subtraction from completing worksheet problems in class, often will not be seen by the student as applicable to the problem of whether or not correct change for a purchase was received from a store clerk. Such connections do not happen automatically. They must be created. The classroom context of the constructivist teacher is designed to reflect the various connections that need to be made among content, learners, and the real-world context.

Constructivist teachers, at times, may borrow from other approaches. For example, you decide during planning that a particular content idea needs the teacher-talk–student-listen approach for a particular group of learners. Transmission-absorption is in conflict with constructivist principles. The decision to use this approach, however, does not eliminate you from the ranks of constructivist teachers. You conclude that a principle rooted in another approach is appropriate in this context. You adapt to the constraints of the particular situation and that *is* a constructivist principle.

Do not interpret these comments to mean that constructivism represents an eclectic approach to teaching—picking and choosing what you will from every approach out there. The result of that particular strategy would be an unconnected collection of teaching tips and techniques, a mixed bag of tricks; a one-from-Column-A and two-from-Column-B type of arrangement. Constructivism is a flexible approach with pivotal principles that connect ideas about teaching and learning and how they should be done. Constructivist teaching still will be interpreted individually by each teacher in working within any community of learners, but its common pedagogical themes connect teacher, learner, content, and context in complex, integrated relationships.

One belief that we hold as part of this approach needs particular emphasis—not all constructions are equal. This applies to both teachers' and students' constructions. Interpretations might be drawn from a particular learning situation that are inadequate or inappropriate for the context of the experience. Reflection is helpful at such times in reinterpreting these experiences for adequacy and appropriateness. (Guidelines for assessing appropriateness of constructions of meaning in physical education are found in subsequent chapters.) Do not conclude, however, that there is only one "correct" construction for every experience. Clearly, there will be multiple constructions of meaning by teacher and students in different learning contexts, but it must be recognized that not every construction is an equally appropriate one.

## *The Individual Constructivist Teacher*

Teachers who teach using the constructivist approach reflect a certain personal identity. The following characteristics help define a constructivist teacher:

1. She is trusting.
2. She shows a willingness to take risks.
3. She has low-ego needs.
4. She demonstrates patience.

Constructivist teachers act in their classrooms in ways that demonstrate these characteristics to students. By doing so, they are being consistent with the views of learning and content within the constructivist approach. Indeed, they could not create constructivist classrooms without these personal characteristics being exhibited.

*Trust.*    Teaching from this perspective requires that you trust that children are capable of making meaning out of their schooling. You value what they bring to the classroom and encourage their contributions to the learning process. Students are more likely to actively participate in their learning when they trust that teachers will not criticize their ideas and will not permit peers to ridicule their learning efforts. Students often come to expect that, when they share their ideas in class, teachers will label them as either "right" or "wrong." They also do not anticipate being rewarded for an idea that appears, at first glance, to be off-track. Consequently, students learn to give short answers, or not to respond at all, to questions or problems posed by the teacher. They do not trust that their incomplete ideas, guesses, half-formed opinions, and divergent thinking will be warmly received by classmates and teacher. They are afraid of being "wrong." The benefit of a trusting environment will be a less fearful and more confident child whose learning can only be enhanced.

*Willing to take risks.*    You must be willing to take risks if you are going to be a constructivist teacher. Courage is needed to start a lesson when you are not sure just exactly where you are headed, how you will get there, or how your students will respond along the way. Even more courage is needed if you give students input as to where and how the lesson goes. A much safer approach is to plan every lesson detail and not deviate from that plan in any way, dismissing how student responses might disrupt your plan.

Giving students input on lessons can be risky. Sometimes you have to hold back and see where they will go. Letting them show you what connections they see as important before you share yours with them could be risky. If their connections are different from yours, how do you handle it? After all, you asked for their input!

Part of being a risk-taking teacher is being willing to accept divergent ideas and novel, non-conforming responses. Students may come up with some perspective that you had not considered before; one to which your students can see that you are not sure how to respond. You must be willing to risk such exposure in front of your students to demonstrate respect for and acceptance of divergent, novel, and non-conforming thinking.

There is one area in which teachers should never be willing to take risks, however, and that area is children's safety. The safety of children should be utmost in the minds of teachers as they interact with their students. The creation of safe learning environments must be a top priority. Teachers need to establish safety rules and demand unquestioned, uniform obedience from students in this area. Children's safety is not an area for risk-taking in any approach.

*Low-ego needs.* Constructivist teachers do not see student–teacher interaction as a competition for control of the classroom. They do not have high-ego needs that can only be satisfied by winning the control battle against students and showing who has more power. Ego needs are satisfied by taking the perspective that "winning" means everyone in the community of learners is working toward a common purpose—meaningful student learning.

*Patience.* Students need time to think about what they are learning. Posing a question to students, then giving an answer almost immediately, limits their opportunities to grapple with the problem posed. They get short-changed in the learning process. Waiting for students to come up with their own questions also takes time. They need time to work with an idea a bit first to find out what questions they have about it. Student innovation, invention, design, revision, discovery—all take time to evolve. When you construct a learning context that encourages such activities, you will most certainly need to evoke your patience fairly frequently. Students may appear to be bored or there may be a lull in the activity level of the class when students are engaged in the thinking process. It takes patience not to rush to the next task in order to alleviate the assumed boredom or the perceived inactivity. Learning takes time and, therefore, requires patience.

There is no single formula for how much time and patience are needed for learning. Generally speaking, material that is new, which students have had little previous experience with, will require more time and patience than material that is familiar. Even material they are familiar with will require more of both if it is being presented in a different context. In addition, content that is progressively more complex and content that is not clearly presented will require additional time and patience. It is difficult to predict precisely the necessary amounts of time and patience for any particular lesson.

# REFLECTION—A KEY IN CONSTRUCTIVIST TEACHING

Reflection is a key activity in constructivist teaching. The dynamic nature of both content and context, as well as the emphasis on student constructions of meaning, focus attention on the need for reflection in the teaching–learning process. It is an activity that takes many forms and occurs at different levels of depth (Posner, 1996; Schön, 1987, 1991; Zeichner & Liston, 1996). In the constructivist approach, reflection is not merely a mechanical monitoring of the learning context or a play-by-play recounting of lesson events. It is more like a living awareness of and a watchful thinking about all the dimensions of the learning experience.

Two interrelated kinds of reflective practice are needed: reflection by the teacher and reflection by the student. Teachers must continually be engaged in reflection. Like students, they are interpreting and constructing meaning for their experience of teaching. They also bring with them their past histories and current knowledge, values, beliefs, and perceptions that give meaning to daily encounters with students. Reflecting on these encounters deepens the understanding and meaning that teachers construct of their experiences. Reflection also plays an important role for students if they are to be responsible for their own learning. Students move toward being self-learners when they become aware of the processes that they use to make sense of new information. As they analyze the ways they make meaning from educational experiences, they are expanding and refining their understanding of how they learn.

Identifying two kinds of reflective practice is not meant to suggest that they have to be done separately. Indeed, they do not. The constructivist classroom is a community of learners including the teacher. Reflection done with others can result in richer and deeper understanding of the educational experience for all.

# DEVELOPING YOUR OWN APPROACH TO TEACHING

How teaching is practiced represents a teacher's personal interpretation of teaching. Interpretations are constantly changing as new teaching experiences are added to previous experiences. You already have had lots of experiences with teaching from the student-in-school point of view (kindergarten through 12th grade) as well as being "taught" by your parents, scout leaders, camp counselors, club advisors, coaches, etc. You probably have not had, however, very much experience with teaching from the perspective of the teacher. Nevertheless, you have begun to form your personal interpretation of teaching, shaping your own approach, so to speak. Although some of the principles of constructivist teaching may already be part of your personal interpretation, we are approaching this discussion as if they would require a change of beliefs on your part. We assume that a large part of your past educational experiences were conducted within a traditionalist environment. If you enjoyed school and felt like you were learning in different situations, then you may think that the traditionalist approach is a highly appropriate one for you to perpetuate and that you do not need to change much about what you already know about teaching. Although Einstein and Infeld (1938) used the following words to describe the relationship between the then new theory of quantum mechanics and the old theory of Newtonian physics, they are applicable to our introduction of a constructivist physical education teacher education program:

> Creating a new theory is not like destroying an old barn and erecting a skyscraper in its place. It is rather like climbing a mountain, gaining new and wider views, discovering unexpected connections between our starting point and its rich environment. But the point from which we started out still exists and can be seen, although it appears smaller and forms a tiny part of our broad view gained by mastery of the obstacles on our adventurous way up (p. 158–159).

Changing beliefs (i.e., climbing a mountain) is a very difficult thing to do. It requires abandoning old ways of thinking and letting go of perspectives that are no longer relevant to the current situation. For change to occur, you must first be uncomfortable or dissatisfied with your present beliefs. Next you must find alternatives that appear to be useful when applied in new contexts. Then you must find ways to make connections between new and old beliefs (Posner, Strike, Hewson, & Gertzog, 1982). We suggest that now would be a good time for you to reflect on your current beliefs about the nature of the teaching–learning process and to consider a change. Perhaps you are beginning to question your beliefs as you are exposed to new ways of thinking about teaching in your teacher education program. Perhaps you are starting to feel a little uncomfortable when you realize that your beliefs about teaching are no longer adequate in light of your new teaching experiences. You look about for alternatives. The constructivist approach is being presented to you as a highly useful set of alternative beliefs. You must look for connections between what you believe about teaching now and what we hope you come to believe about teaching in the future. This can be a difficult and, at times, even painful process but the potential benefits for you and your students are astounding.

# CONSTRUCTING MEANING FOR MOVEMENT EXPERIENCES

Every living being moves. From the beginning of life to the end of life as we know it, we are constantly moving. Even when we stand in one place, or when we sleep, our bodies are moving. We cannot think, breathe, or speak without some type of accompanying body action. Being in motion defines being alive. Milestones in our lives are often noted by movement actions—learning to walk, riding a bicycle for the first time, reaching a time when we lose the ability to perform movements that previously could be performed seemingly without effort. Such milestones are indications of development throughout life and are held to be significant events.

The significance of movement comes from its potential to help us create meaning in our lives. Whether we are moving for utilitarian reasons (reaching for a drinking glass from the cabinet), or for expressive reasons (joyfully performing a dance movement), or for recreational reasons (casting a trout fly into running stream water), or for functional reasons (passing the basketball to a teammate who is positioned closer to the basket), or for any other reason or combinations of reasons, we are satisfying our need to move. Moving gives us the opportunity to establish who we are and to create meaning for our existence.

As social beings, we communicate with others through movement. Research indicates that speech, thought of as the standard method of communication, comprises only 10 percent of human interaction. Nonverbal behavior, of which movement is a large part, comprises the other 90 percent (Hall, 1983). We are able to interact in meaningful ways with others even when speech is not a major component of the interaction. Movement, therefore, provides the foundation both for defining and redefining meaning for ourselves and also for communicating with others.

Movement experiences as part of an elementary school physical education program are rich and unique contexts for children's learning. Children learn about themselves as they learn to move. They come to understand the importance of moving as a way to learn about their worlds and as a way to become fully functioning individuals in their own individual, social, and cultural contexts. They also develop skill in responding to movement demands placed on them by the environment so that not only do they know appropriate responses for all movement situations, but also that they can respond physically by moving in appropriate ways. Movement situations include those that are part of everyday living (e.g., walking down steps, carrying books, getting up from a chair) and those that our culture has defined as relevant in our society (e.g., sports, gymnastics, dance, aquatics). Children gain self confidence as they learn to move skillfully in different types of situations. The meanings that they construct from their movement experiences in physical education class will be affected by their feelings of self confidence.

## Constructing Meaning for Movement Experiences in Physical Education

What we have presented in this chapter is *our construction* of constructivist teaching. Like any other construction, it too is framed by our previous experiences and current understanding. The next chapter focuses on interpreting constructivist teaching for physical education; on applying constructivist principles to physical education as a specific area of the curriculum. As we continue to work with preservice teachers and children in the schools and reflect on that work, we acknowledge that our individual constructions will change because of these experiences. This is to be expected, anticipated, and welcomed. A constructivist approach is an evolving approach. There is no absolute set of beliefs that defines constructivist teaching, no universal meaning, no once-learned set of facts. Each teacher makes individual interpretations of constructivist ideas and puts them into practice in different ways. Most teachers practice constructivism at some level. The difference is in how much.

## *Chapter Summary*

Children are eager for their lives in school to have meaning. As educators, it is our responsibility to respond to that eagerness through the ways in which we design and carryout our work in the schools. The constructivist approach to teaching is identified as a basis for creating meaningful educational experiences for children so that we might meet our responsibility to them.

The constructivist approach to teaching was presented in contrast to the traditionalist approach to highlight its main defining points. Broad goals aligned with constructivist education were presented and elaborated. We described and defined the constructivist classroom, constructivist teaching, and constructivist teachers. We discussed what constructivism *is not* in order to help you better understand what it *is*.

You are being prompted to consider the philosophical tenets of this approach as you go about the task of developing your own approach to teaching. Recognizing that you already have ideas about what teaching should be like from your past experiences of being taught (such recognition is characteristic of the constructivist approach), you are encouraged to reflect on these ideas, the ideas presented in this chapter, and the ideas to which you will be exposed throughout your undergraduate program as you work toward becoming a licensed teacher. Reflection is encouraged as a constant process in your future professional practice and continued professional development.

### References and Reading List

Allison, P. C., & Pissanos, B. W. (1993–94). The teacher as observer. *Action in Teacher Education, 15* (4), 47–54.

Brooks, J. G., & Brooks, M. G. (1993). *In search of understanding: The case for constructivist classrooms.* Alexandria, VA: Association for Supervision and Curriculum Development.

Cropley, A. J. (1992). *More ways than one: Fostering creativity.* Norwood, NJ: Ablex.

Einstein, A., & Infeld, L. (1938). *The evolution of physics.* New York: Simon & Schuster.

Hall, E. T. (1983). *The dance of life: The other dimension of time.* Garden City, NY: Anchor Press/Doubleday.

Lambert, L., Walker, D., Zimmerman, D. P., Cooper, J. E., Lambert, M. D., Gardner, M. E., & Slack, P. J. F. (1995). *The constructivist leader.* New York: Teachers College Press.

Nagel, G. K. (1994). *The Tao of teaching.* New York: Primus Donald I. Fine.

Posner, G. J. (1996). *Field experience: A guide to reflective teaching* (4th ed.). White Plains, NY: Longman.

Posner, G. J., Strike, K. A., Hewson, P. W., & Gertzog, W. A. (1982). Accommodation of a scientific conception: Toward a theory of conceptual change. *Science Education, 66,* 211–227.

Prawat, R. S. (1992). Teachers' beliefs about teaching and learning: A constructivist perspective. *American Journal of Education, 100,* 354–395.

Richardson, V. (Ed.) (1997). *Constructivist teacher education: Building a world of new understandings.* London: The Falmer Press.

Schön, D. A. (1987). *Educating the reflective practitioner: Toward a new design for teaching and learning in the professions.* San Francisco: Jossey-Bass.

Schön, D. A. (Ed.) (1991). *The reflective turn: Case studies in and on educational practice.* New York: Teachers College Press.

Zeichner, K. M., & Liston, D. P. (1996). *Reflective teaching: An introduction.* Mahwah, NJ: Lawrence Erlbaum.

## Note

Constructivism is generally viewed as a theory of *learning* or *meaning-making*. Within a theory of learning, there will be suggestions about, directions for, connections to, and implications concerning how teaching is to be done within that particular theoretical perspective. Our definition of constructivist teaching, therefore, represents those suggestions, directions, connections, and implications grounded in constructivist learning theory.

# CHAPTER 2

# Constructing Meaning in Children's Physical Education

**m**ovement may have particular significance for children. For them, the construction of a definition of self is getting underway. From the beginning, children move to learn about their environment, how they function in that environment, and how others perceive them to function. This learning helps them construct self perceptions. The physical education setting is an instructional environment in which children will learn about themselves while participating in movement experiences. Thus, what goes on in physical education classes is a powerful contributing factor to children's self definitions.

Movement is a very significant part of children's lives, therefore, consideration must be given to what motivates them to move. White (1959) proposed, in his now classic theory of motivation, that we choose to engage in behaviors that compel us toward competence. We want to do and we attempt to do what we think we can do successfully. Being competent means being effective in the environment. For the moving person, this does not mean mere proper execution of physical skills. It means being effective in the movement environment (defined as everything in the surroundings that could possibly affect movement) by accomplishing whatever your movement goal happens to be. If the goal of the task is to pass the basketball to a specific teammate who is closer to the basket than you (and, therefore, has a better chance of scoring), success would be a pass thrown to the teammate, caught in the spot that, at that moment, affords the shooter the best opportunity to make a basket with the least amount of defensive interference for that particular situation. Competence is not simply executing a proper two-hand overhead basketball pass, following all mechanical laws of imparting force; it is getting the ball to the shooter in a way that gives him a chance to make a basket in a particular game situation. Competence is not simply how effectively isolated skills can be performed; it is how effectively one performs those skills in the movement environment.

The distinction between the effective-environmental-performance perspective and the isolated-skill-performance perspective in understanding competence is an important concept to grasp. To further clarify, let's consider the example again. You execute a mechanically correct two-hand overhead pass. You fail, however, to notice an opponent who is close enough to the path of the pass to be able to deflect the ball. The defender moves quickly, redirects the pass off-line, and the ball does not reach your teammate. Despite the fact that the throw was properly executed in terms of mechanics and that you probably "looked good" as you did it, it was not effective in this particular situation because your teammate never received the ball. Your teammate never took the shot or scored a basket. Competence, therefore, was not demonstrated as defined.

A sense of competence becomes a part of an individual's constructed self image. A person is guided by this sense to expect that he will be able to handle whatever demands he comes up against in situations in which he is likely to find himself. He anticipates successfully responding to such demands and also feeling satisfied about doing so. Motivation to act results from the need to move toward and maintain competence, and from anticipated feelings of satisfaction. Acquiring competency, therefore, takes a central role in the constructivist classroom.

As physical education teachers, we ask children to move. How the child approaches an individual movement situation influences his involvement, that is, what he chooses to do and how he moves. It is important for physical educators to understand the individual and social factors that may influence the meaning children construct for involvement in movement situations. Griffin and Keogh (1981, 1982) were among those researchers who explored the constructs of motivation theory specifically in movement settings. Their ideas related to a person's involvement in movement situations, particularly the relationship between competence and confidence. Those ideas are outlined here to expand your understanding of children's meaning making as it occurs in physical education class.

Movement confidence, defined as feeling adequate in meeting the requirements of a movement situation, is seen as a major consideration of a person's involvement in a movement experience. A volleyball player finds himself faced with an excellent overhead set to spike. Confidence in his own ability to spike a volleyball will influence whether or not he chooses to execute a spike at this particular point in the game, how and to what degree of success the spike is performed, and whether or not he will persist at spiking during this game and future games. If his confidence level is high, then he will most likely choose to spike, do it assuredly, and look for more chances to spike during the game. If his confidence level in his ability to spike is low, then he will probably decide to tap the ball over the net instead of spike it, show hesitancy in his movements, and hope no one passes him the ball again during the game.

Confidence levels are influenced by a number of different sources, the most powerful of which is competence in performance. The more often a person achieves success in certain movement situations, the more confidence he will have regarding his ability to perform that movement. The volleyball player who has successfully won points for his team in the past by skillfully executing spikes will have confidence in his ability to spike the next pass that he receives. The competent player believes he will be successful when he attempts to move. He is confident that he will be able to meet the challenge and his level of confidence is determined in part by how competent he perceives himself to be.

It is important to note that movement confidence is not a global trait that represents high expectations for overall movement performance. It is sensitive to the demands of a specific movement context and can vary widely. A confident volleyball player may not be a confident swimmer. More specifically, a confident spiker in volleyball may not be a confident server. Even more specifically, a confident spiker may not be a confident spiker when two highly competent and very tall blockers are in position across the net from him. Movement confidence is influenced by the particular setting in which one is moving.

Movement confidence has been shown to be related to perceived competence. Movement confidence has also been shown to influence participation choice, performance, and persistence in activities. An additional relationship, between participation and competence, is an important aspect of movement involvement that needs our attention. Increased participation will likely result in increased competence; one gets better at what one practices. A competent person is also more likely to perform with ease and to persist at participation further enhancing the opportunity for competence to develop. Movement competence strengthens movement confidence which, in turn, influences participation choice, performance, and persistence in a positive manner, thereby leading to enhanced movement competence and resultant increased confidence. These interrelated ideas clearly show the need for physical educators to emphasize the goal of developing movement competence, or skillfulness, so that self confidence will be enhanced, and to focus their instructional efforts toward this end.

# CONSTRUCTIVIST GOALS FOR PHYSICAL EDUCATION

Understanding the significance that movement can play in children's constructions of meaning in their lives has implications for goal setting in physical education. Program goals are important to have for three reasons. First, they provide direction for the physical education program. They tell us where to head by defining where we want to go. They help us in achieving what we have decided is worth achieving. They guide us toward accomplishing what we set out to do. Without goals, our lessons would lack focus and direction and children's learning would be haphazard at best; nonexistent at worst.

Second, in addition to providing direction for where we want to go, goals help in evaluating where we have been. They are the criteria we use to reflect on our actions as teachers to see if we accomplished what we said was worth accomplishing. Goals help us assess what has occurred in class.

A third reason why goals are important to have is that the act of defining goals is an act that requires reflection, thought, deliberation, self examination, critical analysis, and, ultimately, decision-making. Having goals keeps teaching from becoming a mindless act and curriculum from becoming a random collection of activities. As a teacher, setting goals demands that you give your attention to what you are doing in your program. A program that illustrates careful study and deliberation in the development of goals is a program with the foundation to help children learn.

Keeping in mind these three reasons concerning the importance of having goals for physical education—providing direction, serving as a basis for evaluation, and requiring reflection—review the following statement of goals. These goals were formulated after lengthy and careful reflection, thought, deliberation, self examination, critical analysis, and decision-making. They reflect the direction in which we believe children's physical education should be headed and the criteria against which elementary school physical education programs should be measured.

## Statement of Goals for Children's Physical Education

The goals for constructivist teaching and the description of a constructivist classroom, presented in the previous chapter, are carried through in this statement of goals for elementary school physical education. Physical education should provide sound educational experiences that

1. develop competent movers who move with efficiency in deliberate movement situations and who can adapt their movements to effectively meet the unpredictable and unexpected demands of dynamic movement environments
2. develop understanding of the foundational knowledge upon which movement competence is based
3. assist learners in constructing relevant personal meaning from their movement experiences
4. develop levels of fitness that support a quality life experience

PHOTO 2–1
Within the teacher education program, goals for children's physical education can be discussed, analyzed, and evaluated against constructivist principles.

*Goal 1.* *Develop competent movers who move with efficiency in deliberate movement situations and who can adapt their movements to effectively meet the unpredictable and unexpected demands of dynamic movement environments.* This statement emphasizes movement competency, or skillfulness—as the *major* goal of physical education. Competent movers are those who have skills that can be called upon deliberately in familiar movement situations. A particular folk dance requires a grapevine step with a stamp at a certain phrase of music. Taking weight on hands is selected as the way to dismount from a gymnastics bench. An outfielder catches the softball in straight away center field and must make a forceful overhand throw to get the runner out going home. A competent mover is able to do the deliberate dance step, the deliberate cartwheel, and the deliberate forceful throw in each of these situations.

The goal statement implies, however, that being able to perform specific skills in deliberate situations is not enough to be said to be competent. Skills must be adaptable to unpredictable and unexpected demands. This means a mover must be *versatile* in the performance of specific skills, capable of performing them in a number of different ways. Being skillful at a soccer pass, for example, means that you can adapt your kicking motion to accommodate a bumpy playing field or a sudden rain shower or a rapidly closing opponent or the ever-increasing distance between you and your target. The field, the rain, the opponent, and the distance are all unpredictable or unexpected but the competent mover can adapt his passing skill to effectively meet the demands of the situation and, consequently, get the ball to his teammate under such dynamic, changing game conditions.

*Goal 2.    Develop understanding of the foundational knowledge upon which movement competence is based.* A primary key in developing competence in movement is knowledge about movement. A knowledgeable mover understands how movement is put together to create skills, what about those skills can be adapted, and how they can be adapted to fit different movement environments. Knowing biomechanical principles, for example, contributes to one's knowledge of movement. One important mechanical principle of movement is that the body's center of gravity must be above its base of support in order to maintain balance and not fall. A knowledgeable mover, aware of this principle, is more likely to have success in meeting the teacher's challenge of linking three different balances together in creating a gymnastics sequence than an unknowledgeable mover. The knowledgeable mover understands *which* different combinations of body parts could be placed *where* on the mat to achieve balanced positions, and *how* to move his center of gravity off the first support base to link two, then three, balances together. Understanding the nature of movement contributes to developing movement competence by guiding children toward independence in analyzing and enhancing their own movement capabilities.

*Goal 3.    Assist learners in constructing relevant personal meaning from their movement experiences.* The significance that movement can have in a person's life was discussed in the previous chapter. Movement is one basis from which meaning can be created by the individual. Physical education programs generally have focused on moving for functional purposes—rolling the ball to the target, shooting the puck into the goal, alternating hands in a grand right and left. Meaning derived from functional movement is related to its use in achieving its stated purpose. While learning to move in functional ways should be an integral part of children's physical education, programs that emphasize functional movement to the exclusion of other purposes are programs that limit the possibilities of meaning for children. Movement can also have expressive purposes, being the medium through which feelings are experienced by the mover and communicated to others. In dance, for example, children might be given the opportunity to feel the contrast between stepping very lightly and stepping very forcefully as they move to drum beat accompaniment. Children should have occasion to experience the full range of meaning that can be constructed from participating in different kinds of movement environments.

*Goal 4.* *Develop levels of fitness that support a quality life experience.* Fit human beings are better equipped to live full, rich lives than those less fit (Council on Physical Education for Children, 1998). Achieving and maintaining adequate levels of fitness provide individuals with the basic tools to seek the most possible from their life experiences. Lack of children's fitness and the physical and psychological problems associated with poor fitness levels should be of concern to physical educators (U. S. Department of Health and Human Services, 1996; Youth Fitness, 1997). Physical education class is one area of children's lives where they can acquire skills that give them confidence to participate in physical activities. Participation can lead to improved fitness levels, gains in knowledge about fitness, and opportunities to know what it means to develop one's fitness potential. There are many ways through which fitness can be developed and children must be provided with educational experiences to do so.

## The Physically Educated Person

Recently, the National Association for Sport and Physical Education, an association of the American Alliance for Health, Physical Education, Recreation, and Dance, presented a definition of and outcomes for the physically educated person (see Table 2–1). If the program goals presented in this book are achieved, students who have participated in these programs will be physically educated as determined by our national professional association.

# DESCRIBING THE CONSTRUCTIVIST PHYSICAL EDUCATION SETTING

Goal statements written within a constructivist approach to elementary school physical education embody underlying beliefs about children, learning, and physical education. Which goals are selected and the manner in which they are put into action reflect what a teacher believes to be true about teaching and learning in physical education. Goals and actions mirror beliefs.

Whether conscious or not, intentional or not, beliefs are the bases for goals and actions. Being a professional means operating from a conscious, intentional philosophical base. It is crucial to be *conscious* of one's beliefs,

TABLE 2–1

## NASPE's Statement of Outcomes for Physical Education

DEFINITION AND OUTCOMES OF THE PHYSICALLY EDUCATED PERSON

*A physically educated person has learned skills necessary to perform a variety of physical activities.*

- Moves using concepts of body awareness, space awareness, effort, and relationships
- Demonstrates competence in a variety of manipulative, locomotor, and non-locomotor skills
- Demonstrates competence in combinations of manipulative, locomotor, and non-locomotor skills performed individually and with others
- Demonstrates competence in many different forms of physical activity
- Demonstrates proficiency in a few forms of physical activity
- Has learned how to learn new skills

*A physically educated person is physically fit.*

- Assesses, achieves, and maintains physical fitness
- Designs safe, personal fitness programs in accordance with principles of training and conditioning

*A physically educated person does participate regularly in physical activity.*

- Participates in health-enhancing physical activity at least three times a week
- Selects and regularly participates in lifetime physical activities

*A physically educated person knows the implications of and the benefits from involvement in physical activities.*

- Identifies the benefits, costs, and obligations associated with regular participation in physical activity
- Recognizes the risk and safety factors associated with regular participation in physical activity
- Applies concepts and principles to the development of motor skills
- Understands that wellness involves more than being physically fit
- Knows the rules, strategies, and appropriate behaviors for selected physical activities
- Recognizes that participation in physical activity can lead to multi-cultural and international understanding
- Understands that physical activity provides the opportunity for enjoyment, self-expression and communication

*A physically educated person values physical activity and its contributions to a healthful lifestyle.*

- Appreciates the relationships with others that result from participation in physical activity
- Respects the role that regular physical activity plays in the pursuit of life-long health and well being
- Cherishes the feelings that result from regular participation in physical activity

for how can they be examined if they are unknown? It is critical for one's beliefs to be held *intentionally,* for how can they direct goals and actions if there is doubt about their truth? This program approach is grounded in a conscious, intentional philosophical belief system that describes a constructivist physical education setting. The approach is based on the following beliefs:

- The child is viewed as an integrated, developing whole person.
- Children are to be respected in physical education as the individuals that they are.
- Education of the child for participation in dynamic movement environments must be focused on adaptable, flexible, and versatile ways of moving. Problem-solving and decision-making skills are among the essential skills of adaptability, flexibility, and versatility.
- The individual child participates in physical education as a member of the larger social community of learners.
- Students construct their own meaning from their physical education experiences based on individual, social, and cultural frames of reference.
- Physical education of the child requires a collaborative effort from the child, the parents, different education professionals, and society.

*The child is viewed as an integrated, developing whole person.*    Each child has a sense of who he is in the world. He has a sense of self, of wholeness that says, "This is who I am." The whole is composed of different components that are integrated with one another to complete the whole. The whole, however, is never absolutely complete. The child is a *developing* individual who is constantly changing and growing. It is important to acknowledge and deal with the different components of the developing child's sense of self, but it is equally important to understand that these components are interrelated.

The goals for elementary school physical education were organized around four separate components—movement competency or skillfulness, knowledge, personal meaning, and fitness—that contribute to the developing child's sense of self. The separation is for convenience of discussion and is not meant as support for the view of the individual as a combination of discrete, independent motor (movement competency), cognitive (knowledge), affective (meaning), and physiological (fitness) components. If a person is *moving,* he will also be engaged *cognitively. Fitness* levels will affect how he feels about moving and influence the *meaning* a movement experience has for him. The different components, therefore, do not operate in isolation within the human being as if the others were nonexistent. They are interrelated and impact one another in different ways; some of which are understood, some of which are not. As you plan experiences for your children to meet the goals of your physical education program, you will need to realize that even though you, as the teacher, are emphasizing one component over others, you are impacting all aspects of the child's physical education experience in developing a sense of whole self.

*Children are to be respected in physical education as the individuals that they are.* There is something wonderful about being a child. Childhood is a fascinating "place" to be and an exciting "time" to be one's self. But childhood should not be thought of as a scaled-down version of adulthood. Children are not miniature adults. Think what your class would look like if you believed that children were tiny versions of adults. Games lessons would most probably look like watered-down versions of adult games without regard for the fact that children have different needs from adults. Gymnastics lessons would most probably look like small bodies trying large gymnastics movements without regard for the fact that children's arms and legs might not be long enough or strong enough for what is required in the adult execution of the skill. Dance lessons would most probably look like small people doing repetitive movements in lines until everyone looked exactly the same without regard for the fact that not all children express themselves in the same way.

Childhood has intrinsic value unto itself and should not be seen merely as a training ground for adulthood. Children need to have the opportunity to be themselves and to experience the unique perceptions that come with childhood. They really see things differently from adults. The following humorous story is an example of perception of time, measured by age in years, that is so uniquely a child's. It illustrates how an eight-year-old conceives of time in the future.

When I was in graduate school at the age of 33, my teaching assistantship responsibility was to serve as the demonstration teacher for the lab school of the university's physical education teacher education program. I regularly taught physical education lessons observed by university students and visitors to the lab school to demonstrate different aspects of our program. On this particular morning, I was teaching a games lesson to third graders with approximately 50 university students observing my lesson. The observers were given specific lesson elements to watch for and I, as the teacher, had to make sure those elements were present in the lesson. For part of the lesson, the children were organized into partners. One boy, in the process of getting partners during the lesson, ended up with a girl for a partner (certain doom for third graders). We came to the end of the lesson and the children began individually putting away their equipment and coming to sit down in front of me so we could discuss the lesson focus and what we had been working on that day. This discussion also served to reinforce to the observers what their observational focus had been. Although the girl-boy partnership had worked quietly and productively throughout the lesson, the boy said to me as he was sitting down for the discussion, "I don't like having a girl for a partner." Seeing this as an unexpected opportunity to make a point about gender and participation in physical education both to the children and to the university observers, I asked him why he objected to having a girl for a partner. His reply, "Girls aren't as good as boys." Pressing on, I mentioned that I was a girl and asked him if he thought I could do better than he at what we had been doing that day. His response was "Sure, but that's because you are older." Continuing to build to that moment of insight, I posed my next question, "Well, when you get to be my age, do you think I can still do better than you?" And from the back of the group, as she came to join the discussion, was heard this uniquely insightful child's response, "When he gets to be your age, you'll be dead!"

Teachers must respect children for who they are at every point in time. Even though they are growing toward maturity and our responsibility is to assist with that growth, children need to know that we respect them in the present and that they have every right to enjoy their participation in the present.

*Education of the child for participation in dynamic movement environments must be focused on adaptable, flexible, and versatile ways of moving. Problem-solving and decision-making skills are among the essential skills of adaptability, flexibility, and versatility.* Solving problems and making choices are two skills that children need to cultivate in effectively handling change. Problem solving has a history of going in and out of fashion in education. We believe it should be permanently in fashion. Included in the processes of problem solving are problem finding, planning, abstracting from the particulars to the general, undoing and redoing parts of a solution, and making means into ends (Perkins, 1981). These processes are critical to have in one's behavioral repertoire. Decision-making is also a much needed skill. Whether to pass to a teammate or take the shot oneself is a decision that has to be made a large number of times in game play. Who has the better shot? Who has the better chance to make the shot? Who hasn't had a shooting chance in the game at all? Who wants to take the shot? These questions and many others could all be part of the decision-making process. Children need to learn to evaluate alternatives and choose the best option from among them. They must also learn that decisions have consequences that must be anticipated, planned for, and dealt with. Both problem-solving and decision-making skills support the capability to adapt to change.

*The individual child participates in physical education as a member of the larger social community of learners.* Recognition of the child's unique individuality is a standard tenet of sound educational philosophy. Each child learns and develops at his own rate and is uniquely himself in that regard. School is not, however, a collection of individuals being educated independently from one another. It is a social setting where the group helps determine what is of value. Children recognize that they are a part of a social community and teachers must realize that there are social ramifications for children's participation at school.

> I was preparing to teach a newly mainstreamed kindergarten. Mark, one of the students in the class, functions at a fairly low level. His classroom teacher had assigned Braden to help Mark in school this particular day. It was Braden's job to stay close to Mark and help him stay on task. When the class came to the gymnasium, Braden informed me that he was there to assist me with Mark, particularly to get him to stop when I clapped my hands (my signal for stopping and listening). "You know, Mrs. Asbury," he secretly confided, "Mark really doesn't stop very well when you clap. But don't worry. I'll be right there to help him. You can count on me." And Braden did indeed faithfully carry out his responsibilities during class that day.
>
> The next time the kindergarten came to the gym, Braden was quick to assure me that if I needed his help again he was prepared. "You might need my help with Mark again today, Mrs. Asbury. You just let me know if you do. You can call on me. You and I both know he sometimes needs our help with stopping."

Physical education may be perceived by children to possess even more social significance due to the "public nature" of learning in physical education. It is difficult to move in class and not be seen. You can read to yourself, do math in your head, and hide your science homework, and your classmates will not be able to see your learning efforts. They will be able, though, to see your attempt at a forehand stroke and your miss of a double jump in rope jumping which emphasizes the more visible social nature of the physical education context.

*Students construct their own meaning from their physical education experiences based on individual, social, and cultural frames of reference.* We have been surprised on more than one occasion when we asked our students, "What did you learn in class today?" and they responded with something that we never intended for that lesson and were even more positive that we had not taught that day. Such is the nature of the learning experience. As teachers, we cannot force on students the meaning that educational tasks have for us. They build their own meaning for what we ask them to do in physical education. This is not to say that the teacher plays no role in the meaning students derive from their movement experiences. On the contrary, studies have shown that teachers are powerful influences on what students experience as school (Allison, Pissanos, & Sakola, 1990; Pissanos & Allison, 1993). Teachers must recognize, however, that there is not a one-to-one transfer of meaning from teacher to students. What we think is going on in class may not necessarily be what the students think is happening. And what we think is not happening may very well be thought by the students to be exactly what is happening as the following thought-provoking story illustrates.

> As an elementary school physical education teacher, I have taught in the same school for ten years. I have developed a curriculum that focuses on teaching children to be skillful as games players, as dancers, and as gymnasts. I emphasize their learning of skills in these various curricular areas and I measure my success as a teacher in terms of my children's skillfulness. Like almost all professionals at different times, I questioned whether I was accomplishing this goal. Was I getting through to the students? Were they getting what I was teaching or thought I was teaching? Did they think it was important to have skills in different movement activities? Did they value skillfulness as a goal for physical education? Would the children rather participate in activities simply to have fun?
>
> It was during one of those times of pondering such questions that the opportunity arose to take a one-year leave of absence from my school and assume new responsibilities in a different educational position. The opportunity was one of professional growth and development for me so I made the decision to take the leave. A permanent substitute physical education teacher was hired in my absence. I regretted leaving my children and the program constancy I had established over the years. But the questions lingered and the leave was an opportunity to gain a different perspective.
>
> After the leave, I returned to my elementary school. I was preparing for the new year on one of those days that teachers work before the children start back to class. Terry, the child who had given me the most trouble of all the children about learning skills in physical education class, appeared in my gymnasium door. Terry was the one child in the school that I would have picked to represent my inability to reach each student concerning my goals for physical education. He had been a second grader in the year before my leave. Having been away from my children for an entire year and in an educational environment that was very supportive of my goals for physical education, I wasn't sure I was quite ready for whatever Terry was going to say. I didn't know if I was prepared for his remarks. After all, school had not even officially started for me.
>
> "Ms. Dellinger, I'm so glad you're back. I missed you. We didn't really *do* anything in physical education the whole time you were gone. We just did fun stuff. We played steal the bacon and kickball and stuff like that. We didn't *learn* anything. All of us were just waiting for you to come back because we know you'll *teach* us some skills. We're glad you're back. I can't wait for PE."

It is also important to note that physical education does not mean the same thing to all students. The meaning a student makes of his experiences is influenced by his unique combination of background and purposes that form his frame of reference. Physical attractiveness, gender, skill level, previous experience, ethnicity, size, and goals, for example, all shape and mold the kind of experience a student has in physical education class. Different students have different frames of reference and, therefore, create different meanings for themselves. Accepting this belief demonstrates respect for children and who they are.

*Physical education of the child requires a collaborative effort from the child, the parents, different education professionals, and society.* The physical education of children is a massive undertaking and one that depends on contributions from all who are interested in future generations. No one person can be totally responsible for another's education, and when two or more people are working toward the same goal, collaboration becomes desirable. Collaboration is more involved than cooperation. Cooperation involves working toward similar goals but doing so in an independent manner. Collaboration involves shared decision-making in setting goals and interdependency in reaching these goals (Cervero & Young, 1987). All of the individuals responsible for children's physical education will need to enter into, not simply cooperative relationships, but interdependent collaborative relationships to achieve educational goals.

# FRAMING A DEVELOPMENTAL PERSPECTIVE WITHIN CONSTRUCTIVIST TEACHING

A central principle of the constructivist approach to teaching is recognizing that each child comes to the classroom as an individual who presents himself as his own unique combination of lived experience. As a teacher, when you interact with a student in the teaching–learning environment, you are interacting with a child who comes to you in the present at a particular point in his life span development. His present level of development is framed by his previous experiences, as well as those experiences that will come after his interaction with you that particular day. Acknowledging that a child's behavior in your class reflects a point along his *continuum* of development contributes to your having a developmental perspective toward teaching. A child is a developing being. All of the dynamic systems within the child—anatomical, neural, social-psychological, cardiovascular, moral, postural, perceptual, etc.—are constantly interacting with each other in complex and cooperative ways as the child moves through his life span. Each of these systems has its own continuum of development. Each child will be at different points on each continuum at any given time. Understanding where a child is developmentally in these dynamic systems is essential knowledge for teachers in constructing meaningful experiences for children in physical education.

The brochure, *Looking at Physical Education from a Developmental Perspective: A Guide to Teaching* (National Association for Sport and Physical Education, 1995a), helps to frame the idea of what it means to teach from a developmental point of view. Development implies change; moving along the different dynamic systems continua as one progresses through the life span. Thus, development is a process that leads to behavioral changes in the individual. The process of developmental change is not exclusively a quantitative process. Of course, as children develop, they can jump higher, dribble faster, and swim longer distances than they could previously. But developmental change also means that there are qualitative differences in the ways they jump, dribble, and swim. These movements will *look* different qualitatively as children develop because they are being performed differently than before. There may be a coordinated look to the use of arms and legs in producing height for the jump that could not be seen before. And the dribbling arm may seem to flow as it alternates between the up and down phases of the push. And the swimmer may move more smoothly through the water than before. These are examples of qualitative changes that occur in movement as the individual develops over time.

Developmental change does not occur in isolation. It comes about through the dynamic interplay of person-environment-task. As a child develops a higher and qualitatively different jump over a period of time, it is not *simply* because the child got physically bigger that his jump changed. The environmental conditions under which the jump is performed, the instructional experiences related to jumping tasks, and the goals of particular jumping tasks interact with the child's physical strength in the development of his jumping pattern.

Developmental change is not a haphazard process. It has directionality. Each individual may not follow the exact same directional path to reach a goal, but there will be similarities in the sequential nature of the different individual journeys. Developmental change, therefore, can be said to be sequential.

## Creating Developmentally Appropriate Experiences in Physical Education

Developmentally appropriate teaching practices in physical education enhance the opportunities for children to make meaning of their educational experiences. Such practices are defined as "those which recognize children's changing capacities to move and those which promote such change" (Council on Physical Education for Children, 1992, p. 3). Enhancement occurs when children's levels of development are considered by the teacher in planning and teaching physical education lessons. This requires a knowledge of motor development on the teacher's part, as well as how that knowledge can be used in teaching.

By manipulating person-environment-task relationships, a teacher can try to shape a child's development so it moves toward some goal. We have previously indicated that skillful movement is the major goal for the approach to teaching physical education supported in this text. Thus, teachers' knowledge of motor development is directed to helping children make qualitative changes in their movements that progress toward skillful performance of motor skills. Skillfulness is the most efficient and effective way of accomplishing performance. Nondevelopmental approaches conceive of it as the "adult model" of performing a skill. Looking at performance developmentally means that the teacher does not label as "wrong" any performance that deviates from the adult model. Children are acknowledged for what they can do at a given time, for where they are along the continuum of development toward skillful movement. Their skill attempts are "right" for the demands of the given movement situation (i.e., the environment and the task) and for where they are in their physical and neural development.

## Developmental Sequences

Approaching teaching developmentally encourages you to think of movement along a continuum of change so that it can be ordered, or put in sequence, indicating progress along the way to skillfulness. The concept of a developmental sequence does that for us. A developmental sequence is an ordered description of the qualitative changes that may be observed in children's movement as they make attempts at performing a motor skill over time. Think about a child learning to throw a ball. In comparison to a major league baseball pitcher, a child's initial attempts may only involve the throwing arm in generating force to send the ball away. Later attempts may involve the trunk in a flexion-extension action for force production. Then a step emerges. A backswing starts to come. The series of qualitative changes in the movement continues to occur as the individual progresses toward a skillful, effective forceful throw.

Fortunately for teachers, a number of skills have been ordered into developmental sequences that describe the qualitative changes that occur as children learn these skills under similar environment-task conditions. Developmental research has been conducted to support these sequence orders (e.g., see Roberton & Halverson, 1984). For those skills which have developmental sequences, the sequences are provided at the appropriate places in the book. They have been included to give a richer and more complete understanding of what to expect in how children may respond to the movement content being taught. Unfortunately for teachers, there is a relatively small number of skills, and mostly only games skills, for which we have sequences validated through research.

A lack of validated sequences, however, does not mean that you have to give up the notion of using sequences as teaching tools. Not at all. If you are going to be teaching a skill for which there is no validated developmental sequence, first think about the components of the skill that go into making up the skill. Let's use shooting an arrow in target archery as an example. You would need to consider what the bow hand is doing, what the string fingers are doing, what the shoulders are doing, where the trunk is facing, and what is happening with the head and eyes. The bow hand, string fingers, shoulders, trunk, and head/eyes are the components of shooting in archery. For each component identified, brainstorm about all the different ways that you have seen those movement components done. Viewing videotapes of children doing the skill, reflecting on what you have seen children do as you tried to teach the skill, and observing other teachers teach the skill and the responses they evoke from children are potential sources of information about the different ways the skill components can be done. When you think you have an idea about the full range of possible movements for each component, put them in order of first appearing with experience, to later appearing with experience. For example, considering the range of observed ways of holding a bow, you may order this component of shooting in target archery as follows: all fingers tightly surround bow grip, palm facing archer; all fingers slightly surround grip, palm parallel to target line; bow held without fingers gripping by pulling through thumb-forefinger V, palm parallel to target line. Now you have a hypothesized sequence to use when you teach.

Developmental sequences can be used by teachers as a scheme or model to keep in mind when observing children's movement responses to the instructional tasks that are given. If you know what components of a skill to observe and you have a good idea about how each component progresses, then you can appropriately respond to what you are seeing, formatively assess where children are developmentally, and help move them along the development continuum. Sequence information can also be used in making summative assessments of the qualitative changes in children's progress toward skillfulness.

As you have more opportunities to teach a particular skill, you may find that there are ways of doing some movement components that you had not seen or thought of before. You will have to add to your developmental sequence then. You may also find that a reordering of the sequence is necessary because you now see contributions to skillful performance within a particular component of the skill differently than before. Adding to and reordering of sequences indicate your growth in knowledge of movement and its development. Such growth increases your chances of reaching your goal of developing skillful movers.

## *Interplay of Person-Environment-Task*

Different factors affect the directional paths that children take as they develop toward skilled performance of motor skills. Newell (1986) organized these factors into three categories of constraints in order to more clearly understand their influence on movement. The three categories are:

1. organismic constraints
2. environmental constraints
3. task constraints

A constraint is something that regulates or limits motion within the movement as it is being performed. Constraints come into play in movement at different times and at different levels of regulation. What may be an influential constraint at one point may not be as influential at a later time. And a constraint may affect the overall movement or only one part of it. Becoming more skillful involves accommodating for the constraining factors present in a movement situation. The better the child is able to adapt his movement to the prevailing constraints, the more skillfully he will perform.

Organismic constraints are those factors that are specific to the person as a human organism. Examples of organismic constraints are strength, length of arms, location of center of gravity within the body, height, and body size. Visualize different ways the center of gravity could constrain the ways a child would be able to balance on three different body parts in a gymnastics lesson. Visualize different ways that leg strength could constrain a sustained sinking action in a dance sequence. Your visualizations will help you reflect on the influence of organismic constraints on movement.

Environmental constraints are those factors generally considered external to the individual. Examples of environmental constraints include playing surface, weather, gravitational force, light, ambient temperature, and amount of available space. If you have ever played soccer or field hockey on a bumpy or sloping playing field, then you understand how the environment can constrain movement.

Task constraints can be thought of as environmental constraints that are specific to the goal or outcome of a particular activity. All tasks have goals and one's movements are meant to achieve those goals. The ways a person can move in order to achieve a goal are usually not specified. The way a person actually ends up moving, however, will be constrained by the requirements of the task. Examples of task requirements are the goal of the movement, the rules and conditions that apply to possible movement responses, and the equipment necessary to do the task.

All three categories of constraints—organismic (person), environmental, and task—interact with one another in the dynamic interplay of developing skillfulness in movement. The weight and length of a racket (task constraints) must be considered in relation to the body size and strength of the child (organismic constraints) when giving children instructional experiences with striking. A child whose racket is too heavy for his hand will show earlier levels of the developmental sequence for striking than he might with a lighter racket. He will not feel confident about continuing participation. And his chances for developing skill will be limited unless the interactive nature of factors that constrain movement are recognized. It may be beneficial for you to conceive of teaching as the conscious manipulation of environmental and task constraints in relation to organismic constraints in helping children reach the goal of skillfulness in movement.

## Developmental Task Analysis

It is helpful for teachers to have a tool such as a checklist to examine the interplay of organismic, environmental, and task constraints and to plan for systematic movement experiences. *Developmental Task Analysis* (DTA) (Herkowitz, 1978) provides such a format. DTA examines the task and environmental factors that affect performance of a particular skill. The examination is made in relation to individual children's organismic characteristics so that the relationships between the three categories of constraints can be understood.

DTA has two parts to the analysis. First, task and environmental factors that could affect performance of the skill are identified. In Table 2–2, examples of factors that could influence motor performance of six skills generally taught in physical education are displayed. The examples are not exhaustive but are meant to get you thinking about all the factors that can affect performance of particular skills.

### TABLE 2-2
*Task and Environmental Factor Examples for Selected Skills*

| MOVEMENT SKILLS | TASK/ENVIRONMENTAL FACTORS |
|---|---|
| Throwing | Size of object being thrown<br>Distance to target |
| Dribbling (hand) | Resiliency of dribbling surface<br>Inflation pressure of ball being dribbled |
| Inverted gymnastics balances | Width of base of support<br>Height of center of gravity from balance surface |
| Cartwheel | Equipment/apparatus used for performance<br>Number of hands used for support |
| Rising and sinking in dance | Speed of the actions<br>Combination with additional axial movements |
| Dance locomotion | Evenness of rhythmic pattern<br>Direction dancer is moving |

Second, for every factor identified, an analysis of the factor in terms of levels of difficulty is made. The levels are ordered simple to complex, or easiest to hardest, in relation to performing the skill. In examining the distance-to-target factor for throwing, a target that is close would be the easiest throw, a target that is comparatively a medium distance away would be next hardest, and a target a farther distance away would be the most difficult. In examining the number-of-hands-used-for-support factor in the cartwheel, two hands would be the most simple, then one hand, and no hands would be the most difficult. A fuller example of a Developmental Task Analysis, one for shape-making in dance, is shown in Table 2–3.

As you plan for teaching, you will want to prepare extensive DTAs for movements that you will be teaching in order to identify and give order to all the factors that impact children's motor performance.

This two-part analysis, framed within the organismic constraints of the individual child, gives the teacher guidance in planning for instruction, giving instructional tasks, and providing feedback to students on their perform-

TABLE 2–3

*Developemental Task Analysis for Dance Shape-Making*

| FACTORS | SIMPLE TO COMPLEX | | |
|---|---|---|---|
| Body Parts Used for Support | feet | other lower body parts | upper body parts |
| Level of Shape | medium | deep | high |
| Symmetry | | symmetrical | asymmetrical |
| Accompaniment | none | even metric rhythm | uneven metric rhythm |
| Number of Dancers in the Shape | one | two | three or more |
| Muscle Tension Needed | no specific requirements | maximum tension | minimum tension |
| Time for Getting into the Shape | medium | slow | fast |
| Number of Shapes to be Held | one | two | three or more |
| Idea to be Communicated through the Shape | none | simple emotion | complicated emotion |

ances. DTA, as an application of constraint theory, helps the constructivist physical education teacher to more completely understand the interaction of the child with the content being taught and to more accurately observe their students' attempts at learning that content.

## Chapter Summary

The meaning of movement in the lives of children is highly significant. Children move because they want to be competent. Being competent is directly connected to being confident. Competence and confidence help to construct children's notions of self.

The importance of competence in movement in creating meaning for physical education experiences puts the development of skillfulness at the center of constructivist goals for physical education. Skillfulness, however, is not the only goal. Understanding movement, developing relevant personal meaning, and doing so within the context of a fit lifestyle are all supportive goals for children's development of skillfulness in learning to meet the demands of dynamic movement situations.

How one's classroom would look as the teacher tries to reach these goals is reflected in the beliefs one holds about children, learning, and physical education. The beliefs that reflect a constructivist approach to teaching physical education have been put forth for analysis and reflection to help you acknowledge your beliefs in conscious and intentional ways.

Constructivist teaching has been linked to teaching from a developmental perspective. A developmental perspective has been elaborated to consider the concepts of developmental sequences, the interplay of person-environment-task, and developmental task analysis. It is from a developmental perspective that teachers have the greatest chance to help children become skillful in movement as they make meaning from their physical education experiences.

### References and Reading List

Allison, P. C., Pissanos, B. W., & Sakola, S. P. (1990). Physical education revisited: The institutional biographies of preservice classroom teachers. *Journal of Physical Education, Recreation and Dance, 61* (5), 76–79.

Barrett, K. R., Williams, K., & Whitall, J. (1992). What does it mean to have a "developmentally appropriate physical education program?" *The Physical Educator, 49,* 114–118.

Bressan, E. S. & Weiss, M. R. (1982). A theory of instruction for developing competence, self-confidence and persistence in physical education. *Journal of Teaching in Physical Education, 2* (1), 38–47.

Cervero, R. M., & Young, W. H. (1987). The organization and provision of continuing professional education: A critical review and synthesis. In J. C. Smart (Ed.), *Higher education: Handbook of theory and research, Vol. III* (pp. 402–431). New York: Agathon Press.

Clark, J. E. & Whitall, J. (1989). *What is motor development? The lessons of history. Quest, 41,* 183–202.

Council on Physical Education for Children (1992). *Developmentally appropriate physical education practices for children.* Reston, VA: National Association for Sport and Physical Education/American Alliance for Health, Physical Education, Recreation and Dance.

Council on Physical Education for Children (1998). *Physical activity for children: A statement of guidelines.* Reston, VA: National Association for Sport and Physical Education.

Council on Physical Education for Children and Adapted Physical Activity Council (1995). *Including students with disabilities in physical education.* Reston, VA: American Alliance for Health, Physical Education, Recreation and Dance.

Griffin, N. S., & Keogh, J. F. (1981). Movement confidence and effective movement behavior in adapted physical education. *Motor Skills: Theory Into Practice, 5,* 23–35.

Griffin, N. S., & Keogh, J. F. (1982). A model for movement confidence. In J. A. S. Kelso & J. E. Clark (Eds.), *The development of movement control and co-ordination* (pp. 213–236). Chichester, England: John Wiley & Sons.

Haywood, K. M. (1993). *Life span motor development* (2nd ed.). Champaign, IL: Human Kinetics.

Herkowitz, J. (1978). Developmental task analysis: The design of movement experiences and evaluation of motor development status. In M. V. Ridenour (Ed.), *Motor development: Issues and applications,* (pp. 139–164). Princeton, NJ: Princeton Book.

Keogh, J. & Sugden, D. (1985). *Movement skill development.* New York: Macmillan.

National Association for Sport and Physical Education (1992). *Outcomes of quality physical education programs.* Reston, VA: Author.

National Association for Sport and Physical Education (1995a). *Looking at physical education from a developmental perspective: A guide to teaching.* Reston, VA: Author/American Alliance for Health, Physical Education, Recreation and Dance.

National Association for Sport and Physical Education (1995b). *Moving into the future: National standards for physical education, A guide to content and assessment.* St. Louis, MO: Mosby.

National Association for Sport and Physical Education (1995c). *National standards for beginning physical education teachers.* Reston, VA: Author.

Newell, K. M. (1986). Constraints on the development of coordination. In M. G. Wade & H. T. A. Whiting (Eds.), *Motor development in children: Aspects of coordination and control,* (pp. 341–360). Dordrecht: Martinus Nijhoff.

Perkins, D. N. (1981). *The mind's best work.* Cambridge, MA: Harvard University Press.

Pissanos, B. W. & Allison, P. C. (1993). Students' constructs of elementary school physical education. *Research Quarterly for Exercise and Sport, 64,* 425–435.

Roberton, M. A., & Halverson, L. E. (1984). *Developing children—Their changing movement: A guide for teachers.* Philadelphia: Lea & Febiger.

U. S. Department of Health and Human Services (1996). *Physical activity and health: A report of the Surgeon General.* Atlanta, GA: U. S. Department of Health and Human Services, Centers for Disease Control and Prevention, National Center for Chronic Disease Prevention and Health Promotion.

Waddington, C. H. (1977). *Tools for thought.* London: Jonathan Cape.

White, R. W. (1959). Motivation reconsidered: The concept of competence. *Psychological Review, 66,* 297–333.

Youth fitness: Do young Americans get enough exercise? (1997, September 26). *CQ Researcher, 7.*

Zukav, G. (1989). *The dancing Wu Li Masters: An overview of the new physics.* New York: Bantam.

# 3

# *A Conceptual View of Movement*

*t*he central goal of physical education is to develop skillful movers. This places the content emphasis for physical education on *movement*. The teacher of physical education, therefore, must be very knowledgeable about movement. Teachers must understand what movement is and be able to clearly see it happening in their classes. There are a number of different ways to know movement. One way is to know it conceptually. To know movement conceptually means to understand the structure of movement and how ideas about movement connect with one another. It is knowing movement in the context in which it occurs and understanding the impact of mover and context on one another. A framework is an excellent way to conceptualize and illustrate the structure of movement and its varied connections within the broad perspective of context. In this chapter, a comprehensive overview of movement is presented as a framework for conceptualizing movement.

A comprehensive conceptualization of common, everyday movement is needed by physical education teachers to provide the foundation for understanding movement in the specific contexts of games, gymnastics, and dance as part of the physical education curriculum. Children constantly have movement demands placed on them in all types of situations, not just in physical education class. To help them become more skillful in all types of contexts that demand movement, the teacher first must have an overall understanding of movement within its most general context—daily life. The conceptual framework presented here is a structure for all kinds of movement.

Movement can be thought of as having its own language. To speak a particular language, like the language of movement, you must know vocabulary words specific to the language. To describe ordinary movement actions, an ordinary vocabulary is quite adequate.

*She came into the class, went to her desk, sat down, and got
her books out of her book bag.*

For physical education teachers, however, an ordinary vocabulary is not
adequate. In our efforts to develop skillful movers, we need a systematic, detailed way to talk about movement. This requires a more specialized movement vocabulary.

*She half-walked, half-ran into the classroom, walked
directly to her desk, quickly turned, swung herself into the
seat with her elbows on the desk top, and hurriedly jerked
her books out of her book bag.*

*She walked slowly into the classroom, meandered to her
desk, hesitantly turned, almost suspended, before she sat
down softly in her seat, and then cautiously pulled her books
from her book bag.*

These last two descriptions evoke richer and fuller mental images of
someone coming into a classroom than the first description. Words and
phrases such as *walked directly, swung from her elbows, suspended,* and *sat
down softly* give a richer and clearer description of the movement than the
words *came, went, sat,* and *got.* The more fully an action can be described,
the more fully it can be imaged in the mind's eye. Physical education teachers
need a detailed and clear language to both observe and describe movement
so that their mental images of students' movement responses are as complete as possible. Helping children improve their movement skills is much
easier when the teacher has such a rich descriptive language to use when observing and talking about those skills. The Movement Framework provides
such a language.

The Movement Framework has its origins in the work of Rudolf Laban.
His theories and principles of movement, initially presented for dance, have
been adapted by his students and others for application in educational settings (see Note on page 73). This framework is a continuation of the adaptation process and represents the dynamic, evolving nature of the knowledge
base of the movement approach to physical education.

The Movement Framework is constructed here to present a general cohesive conceptualization of movement. When applied by physical education specialists to the specific movement contexts of games, gymnastics, and dance,
however, the framework would need to be adapted for each different context.
For example, movement in the game of volleyball can be better understood by
adapting the Movement Framework to represent the particular structure of
movement as it occurs in a games environment. Before successful, purposeful
adaptation can occur, however, the basic concept of general movement structure must be thoroughly understood.

# THE MOVEMENT FRAMEWORK

The Movement Framework has four categories for movement description. Figure 3–1 depicts these graphically.

- Body           Describes what the body is doing
- Space          Describes where the body is moving
- Effort          Describes how the body is moving
- Relationships    Describes interactions between/among components of the movement environment

## The Body Category of Movement Description

The body category focuses attention on *what* the body is doing. When asked to describe a person's movement, novice and experienced observers most often will say first what the person is doing. This is a result of needing to put movement in some kind of overall context before describing its specifics. It is a way of orienting oneself as an observer to the overall, generalized picture of the mover and the movement before looking for, talking

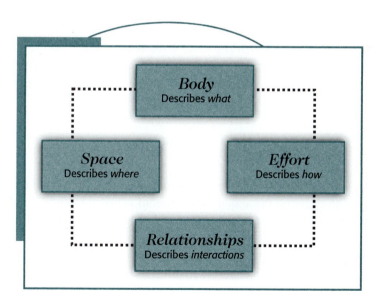

FIGURE 3–1
Basic categories of movement description.

about, or thinking about more specific details. Naming the body activity, therefore, is fundamental to a complete description of movement. Consequently, the body category is given the top center position in the Movement Framework.

## The Space Category of Movement Description

*Where* movement goes when it happens is the focus of this category. Descriptors here help locate the place in space where movement is occurring. The importance of where something occurs is shown in our ordinary vocabulary through phrases like *right here, from here to there, X marks the spot,* and *being in the right place at the right time.* Spatial characteristics are an important part of a full movement vocabulary. The focus in this category on where movement occurs contributes to the thoroughness of movement description.

## The Effort Category of Movement Description

The effort category focuses on *how* movement is performed. Effort is concerned with the active exertion of the body; its *energy* and how it is released. How a moving person blends different effort components defines the efficiency and effectiveness of the movement and gives it its dynamic qualities. Movement does not proceed as a monotone. It does not go in a straight line at an even tempo with the same force being applied all the time. It does proceed as a series of continuous changes in effort qualities that must be noted as part of a systematic, detailed descriptive conceptualization of movement.

## The Relationships Category of Movement Description

Observing the *interactions* that occur between/among different aspects of the general movement environment is crucial to a full understanding of movement. Movement does not occur in a vacuum but in an interactive environment that both acts on the mover and is acted upon by the mover. Likewise, the mover can both adapt to the interactive environment as it acts upon her and change the environment by acting upon it. Noting the relationships among different environmental components becomes the integrating thread of movement description and thus occupies a central position within the Movement Framework.

# THE MOVEMENT FRAMEWORK EXPANDED

The four basic categories of the Movement Framework—body, space, effort, relationships—are expanded at two levels to provide a more specific vocabulary for systematic detailing of movement. At the first level, each category is developed by defining the different dimensions that go together to make up the category. This expanded categorization is shown in Figure 3–2.

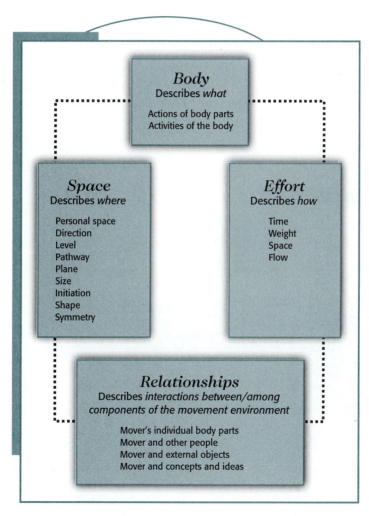

FIGURE 3–2
Basic categories expansion (first level).

At the second level of expansion, each dimension is further developed by presenting the types of movement characteristic of that dimension. Together, Figures 3–3 (body), 3–4 (space), 3–5 (effort), and 3–6 (relationships) present a comprehensive view of movement that illustrates a fully developed conceptualization of movement organized as the Movement Framework. Figures 3–4, 3–5, and 3–6 are found later in this chapter.

## The Body Category Expanded

The body category of movement (Figure 3–3) includes two dimensions: *actions of the body parts* and *activities of the body*. Actions of the body parts delineate what function(s) body parts have in a specific movement. It is important to be able to see the contributions of individual body parts when they are made to the overall action. A body part's particular contribution may appear, disappear, and then reappear in an adapted form as the ever-changing action moves toward completion. The actions of body parts can take the form of *weight bearing, applying force, receiving force,* and *gesturing.*

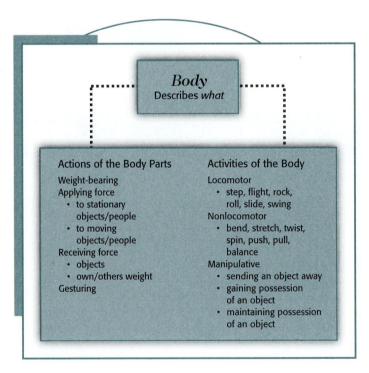

FIGURE 3–3
Body category expanded (second level).

Activities of the body name those activities the body can do. Naming what movement is going on puts movement in an overall context. Activities of the body can be classified as locomotor, nonlocomotor, and manipulative.

*Weight bearing actions.* Body parts act to bear or support the body's weight. When doing so, those parts are the bases of support on which the body balances as it moves. Weight bearing has a second meaning as well. Different body parts are used to support the weight of objects and of other people, and when this occurs, attention should be focused on those parts that are involved in this type of weight bearing.

*Applying force actions.* Body parts can impart force to objects and people. To apply force, the necessary body parts typically retract to help build momentum toward a release of force on the object or person to be moved. The force is released in the desired direction of travel. You want to

PHOTO 3–1
Applying force against the sidewalk to jump over the crack.

jump over a crack in the sidewalk. You bend, or retract, your ankles, knees, and hips then release the force against the sidewalk to propel you upwards, over the crack.

An important consideration is whether the object or person to which force is being applied is stationary or moving. In the previous example, force would be applied to the sidewalk, a stationary object. The stable nature of the surface influences the jump. Surface stability permits most of the force of the jump to be directed upward. If, however, you have ever tried to push off in sand to jump up, you know that the sand moves under your feet. The force being applied does not all go in an upward direction. The result is a jump that is not quite as high as the sidewalk jump.

*Receiving force actions.*    Individual body parts can be involved in receiving the force of objects and the weight of self or others. Force reception, known as force absorption, is accomplished by the sequential giving in the joints of the body parts involved in the absorption. Someone throws you a heavy ring of keys. You catch them by giving in your wrist, elbow, and shoulder in a downward motion. As the force is brought under the receiver's control, it can be either redirected or brought to a moment of stillness. You redirect the force by tossing the keys immediately upward to your other hand or you hold the keys still in your catching hand.

*Gesturing actions.*    Gesturing is expressive movement that communicates meaning through the moving of individual body parts. The arms, legs, a shoulder, a hip, the head, all can gesture to others. A hand extended forward, fingers pointing up, with palm facing out says *stop.* Depending on the context, this stop gesture could communicate "Stop, don't take another step," or "Stop what you are doing. Be quiet. I don't want to hear anymore," or that you are familiar with early choreography for Diana Ross and the Supremes ("Stop, in the name of love, before you break my heart. . . ."). See Photos 3–2, 3–3, and 3–4. Body parts used to gesture have the capacity to express the full spectrum of meaning in movement.

*Locomotor activities.*    Locomotor activities move the body from place to place generally by changing the base of support. Locomotor activities include:

- step
- flight
- rock
- roll
- slide
- swing

PHOTO 3–2
"Stop, don't take another step."

Walking is the most common example of the stepping type of locomotion. Weight is transferred from one foot to the other as the body moves to a new location. Not all step-like actions must be done on the feet. You can move to another place by taking weight onto a series of different body parts like knees to hands to hips.

The body is in flight when no body parts are serving as a base(s) of support. Jumping is an example of flight. Momentary contact is lost with a supporting surface as the body is propelled into the air, moving through space.

PHOTO 3–3
"Stop what you are doing. Be quiet."

· · · · · · · · · · · · · · · · · · · · · · · · · · · · · · · · · · · · · · · · · · · · · · ·

Rocking and rolling are locomotor activities that cause the body to travel from place to place (see Photo 3–5). Rocking involves a back and forth action of weight transference along the same body surfaces. Rolling is weight trans-ference in a continual direction along adjacent body parts, for example, hands to shoulders to hips as occurs when doing a forward roll.

Sliding and swinging are locomotor activities that do not involve a change in supporting body parts. In sliding, body weight is moved to another place while retaining its original base of support. Force must be generated

PHOTO 3–4
"Stop, in the name of love."

for sliding to occur. Think of turning the garden hose on a long strip of plastic laid on the ground, running, taking off, landing on your stomach, and sliding down to the end of the plastic. You would be moving from one end of the plastic to the other while keeping the stomach as the base of support in your sliding action. In swinging, the body's base of support is restricted while free body parts act on or react to gravity. Holding onto the end of a rope anchored to a tree limb that extends out over a lake, then running and jumping off the lake bank, puts the body into a swinging action. You are restricted by your

PHOTO 3-5
Rocking and rolling are locomotor activities that move the body from place to place.

base of support—your hands on the anchored rope—unless, of course, you let go over the water, thereby, ending your swing and putting you into flight (rapidly followed by receiving the force of one's own weight).

*Nonlocomotor activities.* A nonlocomotor activity is movement within one space that does not travel to another space nor alters the base of support. Nonlocomotor activities include:

- bend
- stretch
- twist
- spin
- push
- pull
- balance

Bending draws body parts in close to the body's center. Bending down to pick up an object that has fallen on the floor brings the lower legs in close to

PHOTO 3-6
Bending down to pick up an object brings body parts closer to the body's center.

the thighs which are drawn into the chest, also pulling the shoulders and head inward. Standing up after having grasped the object generates a stretch. Stretching moves body parts away from the center of the body. Twisting involves a rotation of other body parts against a fixed body part(s). Running forward while turning the shoulders back against the hips to wave to someone would result in a twist. Bending, stretching, and twisting can all be done to varying degrees. The body and different body parts, for example, can barely bend, fully stretch, or partially twist. The degrees to which these nonlocomotor activities are occurring, as well as the degrees of presence of all the other components of movement, are important features to notice in a detailed description of movement.

Spinning turns the body to face in new directions. It occurs as the body moves around a central axis while maintaining its supporting body parts.

Pushing directs force away from the body and pulling brings force toward the body. We have push and pull signs on doors to tell us which way to direct the force of our arms against the door to help ourselves go in or out. If you have ever pushed when you should have pulled on a door, then you know what happens when force is applied in an inappropriate direction.

Balancing involves maintaining one's weight over a base of support. Muscle tension permits the body to attain such a balanced state. If the base of support changes or if nonsupporting body parts move freely, balance is threatened. The body can still retain its balance, however, by adjusting its center of gravity (COG) over the supporting base. The body is said to go off balance when it can no longer keep its COG over the original base.

*Manipulative activities.*   This type of activity is used to maneuver objects. Manipulative activities are grouped into the following three categories:

- sending an object away
- gaining possession of an object
- maintaining possession of an object

Sending an object away is accomplished by putting, throwing, and striking. Putting is placing an object out of one's possession. Throwing is most often executed with the hands, though other body parts or pieces of equipment also can be used. In striking, the object to be sent away is not grasped by the person but instead is hit away after a brief moment of contact. Sending objects away can be carried out using varying amounts of force. Hitting a home run is an example of a very forceful striking action. Putting down a fragile glass object on a glass table is an example of sending an object away that requires very little force.

Gaining possession of an object is accomplished by grasping, catching, and collecting. Grasping involves gripping a stationary object and taking hold of it either firmly or gently. Catching is gaining possession of a moving aerial object while collecting is gathering in moving objects approaching along the ground surface. In catching, the object is grasped or held, while in collecting, the object is brought under control but generally not held. Hands are most often used to gain possession of an object, but other body parts and equipment can function in this role.

Once an individual has gained possession of an object (and does not want to send it away), she must maintain possession of the object. Maintenance is possible whether the body is involved in either locomotor or nonlocomotor activities. For example, you carry a cafeteria tray while you walk to a table. You propel a basketball along as you dribble it. You hold a pen in your hand as you write. Carrying, propelling, and holding are ways in which possession of an object can be maintained.

## The Space Category Expanded

Identifying the spatial characteristics of movement is meant to describe where the action is taking place (see Figure 3–4). The movement dimensions that do this are:

- Personal space
- Direction
- Level
- Pathway (air and ground)
- Plane
- Size
- Initiation
- Shape
- Symmetry

***Personal space.*** Personal space is the area immediately around the mover. Its limits are defined by how far the individual mover can extend his/her body in all directions. The concept of one's personal space is always present no

PHOTO 3–7
Maintaining possession of an object (pencil).

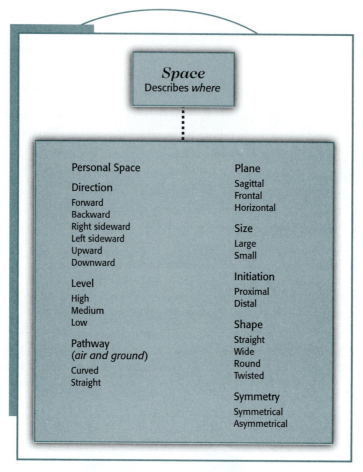

**Space**
Describes *where*

| Personal Space | Plane |
|---|---|
| **Direction** | Sagittal |
| Forward | Frontal |
| Backward | Horizontal |
| Right sideward | |
| Left sideward | **Size** |
| Upward | Large |
| Downward | Small |
| **Level** | **Initiation** |
| High | Proximal |
| Medium | Distal |
| Low | |
| | **Shape** |
| **Pathway** | Straight |
| *(air and ground)* | Wide |
| Curved | Round |
| Straight | Twisted |
| | **Symmetry** |
| | Symmetrical |
| | Asymmetrical |

FIGURE 3–4
Space category expanded (second level)

matter the activity of the body in which the mover is engaged. If a person is in flight (locomotor activity), spinning (nonlocomotor activity), or grasping an object (manipulative activity), a personal space exists around the body.

*Direction.* The direction toward which movement travels can be observed. Directions are identified in relation to where the front of the body faces as the body is moving. The six directions are forward, backward, right sideward, left sideward, upward, and downward.

*Level.* Where a movement is located in relation to the ground/floor surface is defined as the level of the movement. Movement that occurs close to the floor is described as being at a low level, while movement that occurs off the floor or at the upper limits of one's personal space is said to be at a high level. The medium level of movement is between high and low.

*Pathway (air and ground).* As the body moves, it makes designs in space both on the ground and in the air. These designs are called pathways. Pathways are created by the body, individual body parts, or objects being used in the movement. Pathways are either curved or straight.

*Plane.* Movement occurs in three different planes. Planes can be thought of as surfaces that cover different directional points and are best characterized by these three representations:

1. wheel—for the sagittal plane
2. door—for the frontal plane
3. table—for the horizontal plane

A wheel rolling forward or backward illustrates movement in the sagittal plane. Doing a front handspring is an example. Picture a person standing in a really wide door frame. Movement occurring within that frame would occur in the frontal plane. A jumping jack is an example. Think of a table intersecting a person's body perpendicularly, say, around the waist. Movement that occurs on the "surface of the table" is in the horizontal plane. Dusting the table is an example.

*Size.* Where a movement occurs can also be described by the size of the movement. Large movements take up much space and occur far away from the center of the body. Small movements take up little space and usually happen near the body's center.

*Initiation.* Initiation refers to where in the body a movement originates. Initiation points are either proximal (near the trunk) or distal (in the limbs).

*Shape.* Shape is the spatial configuration of the body, both while moving and at rest. Shapes are categorized as follows:

- straight—narrow, one-dimensional such as height
- wide—two-dimensional having both height and width
- round—three-dimensional in a curved configuration
- twisted—three-dimensional in a screw-like configuration

*Symmetry.* Symmetry denotes whether the right and left halves of the body are located in space in identical, or similar, positions. If they are, then the body is said to be symmetrical. If they are not, then the body is said to be asymmetrical. Sitting perfectly straight on a sofa, both feet on the floor, lower arms resting on the thighs would result in a symmetrical shape.

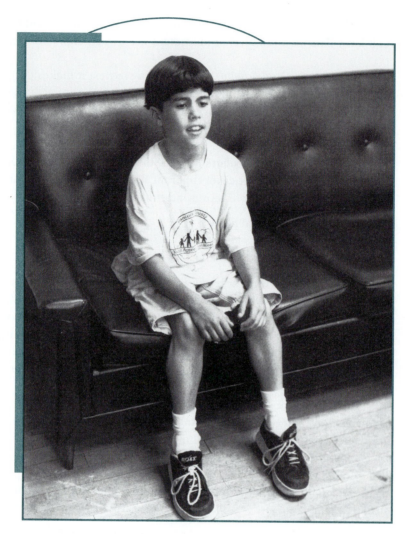

PHOTO 3–8
Symmetrical shape.

Leaning to the right side of the sofa, throwing the left leg up on the sofa seat and the left arm over the back of the sofa, and propping on the right elbow would result in an asymmetrical shape.

## The Effort Category Expanded

Effort descriptors tell how a movement is performed. The effort dimensions of movement give it its energy qualities. These are classified as time,

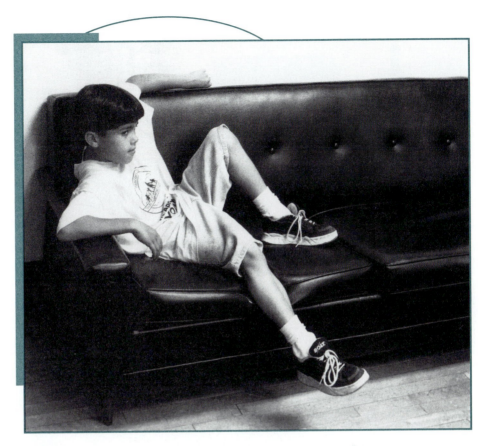

PHOTO 3–9
Asymmetrical shape.

weight, space, and flow. The four effort dimensions are expanded by emphasizing the two extremes of movement for each dimension to facilitate expla-
nation (Figure 3–5). It is recognized that movement occurs all along the
dimensions between the two extremes.

*Time.*    Time describes the speed at which a movement occurs. Fast
movements are quick, over in a hurry, and swift. Slow movements are unhur-
ried, take a long time, and stretch on and on.

*Weight.*    Weight refers to the strength or force with which a movement is done. Strong movements are forceful and aggressive, using a large
amount of force. Light movements, on the other hand, are weightless, gentle,
and delicate. Light movements, however, are not done with lack of muscle

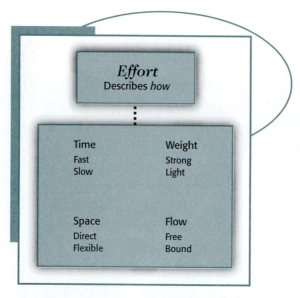

FIGURE 3–5
Effort category expanded (second level).

tension. The individual is deliberately and actively using muscle tension in a light way when moving with light force.

*Space.* Space, as a dynamic component, refers to the direct or flexible use of space. Less space is used with direct movements than with flexible movements as they are straight, undeviating types of movements. Flexible movements are bendable, pliant, or circuitous and, consequently, use more space.

*Flow.* Flow refers to the continuity of movement. Movement that is ongoing and unstoppable is said to be free. A jump is a free-flowing action. Once underway it cannot be stopped. Movements demonstrating bound flow are those that can be stopped. Carefully reaching out to touch a flower blossom is an action characterized as having bound flow.

## The Relationships Category Expanded

The relationships category focuses attention on the interactions that occur between and among the different components of the movement context (Figure 3–6). A person moving in a particular environment will interact with or relate to what is present in that environment while the movement is occurring. The unlimited ways in which these interactions can occur provide

PHOTO 3–10
Free flow characterizes a jumping action.

PHOTO 3–11
Bound flow characterizes the careful reaching toward a flower blossom.

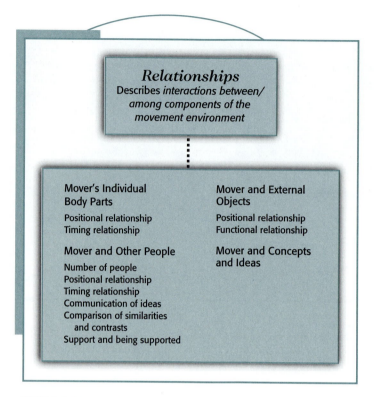

**Relationships**
Describes *interactions between/ among components of the movement environment*

**Mover's Individual Body Parts**

Positional relationship
Timing relationship

**Mover and Other People**

Number of people
Positional relationship
Timing relationship
Communication of ideas
Comparison of similarities
   and contrasts
Support and being supported

**Mover and External Objects**

Positional relationship
Functional relationship

**Mover and Concepts and Ideas**

FIGURE 3–6
Relationships category expanded (second level).

boundless possibilities for movement and the wide ranging individual variations in movement. The fact that the environment itself can be moving also adds to the possibilities for movement. Relationship possibilities are categorized as:

- Mover's individual body parts
- Mover and other people
- Mover and external objects
- Mover and concepts and ideas

*Mover's individual body parts.*    In different types of movement, the positional relationship of individual body parts to one another becomes an important descriptor of the movement. Body parts can be positioned above, below, in front of, over, under, between, around, behind, and beside other parts. The positional relationship needed is generally created by the constraints of the movement being used. For example, a cartwheel necessitates placing the hands beside one another on the mat to take the weight as the body "wheels" over in a sideways movement.

PHOTO 3-12
Note the positional relationship of the hands to each other in this cartwheel photo sequence.

PHOTO 3-13

PHOTO 3–14

PHOTO 3–15

There is also a timing relationship with individual body parts. Different body parts can move at the same time or one after the other. A jump by definition requires both feet to leave the ground at the same time. If they do not, then you could have a leap where one foot leaves the ground first and the other one follows and the first foot lands followed by the other foot.

*Mover and other people.*  When other people are part of the mover's environment, interactions between these individuals will occur. The number of people, and the ways they are grouped together, will influence the type and amount of interactions that occur. These individuals would have positional and timing relationships with one another in the same ways defined in the previous section.

Interactions with others in a movement setting also create the potential for communicating ideas through movement. Movements can be related to what you are trying to say, so to speak. A hug, for example, can have the meaning of support, love, togetherness, or greeting depending on the context in which the hug is given.

When more than one person is moving, their movements can be executed from within the notion of a comparative relationship. This means that all of

PHOTO 3-16
This hug communicates togetherness.

PHOTO 3-17
This hug communicates a greeting.

the movers could be doing the same movement in the same way, for example, three people walking in unison along a sidewalk. They could also be doing different movements at the same time, as when ten players are playing a game of basketball. All of the aspects of movement and their subcategories could be compared among any number of movers to observe and describe the similar and contrasting relationships that exist among them.

Movers can also relate to one another in the role of supporting another person while moving and being supported by another person while moving. Quickly grabbing some one's elbow as you see they are beginning to fall puts you in the role of supporting that person. You are in the role of being supported by another person if you are on belay while rock climbing.

*Mover and external objects.* Objects are almost always a part of the movement environment and the mover must interact and come into relationship with such objects. The relationship is both a positional one and a functional one. Positional relationships have been described previously and are the same with objects as with body parts and with other people. A functional relationship exists between the mover and the purpose, or function, of the object in the environment. The ways in which movers relate to objects have to do with how the object is to be used in the movement. Having a glass of water in your hand, intending to be drunk, will define the movement needed—hand moving up and toward the mouth, then turning to tilt the water out of the glass. The mover must move in relationship to the purpose of the object being present in the environment.

*Mover and concepts and ideas.* Movement also occurs in relationship to things in the environment other than people and objects. Musical accompaniment, rules, and words are examples of concepts and ideas that interact with one's movement. On moving sidewalks and subway escalators, the rule is standees to the right and walkers to the left. If the rule is followed, then it determines at least one type of interaction that exists with others in that particular type of movement setting.

## Chapter Summary

The Movement Framework classifies movement in four broad categories: body describes what, space describes where, effort describes how, and relationships describes interactions. The categories taken together offer a comprehensive view of movement. In classifying a comprehensive concept like movement into narrower categories, however, the danger exists that the broad nature of the concept will be lost. No single movement falls into only one category nor can any one category be excluded from any movement executed. You cannot move your body without moving somewhere, with some effort, and in some kind of relationship. A particular category may be emphasized over the other three for different reasons, but all four are integrally related to one another.

The Movement Framework provides a conceptualization for the structure of movement. It is recognized that this particular concept is not the only way to view movement, but this framework thoroughly and wholly classifies movement so that it can be understood by the teacher of movement. The Movement Framework has been presented as a guide for observing and describing movement. It outlines the possibilities of where a teacher's observational attention could be focused as students respond to lesson tasks. It helps the teacher know what to look at and what to look for during the lesson.

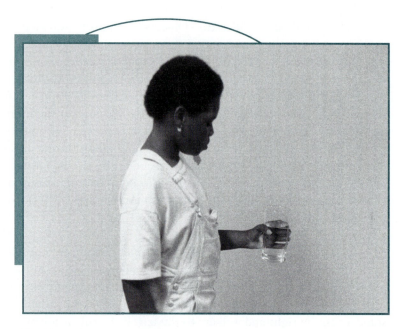

PHOTO 3–18
Movers relate to external objects based on how the object is to be used.

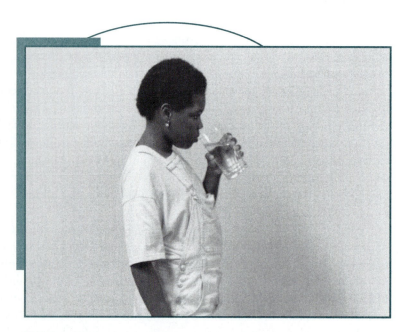

PHOTO 3–19

The framework also generates a rich vocabulary to be used for movement description. These descriptors contribute to the detail of the internal reflective dialog teachers have with themselves as they observe their classes in action. They also contribute to teachers' dialog with children as they help children become more skillful movers. Professional dialog is enhanced as well when colleagues who have similar understandings of movement structure converse with one another to advance their learning.

## Note

The Movement Framework presented here has its roots in Rudolph Laban's original work on a theoretical structure of movement. His colleagues and others have adapted his work and made connections to moving for educational purposes within an educational context. For those interested in a historical perspective, reading Laban's earlier works, and those of his contemporaries, is integral to gaining insight into his ideas about how movement is structured and his movement theories. Enlightening reading includes Laban's *Modern Educational Dance* and *The Mastery of Movement,* Laban and F.C. Lawrence's *Effort,* and Valerie Preston-Dunlop's *A Handbook for Modern Educational Dance.* Educators who have previously applied his theoretical understandings of movement in the movement education textbook literature include Sheila Stanley *(Physical Education: A Movement Orientation),* Joan Russell *(Creative Movement and Dance for Children),* Jennifer Wall and Nancy Murray *(Children & Movement: Physical Education in the Elementary School),* and Bette Logsdon and colleagues in *Physical Education for Children: A Focus on the Teaching Process.*

## References and Reading List

Laban, R. (1975). *Modern educational dance* (3rd ed.) (L. Ullmann, Rev.). London: Macdonald & Evans.

Laban, R. (1980). *The mastery of movement* (4th ed.) (L. Ullmann, Rev.). Estover, Plymouth: Macdonald & Evans.

Laban, R., & Lawrence, F. C. (1974). *Effort: Economy of human movement* (2nd ed.). Estover, Plymouth: Macdonald & Evans.

Logsdon, B. J., Barrett, K. R., Ammons, M., Broer, M. R., Halverson, L. E., McGee, R., & Roberton, M. A. (1984). *Physical education for children: A focus on the teaching process* (2nd ed.). Philadelphia: Lea & Febiger.

Preston-Dunlop, V. M. (1980). *A handbook for modern educational dance* (Rev. ed.). Estover, Plymouth: Macdonald & Evans.

Russell, J. (1975). *Creative movement and dance for children* (Rev. ed.) Boston: Plays.

Stanley, S. (1977). *Physical education: A movement orientation* (2nd ed.). Toronto: McGraw-Hill Ryerson.

Thornton, S. (1971). *A movement perspective of Rudolf Laban.* London: Macdonald & Evans.

Wall, J., & Murray, N. (1994). *Children & movement: Physical education in the elementary school* (2nd ed.). Dubuque, IA: Wm. C. Brown.

# 2

# *The Content of Physical Education*

*m*ovement has been identified as the content of physical education. Movement is the what of teaching. Chapter 3 presented a conceptualization of movement in general within the format of the Movement Framework. This framework is meant to make movement more understandable for teaching.

The framework classifies movement in general though movement always occurs in a particular context. There is an infinite number of contexts in which movement can occur. We carefully walk behind the lawn mower as we strongly push it over the grass in as straight a pathway as we can. We lazily wash the car on a hot summer day, rubbing back and forth, over and over, until the dirt and grime are gone from sight. We gently stroll through the neighborhood walking the dog, alternately generating and releasing pressure on the leash in response to the dog's comings and goings. Although mowing, washing the car, and walking the dog require skill, the particular movement contexts of importance for physical education teachers are games, gymnastics, and dance (see Note on page 79).

Children are aware of the different contexts in which movement occurs in the

physical education setting, as the following story illustrates. The story also shows that children who have experienced a physical education program in which movement is the content focus, and who have a movement vocabulary themselves, sense or understand that it is not the equipment that defines what they learn in physical education, but how they "move" with the equipment that is the essence of their learning.

## *outline*

CHAPTER 4
*Teaching
Educational Games*

CHAPTER 5
*Teaching
Educational Gymnastics*

CHAPTER 6
*Teaching
Educational Dance*

The children were lining up to leave the gym and return to their classroom at the end of the final lesson of a volleyball unit on developing the underhand serve and passing the ball to a teammate. As the children were gathering at the door, one child asked about what we were going to be doing in the next unit. One of her friends chimed in before I could answer, and in her most incredulous voice said, "We just did educational gymnastics. This was a games unit. You know what's next. Educational dance. Mr. Cliffside always rotates between the Big Three." Then a child who had only been in our school for a couple of weeks casually asked if we were ever going to play with scooters and the parachute. I actually felt proud when one of the other students, Jim, turned to the new person and quite seriously asked, "And just what do you really learn by doing scooters and parachutes?"

The shift from being knowledgeable about generalized movement to being knowledgeable about context-specific movement for teaching requires adaptation of the Movement Framework. Each of these three contexts demands that movement be performed differently because each context is unique. There are similarities across the three contexts, but the essence of the movement as it is performed in games, gymnastics, and dance is directly related to what makes a particular movement environment either that of games or gymnastics or dance. Adaptations to the framework could generate the following examples of types of changes:

PHOTO II–1

1. Vocabulary words for observing and describing movement could change. Stretching and bending as general movement terms become rising and sinking in dance, for example. As one rises up from a low level, the body stretches up away from the floor. Rising, in comparison to stretching, is a word that helps capture some of the expression associated with dance movement. Dancers "rise;" they do not merely "stretch."

PHOTO II–2

2. Framework categories could be reorganized and placed differently. Flow is included in the effort dimension in the general Movement Framework. For dance, flow is placed with dance choreography which is a relationship category idea.

3. New content ideas that relate to movement could appear. For example, the forms into which games movement can be organized (conventional and original) do not appear in the Movement Framework. They do appear in the educational games chapter because they are important for understanding different games forms.

Having a fundamental understanding of movement in general is a prerequisite to being able to adapt movement for teaching in context-specific situations. Each of the three chapters on educational games, gymnastics, and dance has its own content framework that is an adaptation of the Movement Framework for its particular context. Other adaptations will be required as you continue to develop your knowledge base and enhance your skills for teaching these movement content areas within the physical education setting.

The overall organizational scheme for each of the three content chapters is the same. First, the specific content area is introduced. Content ideas that have been identified as core content are defined and described. These content pieces are

PHOTO II–3

called the core content for teaching because this is the central, or foundational, content about which you must be knowledgeable in order to be a successful preservice teacher and first-year inservice teacher. The content identified as core

PHOTO II–4

content does not include all movement content with which you would want to be knowledgeable if you are to have an educationally valuable, developmentally appropriate, and safe elementary school physical education program. Core content does include movement content that will provide a base from which your content knowledge can grow as you gain experience with teaching children. The selected content is presented as three adapted Movement Frameworks titled Core Content

Framework for Beginning Teachers—one each for educational games, educational gymnastics, and educational dance.

After the core content is defined, it is divided into units of work. The units give you personal experience with the core movement material in order to help you understand it from a teaching perspective. The units generally adhere to the outline in Table II–1.

## Note

The aquatic environment is perceived to be an important specific movement context for physical education teachers, however, aquatics have not been addressed, in this book for two reasons. Aquatic facilities are not commonly found in elementary schools, making inclusion of aquatic activities in the physical education curriculum less pervasive than one would wish. Also, an excellent text for swimming instruction for physical education teachers already exists:

Langendorfer, S. J., & Bruya, L. D., (1995). *Aquatic readiness: Developing water competence in young children.* Champaign, IL: Human Kinetics.

---

TABLE II–1

*Educational Games, Gymnastics, and Dance Chapters Outline*

| CORE CONTENT SECTIONS | SECTION FOCUS |
|---|---|
| Focus of Content | The core movement content idea identified in the language of the adapted Movement Frameworks |
| Appropriateness of Content | The grade level(s) at which the core content is to be introduced, emphasized, or revisited |
| Ideas from Which Movement Tasks Are Designed | Movement ideas from which tasks could be developed both for you as you work with the core material, and for the children you teach in your field-based experiences |
| Biomechanical Principles Affecting Quality of Performance | Integration of biomechanical principles pertinent to the movement content of the unit; designed to broaden one's knowledge base about movement from the biomechanical perspective |
| Motor Development Principles Affecting Quality of Performance | Integration of motor development principles pertinent to the movement content of the unit; designed to broaden one's knowledge base about movement from the motor development perspective |
| Aesthetic Principles Affecting Quality of Performance (Dance) | Integration of aesthetic principles pertinent to the movement content of the unit; designed to broaden one's knowledge base about movement from the aesthetic perspective |
| Progression | Indicates core content ideas or other movement experiences that should precede or follow the core content; designed to deepen your understanding of the ordering of content for teaching |
| Experiences for Reflection | Educational activities to help you develop your ability to reflect on what, why, and how you are teaching physical education to children; designed to deepen your understanding of movement from a teaching perspective |

# CHAPTER 4

# Teaching
# Educational Games

Our approach to games teaching is guided by our respect for the individual nature of children. To be an integral and valuable part of the total school curriculum, as well as the physical education curriculum, all games experiences must clearly be meaningful and hold educational value for each child.

The National Association for Sport and Physical Education (NASPE) supports programs of elementary school physical education guided by this commitment. They do this by centering their position on the idea of developmentally appropriate practices. Such practices are learning experiences that give "children opportunities to learn motor skills in a way that accommodates their changing characteristics (i.e., their individual differences)" (Barrett, Williams, & Whitall, 1992, p. 115). It is specifically from a developmental perspective, within the constructivist orientation to teaching, that our games approach is designed. Teaching games from a perspective that accommodates children's needs, and at the same time seeks to release their potential for effective movement in the context of a game, is not easy.

Part of the challenge is to recognize that our current thoughts about games teaching have been constructed in relation to past experiences as participants in physical education classes and in youth and adult competitive sports. More recently, the commercialization of sport and the influence of the media have helped shape our views of the games experience. It is important to reflect on one's currently held beliefs and to reexamine them in the light of new ideas, in this case, educational ideas related to the teaching of games.

It is likely that many of our games experiences as children were not consistent with a developmentally appropriate view of physical education, a fact of which, more than likely, we were not aware. Most of us probably were successful at games and played key roles in physical education classes and on teams. These experiences were meaningful to us, but what meaning did our less successful classmates construct from physical education classes and team play? If you reflect on these past experiences now, not only from your personal perspective, but also including your classmates' perspectives as well, you may begin to recognize that many of these games experiences were not consistent with what it means today to teach from a developmental perspective within a constructivist approach.

While all children cannot become, or may not even be interested in becoming, highly skilled games players, all children have a right to an educationally sound games experience during their elementary school years. This right is not reserved just for those who may have a special aptitude toward games playing. Every child's efforts in games should be encouraged. Accepting that all children have the right to educationally sound games experiences creates the need for discussion and reflection on a controversial topic in games education—the issue of competition.

## The Problematic Issue of Competition

Games teaching at the elementary level is one of the most vigorously debated aspects of the physical education curriculum. The central issue running through this debate is the concept of competition. Is it good or bad for children? How best should a teacher deal with competition? While there are numerous games that are cooperative rather than competitive in nature, children do like to play games that have a competitive element in them. Many children are ready for this type of experience and, indeed, can have educationally sound experiences in games that are competitive.

Teaching children how to handle the competitive nature of games is important content to include in a games program, but competition should be experienced by them at their own development levels. In order to understand and perform effectively in competitive situations, clear emphasis needs to be placed on the cooperative and collaborative nature of games.

Games are part of our culture and all children should have the opportunity to learn how to play them to the best of their abilities. We believe that games should be taught from a constructivist educational perspective consistent with developmental theory. School experiences should serve as a base from which children can choose those games they would like to continue to play throughout their lives. Some children will seek highly structured, competitive contexts in which to continue their games playing, whereas others will choose less structured and less competitive contexts.

## Game Playing throughout Life

Informed choices regarding games preferences cannot be made by young adults if their K–5 and 6–12 experiences did not allow them to be active learners in a wide range of game contexts that taught them about games, as well as how to play games. Playing games is not enjoyable or challenging if you do not understand their basic structures and what makes a game "a game." Such understanding needs to start in elementary school. Children experience very special moments when actively taking part in a game that "works" for them. We want as many children as possible to have these experiences—and lots of them—for they can be exhilarating and forever meaningful.

One of the main goals that school physical education holds, and shares with society at large, is the dream that children will keep alive their natural love of activity throughout their lives. Quality physical education programs, through their focus on the development of competent and confident movers, can help children prepare themselves for a lifetime of physical activity. Some children have available to them a range of avenues to achieve this dream outside of schools, but many do not. School programs are available to everyone. As future teachers, you must vigorously accept your share of this responsibility for the accomplishment of this dream. Because children should have participation options open to them, it is important that experiences in all curriculum areas be inviting. It is not critical that all children like all areas of our programs (e.g., games, gymnastics, dance, aquatics, fitness), but it is critical that all have the opportunity to find those areas that hold promise for future and continuous participation.

# THE CORE CONTENT FOR TEACHING EDUCATIONAL GAMES TO CHILDREN

This chapter will challenge you to think differently about some traditional games teaching ideas. Whenever you have a complex curriculum area such as games, it helps to organize your thoughts around a small number of big ideas. You can see the broad picture but still focus on more specific concepts when appropriate. We have identified content in games that is essential for you to understand in order to help children develop as skillful games players. By reflecting on and revisiting this material throughout your teacher education course work and field experiences, you will come to fully understand and be able to use it in constructing your own approach to games teaching.

The content of games has been structured around four broad interrelated ideas or content categories (Figure 4–1):

- game forms
- movement skills
- basic strategies/tactics
- criteria for assessing the educational value of a game

These four broad content ideas contribute to a strong games foundation for children prior to their middle school physical education experience. This content is by no means all the games content that could be taught in schools. It is seen, however, as the essential material for beginning teachers to understand if they are to help children develop their games skills and gain confidence in their game-playing abilities.

## The Games Core Content Framework

> ### Game Forms

Games can be defined as activities in which one or more children engage in cooperative, collaborative, or competitive play, with or without an object, within the structure of certain rules and boundaries. There are two forms that games can take—conventional and original. A conventional game is a game that currently exists in the culture and is available for use by anyone. Physical education and recreation/leisure texts are excellent sources for the wide array of conventional games that we have, as are practicing physical education specialists. In an educational setting, the children, the teacher, or both working together could select which game to play from the available conventional games and modify it as need be. An original game is one that is created at the time that it is played. It can be created and also modified by the children, or the teacher, or both working together.

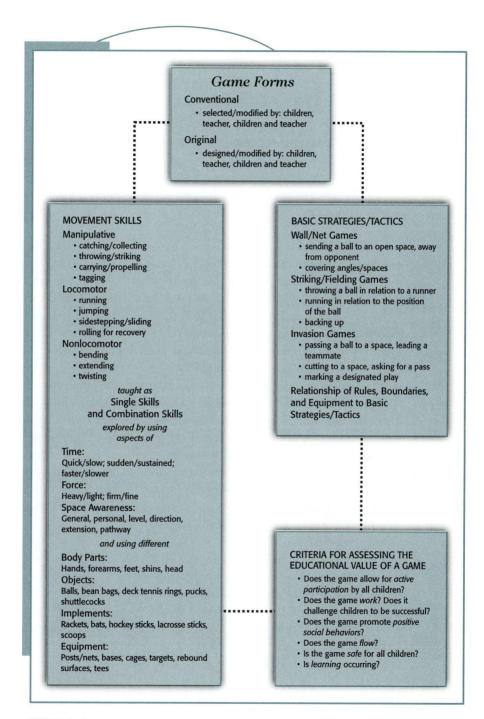

**Game Forms**

Conventional
- selected/modified by: children, teacher, children and teacher

Original
- designed/modified by: children, teacher, children and teacher

**MOVEMENT SKILLS**

Manipulative
- catching/collecting
- throwing/striking
- carrying/propelling
- tagging

Locomotor
- running
- jumping
- sidestepping/sliding
- rolling for recovery

Nonlocomotor
- bending
- extending
- twisting

*taught as*
**Single Skills
and Combination Skills**
*explored by using
aspects of*

Time:
Quick/slow; sudden/sustained; faster/slower
Force:
Heavy/light; firm/fine
Space Awareness:
General, personal, level, direction, extension, pathway
*and using different*
Body Parts:
Hands, forearms, feet, shins, head
Objects:
Balls, bean bags, deck tennis rings, pucks, shuttlecocks
Implements:
Rackets, bats, hockey sticks, lacrosse sticks, scoops
Equipment:
Posts/nets, bases, cages, targets, rebound surfaces, tees

**BASIC STRATEGIES/TACTICS**

Wall/Net Games
- sending a ball to an open space, away from opponent
- covering angles/spaces

Striking/Fielding Games
- throwing a ball in relation to a runner
- running in relation to the position of the ball
- backing up

Invasion Games
- passing a ball to a space, leading a teammate
- cutting to a space, asking for a pass
- marking a designated play

Relationship of Rules, Boundaries, and Equipment to Basic Strategies/Tactics

**CRITERIA FOR ASSESSING THE EDUCATIONAL VALUE OF A GAME**
- Does the game allow for *active participation* by all children?
- Does the game *work*? Does it challenge children to be successful?
- Does the game promote *positive social behaviors*?
- Does the game *flow*?
- Is the game *safe* for all children?
- Is *learning* occurring?

FIGURE 4–1
Games core content framework for beginning teachers.

The material in this category is centered around the manipulative, loco-motor, and nonlocomotor skills taught as single skills and combination skills. Both types of skills are further developed through using aspects of time, force, and space awareness and through using different body parts, objects, implements, and equipment.

*Manipulative.* To gain possession of an object, catching and collecting are the two main skills used. When an object comes to you in the air, you gain possession by catching, whereas collecting means gaining possession of an ob-ject that comes along the ground. In both skills, when there is speed involved, some way of reducing the speed of the object as it is being caught, is required. We usually think of gaining possession of an object in games as done primarily with the hands, but that is too limited a view. Trapping a soccer ball using your legs or feet, receiving a pass with a hockey stick, and receiving a thrown ball using a scoop are examples of collecting and catching without hands.

The main purpose of throwing and striking is to send an object away. Throwing is usually done with the hands and different implements (e.g., scoops, lacrosse sticks). Striking is done with different implements as well as different body parts, especially the hands, head, and feet. Overarm, under-arm, and sidearm patterns are basic to both striking and throwing skills. Many of these patterns, when adapted for use in the context of a particular adult game, have specific names, for example, a lob in tennis, a clear in bad-minton, and a punt or drop kick in football.

Carrying and propelling refer to what games players do when they want to travel with an object and maintain possession of it at the same time. Propelling includes such skills as dribbling a ball with your feet, hands, or a stick. It re-quires you to contact the object repeatedly while moving. Carrying is used in games such as in football and lacrosse where the players must run with the ball, holding it close to their bodies with their hands or cradling it with their sticks.

Hand tagging could be viewed as a specialized form of catching. It is in-cluded here because children can learn a lot about game structure from simple tag games and the act of tagging someone should be considered a skill—a skill requiring a gentle touch with the hand on a safe part of the opponent's body.

*Locomotor.* In playing games, the major locomotor skills needed in-clude running, jumping, sidestepping/sliding, and rolling for recovery. All these skills except the last one require agile footwork and are performed in response to a specific situation (e.g., cutting into a space by running to receive a ball, jumping to intercept a pass, sidestepping/sliding in an attempt to slow down an opponent). In other words, you do not jump just to see how high you can jump. You jump high in order to catch a ball that is traveling high. The agility needed for all these skills requires the ability to keep the body balanced over the feet and to change directions quickly. When thinking about these skills as potential content, it is a good idea to couple them with stopping. Being able to travel is not helpful if the traveling cannot be safely controlled, that is, stopped and started at will.

Rolling for recovery is included in this category of skills as it is a form of traveling, albeit, traveling for safety reasons. You may need to roll for recovery following a catch that has caused you to lose your balance and fall. Forward, backward, sideward, and shoulder rolls all would be possibilities here. This particular content is shared with gymnastics and dance and serves as a tie between the three areas.

*Nonlocomotor.* Nonlocomotor skills are classified as activities of the body. Bending (or curling, or flexing), extending (or stretching) and twisting (or rotating) are actions of the body that occur when performing manipulative and locomotor skills. For example, to sidestep quickly back and forth, the body has to maintain a semicrouched position (partial bending). To catch a ball thrown well out to one's side, a full extension of the arm and upper body, timed to successfully gain possession of the object, is needed. In games, nonlocomotor actions are not usually taught as skills, per se, but are used as vehicles to refine skills and improve the overall quality of the movement being performed. This is not the case, however, in educational gymnastics and educational dance, for they are often used as the major focus of a lesson or series of lessons.

*Single skills and combination skills.* Manipulative and locomotor skills can be taught as single skills (e.g., throwing, catching, foot dribbling) and as combination skills (e.g., running and catching, catching and throwing). When skills are combined, they become a different, more challenging skill than when taught individually. They also become more game-like. The examples given focus only on manipulative and locomotor skills since using nonlocomotor body actions as primary teaching content is not especially useful as was just mentioned.

To have a chance to become effective games players, children must be able to use basic manipulative and locomotor skills (most as combination skills) in a number of different game contexts. Game contexts are dynamic in nature and require children to use their skills in versatile and adaptive

PHOTO 4–1
Combining the two manipulative skills of catching and throwing makes the movement more game-like than performing the movements separately as single skills.

PHOTO 4–2

PHOTO 4–3

PHOTO 4–4

ways. Often they have to use them in ways that they have never actually tried before. Children also must use their skills cooperatively, collaboratively, and competitively in relationship to teammates and opponents. Using selected aspects of time, force, and space awareness as content helps the teacher design more game-like tasks and gives children greater opportunity to become the versatile and adaptive movers required for games playing.

*Time (quick/slow; sudden/sustained; faster/slower).* To be successful games players, children need to vary the time, or speed, of their movement, both in terms of the total body (e.g., when running, sidestepping/sliding) and in terms of individual body parts (e.g., when throwing for distance, the forward rotation of the upper body needs to be done quickly). Variations in speed can range from being very slow, giving the movement a sustained quality, to very quick, giving the movement a sudden quality. Reacting to the speed of an object, like varying the speed of one's movement, is important to success in games. For example, in a game context, children will need to be able to catch and collect balls coming to them at different speeds.

*Force (heavy/light; firm/fine).* Closely related to using speed as content is the concept of using force as content. Time and force are closely related because often as you try to increase the speed of your movement, you have to use more force, and vice versa. Children, who develop finesse in the ways they handle themselves in game contexts, often are demonstrating a unique ability to control the force behind their movements. Children need to learn how to vary the force, as well as the speed of their movements on purpose and in relation to the developing game context. The close relationship between force and time allows teachers two different avenues to get at similar ideas.

Use of maximum force plays a critical role in the development of some manipulative skills; those to which particular attention must be paid when teaching are mentioned specifically. These are throwing for force and striking for distance. Details regarding the role force plays in the development of these skills are addressed later.

*Space awareness (general, personal, level, direction, extension, pathway).* Skilled games players use the space in which their game is played to their advantage. General space refers to all the available space in which the game is allowed to take place. This aspect of space is usually designated by a set of boundaries and varies considerably due to the nature of the game. Learning how to move within a range of boundary sizes is what teaching the use of general space means.

A player's personal space is the space that surrounds the body whether the person is still or traveling. The distances players can reach away from their bodies without falling over are the outer limits of their personal spaces. Skilled games players use this space well, handling objects and implements away from their bodies, as well as close to their bodies, and in all places around them.

Level refers to using the space around you from the lowest to the highest point. Observing a game in progress quickly illustrates how often players must handle objects sometimes at their feet, sometimes above their heads, and the many places in between. It is easier when teaching this material to think of areas of space, such as the space above the children's shoulders as being at a high level, the space between the shoulders and knees as being at a medium level, and the space below the knees as being at a low level.

In any game context, players are consistently required to change the direction of their movements or the direction of an object. The former occurs most often when players are running, jumping, and sidestepping/sliding. It is important to remember when teaching running and change of direction that running is no longer simply running. It is now a different skill. Running forward and then changing direction to run backwards is a skill unto itself.

Changing the direction of a pass is also a different skill from passing straight ahead. It requires a shift in body position and application of force in relation to where you want the ball to go. It is not always easy for children to figure out the shifts and applications.

The concept of extensions within the context of space awareness is similar to the nonlocomotor skills of bending and extending. When playing games, and especially when receiving passes in field and invasion games and shots from across the net in net games, players are often required to extend their bodies or individual body parts or to bend and keep them in close in order to successfully play the ball or game object.

Often in games, especially in those where balls are thrown or struck by hand or with an implement, a specific type of pathway has to be used for a pass to be effective. For example, a puck might have to travel in a flat pathway along the ice or a shuttlecock in an arched pathway in the air. The type of pathway created by a player is usually in response to the game context and what the situation requires.

Skilled games players move in, out, and through space easily. They appear to be "playing" with it. Those children who can use space to their advantage will be more successful in the games program and will more likely enjoy themselves than those children who cannot. These latter children will find this aspect of the content too challenging and may get discouraged. But helping children skillfully use the game space available to them is one of the most exciting aspects of teaching games—and the one with the greatest payoff in their learning to be games players.

*Different body parts, objects, implements, equipment.* It may seem strange to list body parts, objects, implements, and equipment as part of games content. Without using these aspects in developing lessons, however, children will remain unchallenged, their games skills underdeveloped, and their success in actual game playing unachieved. To encourage continuous development, children need many opportunities to develop manipulative and locomotor skills using a range of body parts and using a selected range of objects, implements, and equipment. When you look at advanced soccer or volleyball players, for example, they skillfully use a number of body parts to handle the ball. Knowing when to change the body part to make it easier to succeed is important. If children are playing a net game in which they are hitting a ball with rackets back and forth over a low net, and one or more finds it difficult to handle the racket, it would be important to change the racket to one with a larger head or lighter weight overall, or to change and let them use their hands. The types of objects, implements, and equipment that you provide in your lessons play a critical role in the development of children's skillfulness.

## Basic Strategies/Tactics

Games have been categorized into three different types—wall/net games, striking/fielding games, and invasion games (Werner, 1989). For each type of game, strategies/tactics have been identified that are important for children to be able to use in that game context before they go to middle school. While we have linked specific strategies/tactics to a particular game type here, it is important to recognize that some of these strategies/tactics apply across more than one game type. For example, sending a ball to an open space is used in all but tag games, but for different purposes in the different game categories. Rules, boundaries, and equipment help define the categories of games identified here. Strategies/tactics used in a game, therefore, have a strong relationship to these defining aspects of games.

Strategies/tactics represent what makes a game, a game. Games can be cooperative, collaborative, and competitive in nature. No matter which relationship characterizes them, though, players will have to size up the emerging situation, make decisions about what to do, and then do it. In sizing up the situation, for example, a player may have to decide on whether the situation calls for:

- passing the ball to an open space and away from an opponent
- positioning oneself to cover a space or an angle
- passing the ball ahead of a teammate
- cutting into a space to receive the ball
- marking/staying close to an opponent
- throwing the ball ahead of the base runner
- running away from the ball
- running away from the tagger
- positioning oneself to cut off the runner and make the tag

> ### Criteria for Assessing the Educational Value of a Game

We do not think games teaching has a place in the curriculum unless it is of educational value for each child. Being guided by a commitment to teaching from a constructivist perspective supports this position. Stating this belief and acting on it takes strong willed teachers who are secure in their commitment to games as a form of education. As a place to start, we have identified six criteria that teachers and children can use to evaluate the educational value of any game played in schools.

1. Does the game allow for active participation by all children?
2. Does the game work? Does it challenge children to be successful?
3. Does the game promote positive social behaviors?
4. Does the game flow?
5. Is the game safe for all children?
6. Is learning occurring?

# UNDERSTANDING THE CONTENT FROM A TEACHING PERSPECTIVE

Most of you probably are skilled movers who have come into this field because of a love of activity. You are an active person. You are able to use your skills and tactical knowledge of games playing in contexts that are competitive, cooperative, and collaborative in nature. The importance of maintaining an active life style is a concept that you understand and live. It is from the perspective of an active participant in games and other types of activity that the meaning movement holds for you has been constructed.

The perceptions that you currently possess related to moving and games playing are a great asset. But they now need to be explored to embrace the idea that understanding movement for teaching is different—clearly related, but still different—from understanding movement to move. It is one thing for you to be able to hit a tennis ball back and forth so that your opponent has difficulty returning it, and quite another to teach a fourth or fifth grader to accomplish the same task.

To help you reflect on the material from a teacher's perspective, the games core content has been divided into six units. Each unit of work follows a similar organizational pattern with slight variations when needed. These units of work should not be confused with unit plans that you will be developing for teaching, as they are not constructed in the same way nor are they for the same purpose. Also, the order in which the units is presented is not to be considered a teaching progression. The units are:

## CORE CONTENT 1. MANIPULATIVE SKILLS AS SINGLE SKILLS

Manipulative skills of catching and collecting, throwing and striking, and carrying and propelling taught as single skills explored by using selected aspects of:

> *time:* faster, slower
> *force*: maximum, varying amounts
> *space awareness:* level, extension

in relation to:

> *body parts:* hands, forearms, feet, etc.
> *objects:* balls, bean bags, deck tennis rings, etc.
> *implements:* rackets, bats, hockey sticks, etc.

## CORE CONTENT 2. LOCOMOTOR SKILLS AS SINGLE AND COMBINATION SKILLS

Locomotor skills of running, jumping, sidestepping/sliding, and rolling for recovery taught as single and combination skills explored by using selected aspects of:

> *time:* quick, slow, active pause
> *space awareness:* general, direction

## CORE CONTENT 3. MANIPULATIVE AND LOCOMOTOR SKILLS AS COMBINATION SKILLS

Manipulative and locomotor skills combined–manipulative and manipulative; manipulative and locomotor; locomotor and locomotor explored by using selected aspects of:

*time:* faster, slower
*force:* varying amounts
space awareness: direction, level

in relation to:

*body parts:* hands, forearms, feet, etc.
*objects:* balls, bean bags, deck tennis rings, etc.
*implements:* rackets, bats, hockey sticks, etc.

## CORE CONTENT 4. BASIC STRATEGIES/TACTICS

Basic strategies/tactics for wall/net games, striking/fielding games, invasion games, and tag games as they relate to rules, boundaries, and equipment:

| | |
|---|---|
| **Wall/net games:** | **sending a ball to an open space, away from opponent** |
| | **covering angles/spaces** |
| **Striking/fielding games:** | **throwing a ball in relation to a runner** |
| | **running in relation to the position of the ball** |
| | **backing up** |
| **Invasion games:** | **passing a ball to a space, leading a teammate** |
| | **cutting to a space, asking for a pass** |
| | **marking a designated player** |

## CORE CONTENT 5. GAME FORMS

Two game forms: conventional and original

## CORE CONTENT 6. CRITERIA FOR ASSESSING THE EDUCATIONAL VALUE OF A GAME

Six criteria, in the form of questions, to use when assessing the educational value of a game:

1. Does the game allow for **active participation** by all children?
2. Does the game **work?** Does it challenge children to be successful?
3. Does the game promote **positive social behaviors?**
4. Does the game **flow?**
5. Is the game **safe** for all children?
6. Is **learning** occurring?

## K–5 Progression

To give the big picture of how this content might be emphasized throughout a K–5 program, Figure 4–2, illustrates appropriate times to introduce, emphasize, and revisit the material. The dark green segments represent when this material might be used as the major emphasis in designing lessons.

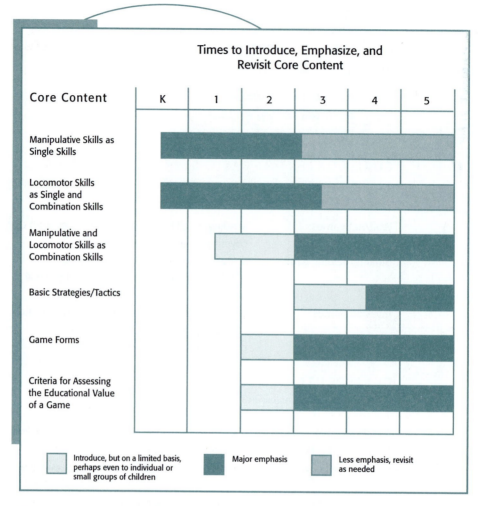

FIGURE 4–2
Suggested games content emphasis by grade level.

The medium green segments suggests when the material might need to be revisited in order to make the tasks less difficult for a class or individual children. The light green segments suggest when the material could be used to redesign a task for an individual or small groups of children to make it more challenging for them.

## Remainder of the Chapter

In the rest of this chapter, the content focus for each of the six Core Content units is explored and developed to help you come to an understanding of these ideas at a level appropriate for a beginning teacher. It is expected that you will expand your knowledge and teaching of games beyond this core material as a result of your continuing professional development.

## *core content*

## Manipulative Skills as Single Skills

### FOCUS OF CONTENT

Manipulative skills of catching and collecting, throwing and striking, and carrying and propelling taught as single skills explored by using selected aspects of:

> *time:* faster, slower
> *force:* maximum, varying amounts
> *space awareness:* level, extension

in relation to:

> *body parts:* hands, forearms, feet, etc.
> *objects:* balls, bean bags, deck tennis rings, etc.
> *implements:* rackets, bats, hockey sticks, etc.

### APPROPRIATENESS OF CONTENT

This material is needed to help children begin to handle basic manipulative games skills and understand movement principles that cut across them. This material is most appropriate with children in K, 1st, 2nd, and sometimes 3rd grade. It becomes appropriate for 4th- and 5th-grade children when more challenging objects, implements and equipment are used such as in collecting using a lacrosse stick and shooting a soccer ball into a goal.

### *Catching and Collecting*

#### IDEAS FROM WHICH MOVEMENT TASKS ARE DESIGNED

- Tossing/catching a 6"–8" ball using the five basic tosses/catches: 1 hand to 2 hands, 1 to the same hand, 1 to the other hand, 2 hands to 1 hand, 2 hands to 2 hands. (Think of this as comparable to the five basic jumps in educational gymnastics and educational dance.)

  > change height of tossed ball (changes force requirements)
  > change type of objects being thrown/caught: balls, bean bags, deck tennis rings

- Catching a 6"–8" ball thrown to arrive just below partner's waist, at knee height, below knees, shoulder height, head height, above head height

  > toss ball to sides to bring out increased extension

- Collecting a ball rolled along the ground directly at partner's feet

**PHOTO 4–5**
Practicing catching with one and two hands.

change the speed of the ball

change the type of ball

roll ball to sides to bring out increased extension

### BIOMECHANICAL PRINCIPLES AFFECTING QUALITY OF PERFORMANCE

*Position of hands (body/body part/implement) prior to catch.* Hands present open surface behind or underneath the object, body behind object, legs relaxed slightly flexed with one foot in front of the other in a ready position; as object picks up speed, hands may need to reach toward it to allow for more give to occur.

*Action of hands (body/body part/implement) at moment of catch.* Hands move toward object just before gently grasping it, immediately giving if necessary.

*Action of hands/arms (body/body part/implement) following catch.* Hands move in direction of object's flight toward body giving with the object; as force of object becomes greater more give may be necessary; giving reduces the speed of the object and helps to absorb force, making it easier to gain possession of the object.

Once the principles are understood and have been fully explored, these ideas can be used to design tasks using the feet and field/ice hockey sticks that have been modified to fit children's heights. In these situations, catching becomes collecting, but the same biomechanical principles apply.

### MOTOR DEVELOPMENT PRINCIPLES AFFECTING QUALITY OF PERFORMANCE

Of the three factors affecting motor development identified by Newell (1986), the effect of equipment and the goals/conditions of the task are important to consider. It cannot be stressed enough that when you or the children toss balls or any object to each other for developing catching and collecting skills, the toss is a critical factor in the receiver's opportunity to learn the skill. The toss sets up the goal and condition of the task. You must treat the toss itself as a skill. If children cannot toss balls to their partners so they can catch them, little opportunity for learning to catch occurs.

Developmental sequences of catching (Roberton & Halverson, 1984), shown in Table 4–1, are helpful as an observation tool to train yourself to observe specific movement components and to interpret your observations developmentally. These sequences represent how catching develops over time from children's initial attempts to their most advanced performances. They can be a major means for assessing children's progress.

## PROGRESSION

Tasks designed in which the object does not bounce or roll and is tossed gently by the children themselves are the easiest. The more difficult tasks involve catching with parts other than the hands, objects that bounce or roll, objects that travel with more speed or force, and implements that are longer or heavier. Use any of the tasks outlined previously as long as they challenge children to further develop their catching and collecting skills. Your task selection should be based on observation and assessment of their progress, especially in controlling the force and accuracy of their tosses. By knowing what to look for and accurately interpreting what factors are affecting children's movement patterns, you will be able to design your own task progression as it relates specifically to the children you teach.

## EXPERIENCES FOR REFLECTION

1. Make a checklist based on the developmental sequences for catching with the components and steps going down the left side of the page and the type of ball, condition, etc. along the top. Find three children of different ages below the age of eight, and observe each of them catch balls of at least two different sizes tossed by you or another person. Assess each child's developmental level using your checklist. Summarize the results and reflect on your data. What are the differences and similarities among these children? How might you interpret your findings?
2. With another classmate, discuss how understanding the developmental sequences designed for catching helps you assess progress in catching in different situations, for example, catching balls of different types or balls being thrown at different speeds or using different implements.
3. Write a short essay focused on how the principles of preparation, moment of contact, and follow through apply across all catching and collecting skills no matter the situation in which they are being performed. What is the relationship between these principles and developmental sequences? Discuss your essay with another member of the class.

## *Throwing and Striking*

### IDEAS FROM WHICH MOVEMENT TASKS ARE DESIGNED

- Throwing a bean bag or yarn ball hard against a wall (overarm, underarm) at a spot that results in releasing the object at a 45° angle
- Throwing a yarn ball (overarm, underarm) so that it rebounds off the wall back to the thrower

    vary the distance thrower is from wall
    change to throwing with partners

**TABLE 4–1**

*Developmental Sequences for Catching*

. . . . . . . . . . . . . . . . . . . . . . . . . . . . . . . . . . . . . . . . . . . . . . . . . . . . . . . . . . . . . .

**PREPARATION: ARM COMPONENT**

*Step 1*    The arms await the ball toss, outstretched with elbows extended.

*Step 2*    The arms await the ball toss with some shoulder flexion still apparent but flexion now appearing in the elbows.

*Step 3*    The arms await the ball in a relaxed posture at the sides of the body or slightly ahead of the body. The elbows may be flexed.

. . . . . . . . . . . . . . . . . . . . . . . . . . . . . . . . . . . . . . . . . . . . . . . . . . . . . . . . . . . . . .

**RECEPTION: ARM COMPONENT**

*Step 1*    The arms remain outstretched and the elbows rigid. Little to no "give" occurs, so the ball bounces off the arms.

*Step 2*    The elbows flex to carry the hands upward toward the face. Initially, ball contact is primarily with the arms, and the object is trapped against the body.

*Step 3*    Initial contact is with the hands. If unsuccessful in using the fingers, the child may still trap the ball against the chest. The hands still move upward toward the face.

*Step 4*    Ball contact is made with the hands. The elbows still flex but the shoulders extend, bringing the ball down and toward the body rather than up toward the face.

. . . . . . . . . . . . . . . . . . . . . . . . . . . . . . . . . . . . . . . . . . . . . . . . . . . . . . . . . . . . . .

**HAND COMPONENT**

*Step 1*    The palms of the hands face upward. (Rolling balls elicit a palms-down, trapping action.)

*Step 2*    The palms of the hands face each other.

*Step 3*    The palms of the hands are adjusted to the flight and size of the oncoming object. Thumbs or little fingers are placed close together, depending on the height of the flight path.

. . . . . . . . . . . . . . . . . . . . . . . . . . . . . . . . . . . . . . . . . . . . . . . . . . . . . . . . . . . . . .

**BODY COMPONENT**

*Step 1*    No adjustment of the body occurs in response to the flight path of the ball.

*Step 2*    The arms and trunk begin to move in relation to the ball flight path.

*Step 3*    The feet, trunk, and arms all move to adjust to the path of the oncoming ball.

. . . . . . . . . . . . . . . . . . . . . . . . . . . . . . . . . . . . . . . . . . . . . . . . . . . . . . . . . . . . . .

*Note:* These sequences have not been validated. They were hypothesized by Harper.[121]

Reprinted by permission from Roberton & Halverson, 1984.

vary the distance between partners

change ball being thrown

throw ball slightly to the right and left of the partner (this will be the beginning of combining manipulative and locomotor skills)

- Striking a yarn ball off a tee toward a wall so that it hits the wall hard

  vary the distance tee is from wall

- Kicking a stationary 8" ball or a hand held ball (i.e., punt) against a wall

  vary the amount of inflation of the ball
  vary distance kicker is from wall

- Striking a balloon in an upward direction using different body parts

  use parts on both sides of the body
  use both upper and lower body parts

- Striking a balloon continuously using different body parts

  change the height the balloon is to be struck
  vary the object to be struck
  change the striking surface to short handled, light paddles

- Striking a balloon back and forth with a partner keeping it from touching the ground

  use different body parts
  vary the object to be struck
  change the striking surface to short handled, light paddles

- Using hands, striking a beach ball back and forth with a partner, letting it bounce in between

  use both left and right hands
  vary the object to be struck
  strike slightly to the right and left of partner (the beginning of combining manipulative and
    locomotor skills)
  change the striking surface to short handled, light paddles

### BIOMECHANICAL PRINCIPLES AFFECTING QUALITY OF PERFORMANCE

There are three throwing and striking patterns with which children need to become familiar—overarm, underarm, and sidearm. In the overarm pattern, the arm primarily moves in the space above the shoulder; in the underarm pattern it moves below the shoulder and in the side arm pattern it moves even with the shoulder. Using the shoulder joint as the reference point, these three places in space are referred to as moving above, below, and at the horizontal. Linking these patterns with actual skills used in sports (e.g., overarm serve in tennis, underarm pitch in softball, forehand in tennis) often helps children see their importance. Kicking is a specialized form of striking that uses the lower limbs.

Biomechanical principles are discussed assuming that maximum force is needed. When applying these principles to throwing and striking skills when maximum force is not needed, the teacher's focus shifts to helping children produce the right amount of force for the situation. The same principles apply however. It is helpful to view all throwing and striking skills biomechanically as having three phases—preparation, contact, and follow through.

*Preparation.*    In throwing and striking there is a preparation or "wind up" phase followed by a sequential unwinding of body parts.  In the overarm throw, for example, preparation would include full rotation away from the direction of the throw with the hand, arm, upper body, and hips. To achieve the greatest range of motion, the legs should be in a stride position with the forward leg opposite to the throwing arm.

*Contact.*    Force is applied to the ball through sequential unwinding of all body parts and implements. The greater the range of motion and the speed of the body parts through space, the greater the force created. To direct the ball where you want it to go, force must be applied through the center of the ball in the intended direction. The amount of force needed is dependent on the purpose of the throw or strike and the weight of the ball.

*Follow Through.*    After release or contact, the hand or implement or foot continues in the intended line of direction. This motion contributes both to speed and accuracy. If a lot of force is being used, following through also inhibits potential injury.

**PHOTO 4–6**
From biomechanical and developmental perspectives, compare the deepest point of the preparation or "wind up" phase of the overarm throw for force across the three children in Photos 4–6, 4–7, and 4–8.

PHOTO 4–7

### MOTOR DEVELOPMENT PRINCIPLES AFFECTING QUALITY OF PERFORMANCE

As with catching and collecting, knowledge of Newell's (1986) three-factor constraint model is important when teaching throwing and striking. You will have no difficulty assessing children's progress if you can observe how the goal/condition of the task (e.g., strike the balloon just above your head; throw hard against the wall) and the equipment used (e.g., size and weight of ball) are affecting the movement response. Once you can assess this, you can restructure the task to fit the recognized need (see Photo 4–9).

Developmental sequences for throwing for force, sidearm and overarm striking for force, and kicking for force have been previously devised (Roberton & Halverson, 1984). See Tables 4–2 through 4–9.

This information is particularly helpful as an observation tool to train yourself to observe specific movement components. These sequences represent how throwing and striking patterns develop over time from children's initial attempts to their most advanced performances.

PHOTO 4–8

Throwing and striking are skills that impart force to an object either with individual body parts or an implement. These skills will be easier to understand, teach, and assess if you teach them sometimes requiring maximum force (MF) and, at other times, with varying amounts of force (VF). When you are focused on helping children develop the most advanced or mature pattern in specific components, you teach for MF. This is because the most mature pattern in these skills requires maximum range of motion of body parts used in a context-specific time/force/space sequence. When you want children to control the amount of force they use for a particular purpose in throwing and striking, you teach for VF. The direction and distance necessary for these throws and strikes will vary according to the emerging game situation.

Exhibiting a mature pattern in throwing for force takes a long time to develop. Motor development researchers believe that the more mature a pattern is, the more options children will have available to them when playing in different game contexts. In terms of teaching force production, we have every reason to believe that working with both concepts at the same time—maximum force and varying force—can be emphasized interchangeably.

PHOTO 4–9
What might the teacher have observed in the children's movement responses that suggested a restructuring of the throwing task (moving some children farther from the wall)?

· · · · · · · · · · · · · · · · · · · · · · · · · · · · · · · · · · · · · · · · · · · · · · · · · · · · · · · · · ·

### PROGRESSION

Tasks designed for children to work alone, with objects that do not bounce or roll and are light are the least complex. The more difficult tasks involve objects that bounce or roll and travel with more speed and force, and implements that are longer or heavier. Because some of these tasks focus on using maximum force, be alert to the safety of the environment in which these tasks are performed. If you know what to look for and can interpret how person-environment-task constraints are affecting children's movement patterns, you will be able to design your own progression as it relates to your specific children.

### EXPERIENCES FOR REFLECTION

1. With a partner, make a checklist based on the developmental sequences for one or more of the throwing- or striking-for-force skills. Use the same format as you did for catching. Find four children, two boys and two girls, of the same age and video tape them performing the skill you are assessing. Using the video and slow motion playback, assess each child's developmental level using your checklist. Reflect on your data and summarize the results. What are the differences and similarities between these children? How might you interpret these findings?

TABLE 4–2

*Developmental Sequences for Backswing, Humerus, and Forearm Action in the Overarm Throw for Force*

**PREPARATORY ARM BACKSWING COMPONENT**

*Step 1*   **No backswing.** The ball-in-the-hand moves directly forward to release from the arm's original position when the hand first grasped the ball.

*Step 2*   **Elbow and humeral flexion.** The ball moves away from the intended line of flight to a position behind or alongside the head by upward flexion of the humerus and concomitant elbow flexion.

*Step 3*   **Circular, upward backswing.** The ball moves away from the intended line of flight to a position behind the head via a circular overhead movement with elbow extended, or an oblique swing back, or a vertical lift from the hip.

*Step 4*   **Circular, downward backswing.** The ball moves away from the intended line of flight to a position behind the head via a circular, down and back motion, which carries the hand below the waist.

**HUMERUS (UPPER ARM) ACTION COMPONENT DURING FORWARD SWING**

*Step 1*   **Humerus oblique.** The humerus moves forward to ball release in a plane that intersects the trunk obliquely above or below the horizontal line of the shoulders. Occasionally, during the backswing, the humerus is placed at a right angle to the trunk, with the elbow pointing toward the target. It maintains this fixed position during the throw.

*Step 2*   **Humerus aligned but independent.** The humerus moves forward to ball release in a plane horizontally aligned with the shoulder, forming a right angle between humerus and trunk. By the time the shoulders (upper spine) reach front facing, the humerus (elbow) has moved independently ahead of the outline of the body (as seen from the side) via horizontal adduction at the shoulder.

*Step 3*   **Humerus lags.** The humerus moves forward to ball release horizontally aligned, but at the moment the shoulders (upper spine) reach front facing, the humerus remains within the outline of the body (as seen from the side). No horizontal adduction of the humerus occurs before front facing.

TABLE 4-2 *(CONTINUED)*

## Developmental Sequences for Backswing, Humerus, and Forearm Action in the Overarm Throw for Force

**FOREARM ACTION COMPONENT DURING FORWARD SWING**

*Step 1* **No forearm lag.** The forearm and ball move steadily forward to ball release throughout the throwing action.

*Step 2* **Forearm lag.** The forearm and ball appear to be "lag," i.e., to remain stationary behind the child or to move downward or backward in relation to him/her. The lagging forearm reaches its furthest point back, deepest point down, or last stationary point before the shoulders (upper spine) reach front facing.

*Step 3* **Delayed forearm lag.** The lagging forearm delays reaching its final point of lag until the moment of front facing.

*Note:* Validation studies [58,60,61,62,89] support these sequences for the overarm throw with the exception of the preparatory arm backswing sequence which was hypothesized by Roberton[69] from the work of Langendorfer[93]. Langendorfer[64] feels the humerus and forearm components are appropriate for overarm striking (see text).

Reprinted by permission from Roberton & Halverson, 1984.

TABLE 4-3

## Developmental Sequences for Action of the Feet in Forceful Throwing and Striking

*Step 1* **No step.** The child throws from the initial foot position.

*Step 2* **Homolateral step.** The child steps with the foot on the same side as the throwing hand.

*Step 3* **Contralateral, short step.** The child steps with the foot on the opposite side from the throwing hand.

*Step 4* **Contralateral, long step.** The child steps with the opposite foot a distance of over half the child's standing height.

*Note:* This sequence hypothesized by Roberton[69] from the work of Leme and Shambes,[95] Seefeldt et al.,[75] and Wild.[96]

Reprinted by permission from Roberton & Halverson, 1984.

## TABLE 4–4

### Developmental Sequences for Trunk Action in Throwing and Striking for Force

. . . . . . . . . . . . . . . . . . . . . . . . . . . . . . . . . . . . . . . . . . . . . . . . . . . . . . . . . . . . . . . . . .

*Step 1*    **No trunk action or forward-backward movements.** Only the arm is active in force production. Sometimes, the forward thrust of the arm pulls the trunk into a passive left rotation (assuming a right-handed throw), but no twist-up precedes that action. If trunk action occurs, it accompanies the forward thrust of the arm by flexing forward at the hips. Preparatory extension sometimes precedes forward hip flexion.

*Step 2*    **Upper trunk rotation or total trunk "block" rotation.** The spine and pelvis both rotate away from the intended line of flight and then simultaneously begin forward rotation, acting as a unit or "block." Occasionally, only the upper spine twists away, then toward the direction of force. The pelvis, then, remains fixed, facing the line of flight, or joins the rotary movement after forward spinal rotation has begun.

*Step 3*    **Differentiated rotation.** The pelvis precedes the upper spine in initiating forward rotation. The child twists away from the intended line of ball flight and, then, begins forward rotation with the pelvis while the upper spine is still twisting away.

. . . . . . . . . . . . . . . . . . . . . . . . . . . . . . . . . . . . . . . . . . . . . . . . . . . . . . . . . . . . . . . . . .

*Note:* Validation studies support this sequence.[60,61,62,64,89]

Reprinted by permission from Roberton & Halverson, 1984.

## TABLE 4–5

### Developmental Sequences for Punting

. . . . . . . . . . . . . . . . . . . . . . . . . . . . . . . . . . . . . . . . . . . . . . . . . . . . . . . . . . . . . . . . . .

**BALL RELEASE: ARM COMPONENT**

*Step 1*    Hands are on the sides of the ball. The ball is tossed upward from both hands after the support foot has landed (if a step was taken).

*Step 2*    Hands are on the sides of the ball. The ball is dropped from chest height after the support foot has landed (if a step was taken).

*Step 3*    Hands are on the sides of the ball. The ball is lifted upward and forward from the waist level. It is released as or just prior to the landing of the support foot.

*Step 4*    One hand is rotated to the side and under the ball. The other hand is rotated to the side and top of the ball. The hands carry the ball on a forward and upward path during the approach. It is released at chest level as the final approach stride begins.

. . . . . . . . . . . . . . . . . . . . . . . . . . . . . . . . . . . . . . . . . . . . . . . . . . . . . . . . . . . . . . . . . .

TABLE 4-5 *(CONTINUED)*

## *Developmental Sequences for Punting*

**BALL CONTACT: ARM COMPONENT**

*Step 1*    Arms drop bilaterally from ball release to a position on each side of the hips at ball contact.

*Step 2*    Arms bilaterally abduct after ball release. The arm on the side of the kicking leg may pull back as that leg swings forward.

*Step 3*    After ball release, the arms bilaterally abduct during flight. At contact the arm opposite the kicking leg has swung forward with that leg. The arm on the side of the kicking leg remains abducted and to the rear.

**LEG ACTION COMPONENT**

*Step 1*    No step or one short step is taken. The kicking leg swings forward from a position parallel or slightly behind the support foot. The knee may be totally extended by contact or, more frequently, still flexed 90° with contact above or below the knee joint. The thigh is still moving upward at contact. The ankle tends to be flexed.

*Step 2*    Several steps may be taken. The last step onto the support leg is a long stride. The thigh of the kicking leg has slowed or stopped forward motion at contact. The ankle is extended. The knee has 20 to 30° of extension still possible by contact.

*Step 3*    The child may take several steps, but the last is actually a leap onto the support foot. After contact, the momentum of the kicking leg pulls the child off the ground in a hop.

*Note:* These sequences, hypothesized by Roberton,[69] have not been validated.

Reprinted by permission from Roberton & Halverson, 1984.

2. With another classmate, question each other on how you think that understanding the developmental sequences designed for throwing and striking for force help you assess progress in these skills when you are trying to teach children how to use different amounts of force?

3. Write an essay and share it with another classmate on how you think the principles of preparation, contact, and follow through apply across all throwing and striking skills no matter the situation in which they are performed. What is the relationship between these principles and developmental sequences?

## *Carrying and Propelling*

These two manipulative skills are so closely tied with running and sidestepping/sliding that we consider them to be combination skills. It is so rare for these skills to be used in a game or game-like context without traveling, that it is best to teach them as combination skills right from the start. If needed, they can be taught as single skills for brief moments when first introduced.

*core content*                                                    ⟨ *2* ⟩

## Locomotor Skills as Single and Combination Skills

FOCUS OF CONTENT

   Locomotor skills of running, jumping, sidestepping/sliding, and rolling for recovery taught as single and combination skills explored by using selected aspects of:

   *time:* quick, slow, active pause
   *space awareness:* general, direction

   Jumping is not included here as it is introduced as a game skill in combination with catching. Jumping as a single skill is presented in some detail in Chapter 5.

APPROPRIATENESS OF CONTENT

   This material is most appropriate for younger children who are still trying to gain control over their bodies while running, jumping, and traveling on their feet by other means.  This material may be more easily taught in educational gymnastics since the goal of general body management is so central to gymnastics experiences. In games, the ability to travel on your feet, starting and stopping with quick changes of direction, is critical to successful games playing. The locomotor skills that are used, however, are used in response to the emerging context of the game. Thus, teaching these skills outside of a game-like or actual game context should not be a major emphasis. Certainly, if children demonstrate difficulty with running and changing directions, for example, you would design tasks focused on meeting this need. Rolling for recovery can be taught when all of the children in a class can do a sideways (safety) roll, one of the skills recommended to be taught early in educational gymnastics.

### *Running, Sidestepping/Sliding as Single and Combination Skills*
#### IDEAS FROM WHICH MOVEMENT TASKS ARE DESIGNED

- Running easily throughout the general space, keeping away from everyone else

   change speed by accelerating and decelerating
   change direction: forward, backward and sideward (this becomes sidestepping/sliding)
   change amount of space used

- Running, sidestepping/sliding, and pausing

   change speed by accelerating and decelerating
   change direction: forward, backward and sideward (this becomes sidestepping/sliding)
   pause after periods of varying duration of running, sidestepping/sliding

- Running forward, backward; sidestepping quickly to the left and right

   mixing direction of run; sidestep
   change speed by accelerating, decelerating, and actively pausing

PHOTO 4–10
Sidestepping/sliding with a pause.

· · · · · · · · · · · · · · · · · · · · · · · · · · · · · · · · · · · · · · · · · · · · · · · · · · · · ·

- Traveling and changing direction in relation to an outside influence (i.e., a teacher running easily toward different children who quickly change direction to get out of the way)

    vary the speed of traveling
    change speed at which the outside influence is running

### BIOMECHANICAL PRINCIPLES AFFECTING QUALITY OF PERFORMANCE

*Center of gravity and balance.*   As children are traveling using different speeds and directions, their main task is to keep their centers of gravity over their bases of support. If they cannot do this, they will fall over. The larger their bases of support, the more stable their bodies. Stopping quickly requires a larger base than stopping slowly. Changing directions quickly requires a shift of gravity in the direction of the next move along with a firm push against the surface on which the children are moving and away from the new direction.

*Production and absorption of force.*   When traveling on the feet at varying speeds, the hips, knees, and ankle joints are in a continuous state of producing and absorbing force. Done effectively, these actions cushion the body and prevent injuries. With the material in this unit of work, the main goal for children is

PHOTO 4–11
Running forward to a cone, then sidestepping quickly to either side.

. . . . . . . . . . . . . . . . . . . . . . . . . . . . . . . . . . . . . . . . . . . . . . . . . . . . . . . . . . . . . .

traveling with directional and speed changes, stopping while demonstrating a resilient quality in their footwork, and controlling their centers of gravity over their feet and not falling over.

### MOTOR DEVELOPMENT PRINCIPLES AFFECTING QUALITY OF PERFORMANCE

Of Newell's (1986) three factors affecting motor development, the environment and clothing play central roles in how well this material can be taught and learned. For example, the size of the space in which the children are traveling will affect their responses, as will the type of surface on which they are traveling. Their shoes will also considerably affect their traveling. In fact, some shoes on certain floor surfaces (e.g., leather against wood, rubber against rubber) pose risks for potential injuries because of the resulting traction problems.

As with the manipulative skills discussed previously, developmental sequences have been hypothesized for running (Roberton & Halverson, 1984) (Table 4–6). These sequences can be particularly helpful for they allow you to see which aspects of the running pattern give children the most difficulty in different game-like situations.

Sliding is a sideways gallop. Children's early efforts display stiff knees with the arms often held in an "inefficient guard position" (Haywood, 1993, p. 95). In a more mature slide, the knees are relaxed and there is a springy quality to the movement. The arms are relaxed and ready to be used in the next task (Haywood, 1993).

TABLE 4–6

## Developmental Sequences for Running

### LEG ACTION COMPONENT

*Step 1*  The run is flat-footed with minimal flight. The swing leg is slightly abducted as it comes forward. When seen from overhead, the path of the swing leg curves out to the side during its movement forward. Foot eversion gives a toeing-out appearance to the swinging leg. The angle of the knee of the swing leg is greater than 90° during forward motion.

*Step 2*  The swing thigh moves forward with greater acceleration, causing 90° of maximal flexion in the knee. From the rear, the foot is no longer toed-out nor is the thigh abducted. The sideward swing of the thigh continues, however, causing the foot to cross the body midline when viewed from the rear. Flight time increases. After contact, which may still be flat-footed, the support knee flexes more as the child's weight rides over the foot.

*Step 3*  Foot contact is with the heel or the ball of the foot. The forward movement of the swing leg is primarily in the sagittal plane. Flexion of the thigh at the hip carries the knee higher at the end of the forward swing. The support leg moves from flexion to complete extension by takeoff.

### ARM ACTION COMPONENT

*Step 1*  The arms do not participate in the running action. They are sometimes held in high guard or, more frequently, middle guard position. In high guard, the hands are held about shoulder high. Sometimes they ride even higher if the laterally rotated arms are abducted at the shoulder and the elbows flexed. In middle guard, the lateral rotation decreases, allowing the hands to be held waist high. They remain motionless, except in reaction to shifts in equilibrium.

*Step 2*  Spinal rotation swings the arms bilaterally to counterbalance rotation of the pelvis and swing leg. The frequently oblique plane of motion plus continual balancing adjustments give a flailing appearance to the arm action.

*Step 3*  Spinal rotation continues to be the prime mover of the arms. Now the elbow of the arm swinging forward begins to flex, then extend during the backward swing. The combination of rotation and elbow flexion causes the arm rotating forward to cross the body midline and the arm rotating back to abduct, swinging obliquely outward from the body.

*Step 4*  The humerus (upper arm) begins to drive forward and back in the sagittal plane independent of spinal rotation. The movement is in opposition to the other arm and to the leg on the same side. Elbow flexion is maintained, oscillating about a 90° angle during the forward and backward arm swings.

*Note:* These sequences have not been validated. They were hypothesized by Roberton[69] from the work of Wickstrom[74] and Seefeldt, Reuschlein, and Vogel.[75]

Reprinted by permission from Roberton & Halverson, 1984.

## PROGRESSION

Taken together, these skills can be thought of as footwork specific for game contexts. Skilled games players can maneuver themselves quickly throughout a given area by means of running and sidestepping/sliding as they position and reposition themselves in relation to game objects, teammates, and opponents. It is easier for children to move with control slowly than quickly. This implies using speed as a key ingredient for progression. With this material, we suggest that you start with it altogether, that is, running and sidestepping/sliding with changes of direction and speed. Begin with an easy pace, then encourage children to increase speed while being sure they maintain body control.

If you see specific difficulties, such as children's arms beginning to come up, their knees becoming stiff, or their balance consistently being lost, then go back and design tasks focused on these skills as single skills. Locomotor skills are a major portion of the educational gymnastics and educational dance curriculums and, with careful teaching, can be adapted to the games environment.

### EXPERIENCES FOR REFLECTION

1. With a classmate, go to a playground where preschool-aged children are playing and observe the locomotor patterns of at least four different children. Include in your sample differences in race, gender, and physical and cognitive abilities. Focus on what the children's running, stopping, and changes of direction look like. With your classmate, describe what you see and identify the developmental levels observed. Reach consensus through discussion. What questions arise as a result of this experience?

2. Go to a high school or university soccer, basketball, or baseball game and observe the locomotor actions of the players. Compare their movement patterns with your knowledge of the development of running and sliding. Are you seeing any differences among these players? If so, why do you think you are seeing them? If not, why not? Do any of these players exhibit differences unique only to them? If so, what are they and why do you think this is occurring?

## *Rolling for Recovery (as a Single Skill and Combined with Catching)*

In many games, players sometimes lose their balance and fall as they "go for" an object that appears out of reach. In these instances, rolling becomes a safety skill to prevent injury. Below are some ideas for teaching children how to do this. The ideas for tasks are presented with the assumption that the children already know how to do a sideways safety roll from their gymnastics lessons and dance lessons. The roll is now being modified to fit a new situation.

### IDEAS FROM WHICH MOVEMENT TASKS ARE DESIGNED

Because there is a potential safety risk associated with the idea of rolling and recovery, actual tasks are presented in a suggested progression. We acknowledge that there may be other and better progressions, but this one has been used frequently and works well.

- Slowly, do a sideways safety roll across the mat (see Chapter 5, Teaching Educational Gymnastics, Core Content 1)

    repeat this task until it can be done smoothly from a standing position and from a walk (i.e., the combination skill of walking and rolling) increase the speed of the roll giving children the option to do this when they feel that they are ready to go faster

- Place a bean bag on the mat on a spot that, when you lower yourself to begin the roll, you can easily pick it up and complete the roll

    repeat this task until it can be done smoothly from a standing position and from a walk
    increase the speed of the roll giving children the option to do this when they feel that they are ready to go faster

- Toss a bean bag slightly out in front of you but in a spot that just pulls you off balance enough to force you to lower yourself and go into a sideways safety roll

    repeat this task until it can be done smoothly from a standing position and from a walk
        (i.e., the combination skill of walking, catching, and rolling)
    repeat this task but toss the bean bag slightly farther away from you each time
        (this will lead to a faster roll because the children have to extend farther)
    increase the speed of the entire task giving children the option to do this when
        they feel that they are ready to go faster

- Toss a bean bag out in front of you and high, causing you to have to jump up and out to catch it (i.e., the combination skill of jumping, catching, and rolling)

    adapt progression already given
    use a yarn ball, bean bag ball, or small, soft football
    strike the ball just before rolling instead of catching it

### BIOMECHANICAL PRINCIPLES AFFECTING QUALITY OF PERFORMANCE
See Chapter 5, Teaching Educational Gymnastics, Core Content 1.

### MOTOR DEVELOPMENT PRINCIPLES AFFECTING QUALITY OF PERFORMANCE
See Chapter 5, Teaching Educational Gymnastics, Core Content 1.

### PROGRESSION
The tasks are presented in a suggested sequence because this skill is fairly complicated and presents some risks. Basically the progression involves first reestablishing the basic pattern of the sideways safety roll from a stationary position. From then on, it is done from a moving position, at faster speeds, with a bean bag placed on the mat, and finally from catching a tossed bean bag or ball, first close to the body and then increasingly farther away. For those children able and ready, they can be challenged to make this sequence more game-like by using a soft football, striking a beach ball with the hand and striking a soft ball with a racquet. These last ideas require advanced manipulative skills.

### EXPERIENCES FOR REFLECTION
1. Discuss in class why this specific combination of skills might be or might not be important for children to experience. At the end of the discussion, state whether you would or would not include it in your program. Justify your answer.

2.  In small groups, using your knowledge from the developmental sequences of catching and forward rolling (see Chapter 5), discuss what steps you think children go through to become skillful with this combination of skills. Can you support your answer? Which steps do you think will give children the most difficulty? Why? Share your thoughts with another group.

*core content*

## Manipulative and Locomotor Skills as Combination Skills

### FOCUS OF CONTENT

Manipulative and locomotor skills combined—manipulative and manipulative; manipulative and locomotor; locomotor and locomotor explored by using selected aspects of:

> *time:* faster, slower
> *force:* varying amounts
> *space awareness:* direction, level

in relation to:

> *body parts:* hands, forearms, feet, etc.
> *objects:* balls, bean bags, deck tennis rings, etc.
> *implements:* rackets, bats, hockey sticks, etc.

### APPROPRIATENESS OF CONTENT

Tasks combining manipulative and locomotor skills, carefully selected for children's individual differences, could begin late in the second grade. They are a major part of lessons in grades 3 through 5, interacting continuously with the material in Core Content 4 and 5.

This material is more challenging than previous core content units because it combines skills under more complex situations. Locomotor skills are combined with other locomotor skills. Locomotor skills are combined with manipulative skills. Manipulative skills are combined with other manipulative skills. Instead of focusing on simply catching, for example, children will now try to run, catch, and then pass, letting all three skills flow together to become one skill.

**IDEAS FROM WHICH MOVEMENT TASKS ARE DESIGNED**

Combining locomotor and manipulative skills requires complex organizational patterns because children need more space and need to go faster to perform such combinations. Workable safe organizational patterns are included with the task ideas as they are presented.

Organizational Pattern:   random
keeping within a 6' X 6' area
children working alone
all children active or half on/half off

- Tossing balls/bean bags to move forward, backward, and to both sides within a 6' X 6' personal area to catch at shoulder height (Skills combined: running, sidestepping/sliding, throwing, catching)

    place ball farther and farther away (Skills combined: running, sidestepping/sliding, throwing, catching, extending)
    use right and left hands
    change the ball type
    use scoops or children's-sized gloves
    place ball so you have to jump to catch it

- Tapping a ball forward, backward, and to each side with a field/ice hockey stick within a 6' X 6' area (Skills combined: propelling, running, sidestepping/sliding)

    use larger or slower rolling ball
    use feet instead of stick
    use a hand dribble
    use smaller or bouncier ball

PHOTO 4–12
Tossing a ball to elicit a jump when catching.

PHOTO 4–13
Traveling through space tapping a ball in different directions with a hockey stick, keeping the ball close to the stick.

● ● ● ● ● ● ● ● ● ● ● ● ● ● ● ● ● ● ● ● ● ● ● ● ● ● ● ● ● ● ● ● ● ● ● ● ● ● ● ● ● ● ● ● ● ● ● ● ● ● ● ● ● ● ● ●

**Organizational Pattern:**   random
                                  using entire space
                                  children working alone
                                  all children active or half on/half off

- Traveling through the entire space by tapping a ball forward, backward, and to the sides with a field/ice hockey stick, keeping it close to the stick and away from everyone (Skills combined: propelling, running, sidestepping/sliding)

    stop on signal or with uncontrolled ball
    vary the speed of traveling
    accelerate, decelerate
    change type of ball
    use feet instead of a stick
    change to hand dribbling
    use right and left hands

- Traveling with the ball while moving continuously in a forward direction. Once children are able to safely get their "feet around" when trying to move into open spaces, the teacher can move throughout the space toward different children gently trying to tag each one's ball. As the teacher moves toward a child's ball, it becomes the child's task to maneuver the ball in such a way as to avoid the teacher's attempt to tag the ball. We call this being a "gentle nuisance." Children can often play this role and, when they do, it is a great opportunity to introduce some basic defensive concepts, for example, moving toward the player with the ball (Skills combined: propelling, running, sidestepping/sliding)

> change to a slower rolling ball if needed
> change to foot dribbling
> change to hand dribbling
> use right and left hands
> increase speed while traveling with the ball
> increase and decrease speed of the gentle nuisance

*Questions for the Children (Q4C).*   The manner in which these tasks are performed, especially those in the last group, presents a perfect chance to integrate cognitive learning with motor learning by discussing with the children what aspects of their skill development need improving. For example, they might be asked, "When I came toward you, what did you need to do to maintain control over the ball and still get around me?" Select together which aspects of their answers to work on.

**Organizational Pattern:**   random
> using entire space
> children in groups of two or three facing each other
> all children active or half on/half off

- Tossing bean bag balls to a receiver, with the goal of making the receiver move forward, backward and to the sides in order to catch. For safety reasons, encourage tossing so the receiver has to move backward after bringing the receiver forward (Skills combined: catching, throwing, running, sidestepping/sliding)

> toss object so receiver has to move faster
> toss object so receiver must give more
> toss object so receiver has to jump to catch it
> change type of ball
> change type of object being caught
> use implements to catch

- Rolling a ball to the receiver who has a field/ice hockey stick, with the goal of making the receiver move forward and to each side to collect the ball (Skills combined: collecting, throwing, running, sidestepping/sliding)

> roll ball so receiver has to move faster
> roll ball so receiver must give more
> change type of ball
> change to collecting with feet
> use implements to collect a rolling ball

**Organizational Pattern:**   traditional wave including the cross diagonal
> alone and in groups of two or three

- Tossing the ball to self with one hand to be caught in front at shoulder height with the other hand or both hands together, using easy running straight across the space, so that running stride is not broken (Skills combined: throwing, catching, running, coming to a controlled stop)

  > vary the speed of running
  > accelerate, decelerate
  > place toss farther ahead
  > place toss slightly out to both sides
  > use right and left hands for tossing and catching
  > change type of ball
  > use different objects
  > use implements for catching

- Beginning side-by-side running forward in twos or threes, tossing a bean bag ball back and forth so each player must catch it in front with either hand or both hands, shoulder height, without breaking stride (Skills combined: throwing, catching, running, jumping, coming to a controlled stop). You are also introducing a basic offensive strategy used in invasion games—making a lead pass

  > place toss slightly ahead of receiver
  > place toss above receiver's head to elicit a jump and catch
  > change object
  > use implements for catching
  > change to passing using feet
  > change to passing using field/ice hockey sticks
  > note how many completed tosses/catches you can do

  *Q4C:* Collecting with a field hockey stick requires you to present the flat side of the stick to the ball prior to collecting it. How will you do this?

**Organizational Pattern:** random
> using entire space
> children in groups of two or three facing each other
> all children active or half on/half off

- Striking a light 8" plastic ball back and forth to each other using the palm or heel of the hand, so that partner has to move forward, backward, and to both sides to receive, letting it bounce once before striking it back (Skills combined: striking, running, sidestepping/sliding, starting and stopping)

  > use hand on side to which the ball is coming
  > use a backhand pattern
  > change the height of the ball by striking it upward
  > work against a wall or to a partner who catches
  > strike with rackets of varying handle lengths
  > change ball size, weight, and bounce

- Tossing a bean bag or bean bag ball in front so it drops short, requiring partner to reach forward and go into a roll and recover onto feet

use mats as needed

toss to both sides

toss object so partner has to jump up forward or sideward before landing

**BIOMECHANICAL PRINCIPLES AFFECTING QUALITY OF PERFORMANCE**

The biomechanical principles identified in Core Content 1, Manipulative Skills as Single Skills, apply for these tasks as well. For example, in teaching a task that combines running, passing, and receiving a ball using a field hockey stick, the principles affecting quality of performance outlined for catching and collecting, and for throwing and striking are applicable. Critical features of the movement taught in tasks designed from the material in this unit and reflective of these biomechanical principles are presented in the following section.

CATCHING AND COLLECTING

1. Position body and hand(s), feet, hockey stick, or scoop behind oncoming ball whenever possible.
2. Reach toward object with hand(s), feet, hockey stick, or scoop.
3. Watch that object, just prior to being touched, is positioned in a spot in relation to the body, feet, hockey stick, or scoop so it can be easily caught or collected, not too close nor too far away from the body.
4. As contact is made with object, give with initial contact.
5. Reposition after catching and collecting so that the ball can be released fairly quickly.
6. Of the implements used, the field hockey stick is the most challenging since only one side of the stick can be used. This requires quick footwork to position the body and stick toward the oncoming object. A slower rolling object is often helpful.

PROPELLING

1. Keep weight over feet with quick footwork.
2. Use just the right amount of force to keep continuously tapping the object.
3. Tap in the direction the object is going. Tap through the center of the object. Keep follow through short.

THROWING

1. Encourage a preparation that allows the right amount of force to be applied as the range of motion needed will vary from situation to situation.
2. Release through the center of the object in the intended direction. Hand follows through in the same direction.

STRIKING

1. Encourage a preparation that allows the right amount of force to be applied as the range of motion needed will vary from situation to situation.
2. Contact through the center of the object in the intended direction. Hand/racket follows through in the same direction.
3. Position body so racket can contact the ball out in front and to the right and left of the body in a natural swinging motion. Usually the body faces sideways to the oncoming ball.

## MOTOR DEVELOPMENT PRINCIPLES AFFECTING QUALITY OF PERFORMANCE

As pointed out in Core Content 1, how a ball is tossed and the type of equipment used continuously affect children's efforts at performing motor tasks. Their shoes and the surface will also have an effect on their performance.

In observing children trying to catch balls tossed ahead of them without success, you will have to decide the causes of their unsuccessful catches and then redesign tasks based on that information. Is the ball being tossed too far ahead? Is the ball or implement the wrong size or weight? Is the space so limited that the child cannot accelerate? At this point, you are using knowledge from biomechanics and motor development together as integrated knowledge. It might help if you think of it in this way—developmental and biomechanical principles assist you in interpreting the levels at which children are performing, while Newell's constraint theory helps you in interpreting why they might be performing at these levels.

## PROGRESSION

The easiest tasks are those that use less space and are performed alone. As you change tasks so that children have to use more space and speed and then begin to work with one another, the tasks become more difficult. Tasks involving throwing and catching are easier than tasks involving propelling and striking. Hands are easier to catch with than a scoop. Propelling tasks with feet and hands are easier than ones with a hockey stick. In collecting tasks, using the feet is easier than using a hockey stick. Catching off balance and rolling are difficult and have some inherent risks in doing them. Rolling to recover is easier from a standing position than jumping forward and being clearly off balance.

All tasks become more difficult when you increase the distance between children when they are working in groups or when tasks require them to change their directions or handle balls in the space above their heads. Adding speed to these tasks also increases the difficulty.

## EXPERIENCES FOR REFLECTION

1. In small groups in your class, discuss which of the biomechanical principles you think are the most critical to effective performance of the material in this unit. Why do you say this? Share your answers with the class.

2. Videotape a group of children performing tasks designed from the material presented in this unit. Be sure to have represented in your group different genders, races, and levels of motor ability. View the tape and answer together, "How does understanding the development of catching and collecting skills and throwing and striking skills help you to observe and to assess progress in children's ability to perform these tasks?" Summarize differences and similarities across children.

3. Using the same tape, select critical features identified under the biomechanical principles section as criteria for assessment. Reflect on these two questions: "To what degree do these children meet the criteria?" and "For those children demonstrating some difficulty, how might I help them?"

4. Observe a middle school game of basketball, tennis, volleyball, soccer, or touch football. Try to find all those children who are able to demonstrate a mature level of performance of the biomechanical principles outlined in this chapter. Keep a record of your observations. When you have completed this task, summarize your observations and reflect on them. What do they mean to you? If possible, compare games of single and mixed genders. Does anything change?

## Basic Strategies/Tactics

### FOCUS OF CONTENT

Basic strategies/tactics for wall/net games, striking/fielding games, invasion games, and tag games as they relate to rules, boundaries, and equipment:

| | |
|---|---|
| **Wall/net games:** | sending a ball to an open space, away from opponent |
| | covering angles/spaces |
| **Striking/fielding games:** | throwing a ball in relation to a runner |
| | running in relation to the position of the ball |
| | backing up |
| **Invasion games:** | passing a ball to a space, leading a teammate |
| | cutting to a space, asking for a pass |
| | marking a designated player |

It is difficult to write about this content separately from the material in Core Content 1, 2, and especially 3 because they are so interrelated. It is important to recognize this interrelatedness when you teach. For example, you might begin a lesson with a small-sided game focusing on a particular strategy/tactic. Then, if it is needed, you might leave the game temporarily and work on some combination skills, or even a single skill, that appears to be too immature for effective use in the game.

Teaching games in schools has traditionally emphasized the teaching of individual skills in artificial organizational drill patterns without careful consideration for the contextual nature of the games themselves (Bunker & Thorpe, 1986). When you consider the effect that the contextual nature of games has on how skills are actually performed in the game, there is direction for how games skills are taught. John Lawther (1951) in his book, *The Psychology of Coaching,* spoke of this idea as giving "meaning" to the skill "in the sport" (p. 122). In describing throwing in baseball, he pointed out, "Each throw has a specific nature in terms of the game situation" (p. 122). He further elaborated this idea by saying, "Throwing taught as an act divorced from the game has extremely vague meaning in terms of sports use" (p.122).

When considering the context in which a game is played, a different notion of the relationship between game strategies/tactics and skills emerges. Lessons would be centered around the playing of small-sided games that focus on specific strategies/tactics. Practice of skills would grow out of demonstrated needs identified by the children and guided by their teachers (Griffin, Mitchell, & Oslin, 1997; Thorpe, Bunker, & Almond, 1986; Turner & Martinek, 1995). Ideas for implementing this approach appear regularly in our literature under labels such as Games for Understanding, Teaching for Understanding, Games Centered Approach, or Tactical Games Approach.

### APPROPRIATENESS OF CONTENT

The material in this unit can be used with different levels of sophistication beginning with the 3rd grade. It is emphasized in 4th and 5th grades.

**IDEAS FROM WHICH MOVEMENT TASKS ARE DESIGNED**

A different format is used to present the material in this unit as strategies/tactics are the focus rather than movement skills. For the strategies/tactics identified, ideas for game-like tasks and games are described. Suggestions are given for how the game-like tasks and games can be taught and modified to be more or less complex and, where appropriate, how they relate to Core Content 1–3. Most of the games included here are considered conventional games. A more thorough discussion of original games is included as part of Core Content 5, Game Forms.

Game-like tasks are being suggested as the primary means to introduce children to a particular strategy or tactic. A game-like task becomes a game once it is put into the structure of certain rules and boundaries. In teaching both game-like tasks and games, the focus is clearly on the interplay between strategies/tactics and the necessary combination motor skills.

## Wall/Net Games

Examples of familiar adult games in this category include badminton, tennis, volleyball, squash, and racket ball.

### Game-Like Task

| | |
|---|---|
| Strategies/Tactics: | Sending ball to an open space, away from opponent |
| | Covering angles/spaces |
| Equipment: | Short handled, light weight racket |
| | Medium weight ball that bounces |
| | Net or rope held taunt 3' to 4' high |
| | Rectangular playing area approximately 10' X 20' (or smaller) |
| Task: | Two children, using an underarm pattern, striking the ball with a racket back and forth trying to make the ball land in spaces forward of each other as well as to the sides and behind. |
| Possible Modifications: | Increase group size to two per side |
| | Change size, weight, texture of object being struck |
| | Change height of net |
| | Use palms or hands instead of racket |
| | Increase/decrease the space available |
| | Shift striking to a wall space |
| | Change the manipulative activities to throwing and catching |
| | Without the net, shift to passing and receiving using feet and a soccer ball or a field/ice hockey stick and ball |
| Discussion: | Before this task is tried, let the children rally back and forth to get a feel for the situation. If the skill combinations seriously break down, leave the game-like task and design a task(s) that focuses on the combination skills giving them the most difficulty. Otherwise, keep focusing on the basic |

| | strategies/tactics by asking the children questions that encourage them to think through the situation, and have them "try it again." |
|---|---|
| Q4C: | Where are the empty spaces?  How might you strike the ball so it lands in those spaces? |
| | How might you first move your partner forward, then backward, to either the right or left sides? |
| | After you have struck the ball, where do you think the best place would be to position yourself as you get ready to respond to your partner's hit? How might you tell where your partner's ball will come to you? |
| | If a ball comes to your right side (child is left-handed), what is the best way to position yourself to return it?  How will you make it go in different directions so it forces your partner to move? |
| Game Alert: | This task can be shifted easily to the status of an original game either by making one up yourself or guiding the children to do so.  For example, you could design a cooperative game by counting how many successive hits over the net are completed, each one clearly making the partner move to get the ball. From here, you could introduce the concept of placing the ball so your partner cannot get to it, all the time helping the children see the role that boundaries play in relation to where the opponent is.  Rules to be decided by you or with the children might include who starts the game and how scoring might be kept. |
| | If you change the manipulative skills and implements used, the previous comments still apply. The game-like tasks and games, especially those using a field/ice hockey stick or lacrosse stick, are more challenging as their single and combination skills are more complex. In working with these tasks and games, it is likely that you will have to return to and refine a number of combination skills and quite possibly some single skills. |

## Game: 2 versus 2 Modified Deck Tennis*

| Strategies/Tactics: | Sending ball to an open space, away from opponent |
|---|---|
| | Covering angles/spaces |
| Equipment: | One rubber ring for four children |
| | Standards and nets or ropes used as nets |

*Adapted from "Quiot, or Deck Tennis" (Lenel, 1969, pp. 111–112, 115).

| | |
|---|---|
| Goal of Game: | Players 1 and 2 play against players 3 and 4. Player 1 starts serving followed by 2, 3, and 4 in turn. The server continues serving from alternate sides until a point is lost (ring touches ground). Each player starts serving from behind a designated line. |
| Area: | Neutral ground either side of net<br>Boundary lines<br>Playing area approximately 10' X 20' |
| Initial Rules: | Ring must travel horizontally from below without wobbling<br>Ring must be thrown with the same hand used to catch it<br>Ring may be caught with either hand, but may not touch body<br>Only the serving side scores if opponent does not catch the ring, uses two hands or the body, or ring falls outside boundaries |
| Rules Still to Be Decided: | Who starts the game<br>The order for serving<br>Who plays the ring if it is coming between two teammates<br>Number of points that make up a game<br>What happens if the ring touches the net<br>What happens if the ring drops on a boundary line in neutral territory |
| Rules That Might Need Modification as Play Progresses: | Scoring (e.g., score a point every time either side catches ring)<br>Boundaries |
| Discussion: | Have children begin playing this game cooperatively, seeing how many consecutive catches they can do before shifting to 2 versus 2. Let them get a feel for the ring, net, and playing area. Gradually introduce initial rules. Once the children are playing the game as originally planned, decide together any additional rules as the groups show a readiness for them. |
| Q4C: | How do you draw your opponent out of position?<br>If your partner is drawn toward the middle of the net, where should you position yourself to anticipate the return?<br>How can you direct the ring so it does not go too far? too short? too wide?<br>Where are the best places to serve the ring?<br>Do you need to change your boundaries? |

If the children cannot handle the strategies/tactics because they are having difficulty passing and catching the ring, then change the ring to an object they can catch, then continue. The content with which you are working is strategies/tactics. It is this content that you want the children to understand and demonstrate. Keep modifying aspects of the game until the children can focus on and handle the strategies/tactics.

If the skill combinations inherent in this game break down, then consider leaving the game for the moment and designing tasks to focus specifically on the combination skills in question (Core Content 3). Then go back to the game. When skills break down in game play, it can be very frustrating and can often lead to teachers giving up because they thought, "Well, that game certainly didn't work!"

As children gain skill in playing this game, other changes that might be tried include four children per side, having a larger playing area, and striking a ball (e.g., a beach ball) instead of throwing a ring. As modifications are applied, remember to keep the children focused on the strategies/tactics and what changes they might have to make in their skills to accommodate them.

Q4C:     When striking a beach ball, what will you have to do to direct the ball into a space?

Do we need to change any of the rules used with the ring, now that we are striking a beach ball?

## *Striking/Fielding Games*

Examples of familiar adult games in this category include baseball, softball, and cricket.

### *Game-Like Task*

| | |
|---|---|
| Strategies/Tactics: | Throwing a ball in relation to a runner |
| | Running in relation to the position of the ball |
| | Backing up |
| Equipment: | 6"–8" medium weight, firm texture ball |
| Task: | Players 1, 2, and 3 on the outside 10'–15' apart, player 4 in the inside standing in front of one outside player. Players 1, 2, and 3 pass the ball among themselves, trying to get it to the player closest to player 4. Player 4 moves away from the ball forcing players 1, 2, and 3 to pass quickly in different directions. |
| Possible Modifications: | Increase number on the inside or outside by one |
| | Change the ball |
| | Change the size of the inside space |
| | Limit the throwing pattern used |
| Discussion: | While the task structure is not in the traditional striking/fielding organization (batters and fielders), it clearly helps children focus on the key strategies/tactics of throwing a ball in relation to a runner, running in relation to where the ball is being thrown, and the idea of backing up. When modified to include more players inside and outside, the task becomes more difficult cognitively, as the children have to make decisions toward which runner they want to throw the ball. |

| Q4C: | If you cannot throw the ball the full distance across the playing area, what else could you do so our playing does not slow down? |
| | If a ball gets outside the playing area, how can you get it back quickly? |
| Game Alert: | This task structure is easily adapted to game status. As children work with the task, rules could be made, for example, related to changing runners, types of passes, scoring, and boundaries. Once the children can use the strategies/tactics central to this task, the challenge of touching or tagging the runner with the ball below the waist (ball remains firmly in the hands) could be added. This addition sets off a new round of discussions as the rules used in earlier versions may need to be revised. It also stresses more thinking on the part of the runner which affects how the throwers have to react. |
| Q4C: | If runners decide to stand in the space between the outside players, how might the outside players move to be in a better position to tag them? |
| Game Alert: | The addition of tagging the runner demonstrates dramatically to the children how different rules can affect the structure of a game. This moment would be a good time to discuss some of the changes that are being proposed or that have been made recently in particular sports (e.g., size of the women's basketball, composition of tennis balls for grass courts, three-point basket line). |

## Game: 3 versus 3 Throwing Base Ball*

| Strategies/Tactics: | Throwing a ball in relation to a runner |
| | Running in relation to the position of the ball |
| | Backing up |
| Equipment: | One 6" ball, three bases, a home plate, and a pitcher's line |
| Goal of Game: | The "batter" throws/rolls the ball into the field within the triangle set up by the bases (Figure 4–3). Player runs outside the bases in turn and may stop at each one. A point is scored when the player reaches home plate. The fielders field the ball and throw it to the pitcher who must touch the pitcher's line and call "Stop!" Any batter running between the bases at this moment is out. Base runners may start running as soon as the ball has left the hands of the |

*Adapted from "5-A-Side Kicking or Throwing Rounders" (Lenel, 1969, pp. 124–125, 129).

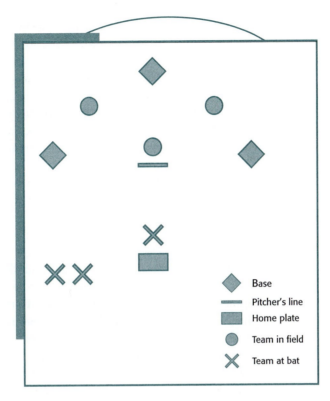

FIGURE 4–3
Field of play for throwing base ball.

| | |
|---|---|
| ◆ | Base |
| — | Pitcher's line |
| ▬ | Home plate |
| ● | Team in field |
| ✕ | Team at bat |

| | batter currently at bat. There may be no more than two batters at a base at one time. |
|---|---|
| Initial Rules: | The ball must not be thrown/rolled outside the triangle |
| | Batters run outside the bases |
| Rules Still to Be Decided: | Length of innings |
| | Fielders positioning at the start of the game |
| | Need for a captain |
| | Whether the batter can continue if fielder catches a fly ball |
| | What happens if the batter runs inside a base |
| Rules That Might Need Modification as Play Progresses: | Scoring (e.g., should passing a base be counted as a score?) |
| | Dimensions of the playing area |
| | Throwing the ball to a base rather than to the pitcher's line for an out |
| Discussion: | This game focuses primarily on running in relation to ball position and backing up. If you changed how an out can be made by throwing the ball to a base, throwing in relation to |

a runner becomes important. As before, let the children get the feel of the game before you start guiding them toward making additional rules or changing the game. Depending on how successful they are in playing this game, they may find that three per side is too few. If this occurs, see if they can work out what number they need but still keep the game active and use the same strategies/tactics. Discussing this aspect will often result in the children having to reexamine some of the other rules as well.

| | |
|---|---|
| Q4C: | When should the runners on the base begin to run? |
| | Where should the batter throw or roll the ball to gain an advantage? |
| | Where should the fielders stand just before the batter throws or rolls the ball? |
| Game Alert: | Remember that you are teaching strategies/tactics and need to tailor your guidance to meet this objective. As with the games previously presented, changes could be made with how the children start the game. For example, they could kick the ball keeping it close to the ground or even strike it from their hand. This could evolve into using a short handled racket or small bat. If the ball is to be changed, think through the rules governing how to put it in play. You do not want the ball to be too difficult for the fielders to handle. |

## Invasion Games

Examples of familiar adult games in this category include basketball, team handball, ultimate Frisbee soccer, football, field/ice hockey, and lacrosse.

## Game-Like Task

| | |
|---|---|
| Strategies/Tactics: | Passing a ball to a space, leading a teammate |
| | Cutting to a space, asking for a pass |
| Equipment: | Ball of appropriate size, weight, texture |
| Task: | Three children, continuously traveling throughout the space, passing the ball to each other, so that the receiver must catch the ball ahead of his path. |
| Possible Modifications: | Increase group size to four or five |
| | Change size, weight, texture of object |
| | Increase/decrease the space available |
| | Change to using feet, field/ice hockey stick |
| Discussion: | Before this task is presented, let the children try it without focusing on passing ahead or cutting into a space. |
| | Emphasize throwing the ball so the receiver can catch it. |

PHOTO 4–14
One way to modify a game-like task is to increase the group size (from 2 versus 2 to 3 versus 3).

This will give you an idea of how familiar they are with basic skill combinations (e.g., running and changing directions, accelerating and decelerating, throwing and catching).

When you begin to focus on where to pass and cut, if skill combinations seriously break down, design a task that focuses on those particular skills (Core Content 3).

Otherwise, keep focusing on the basic strategies/tactics by asking the children questions that encourage them to think through the situation "and try again."

Q4C: As the receiver, where do you have to cut to receive a pass that leads you?

How might you ask for the pass to help the passer?

As the passer, where do you want your receiver to cut?

Where are you trying to pass the ball?

Game Alert: This task can easily be shifted to the status of a competitive game by adding a defender and playing 2 versus 1 Keep Away as described in the next section. Further, you could make up a cooperative game in which the object became the number of successive passes with no pass backs (passing the ball back to the last thrower) before the ball touches the floor. With input from the children, both of these ideas could be developed into challenging and interesting games using passing ahead and cutting into a space as basic strategies/tactics.

## Game: 2 versus 1 Keep Away

| | |
|---|---|
| Strategies/Tactics: | Passing a ball to a space, leading a teammate |
| | Cutting to a space, asking for a pass |
| | Marking a designated player |
| Equipment: | Ball of appropriate weight and size |
| Goal of Game: | Two children are passing the ball between them while a third is trying to intercept it. |
| Area: | Approximately 10' X 10' |

PHOTO 4–15
2 versus 1 game of keep away.

PHOTO 4–16

| | |
|---|---|
| Initial Rule: | No contact |
| Rules Still to Be Decided: | Whether player with the ball can run with it |
| | How players change over |
| | Scoring if desired |
| | Penalty for breaking the no contact rule |
| | What happens when the ball is intercepted |
| Rules That Might Need Modification as Play Progresses: | Scoring if desired |
| | Boundaries |
| | Rules governing player with the ball |
| Discussion: | The first decision to be made is how will you handle those rules still to be decided. Will you take the responsibility for integrating them into the games or will you involve the children in making these decisions? Bringing the children into this process is what we encourage as it helps them learn about games, for example, the relationship between scoring possibilities and boundaries and how to balance opportuni- |

ties for both offense and defense so the game does not get too one-sided. No matter which direction you take, begin by continuously scanning all the games going on during the lesson. Base your next move on these observations. Observe long enough to give the children a fair chance to get a feel for the game. Of course, you must interrupt for safety reasons if needed. If you decide you want to help the children to improve the game directly, you could bring them all in, identify one key point that you want them to work on, and invite them to return to their games and try it. If you decide you want to involve the children's perspective in the improvement of their games, you could ask each group to sit down and reflect on this comment: "Many of you seem to be holding the ball so long when passing it that the receiver does not know where to go. What could the passer and the receiver do to help change this situation? Talk together about this for a moment, decide what you want to try, and then have a go at it."

## Game 2: 3 versus 2 Alamance End Ball

| | |
|---|---|
| Strategies/Tactics: | Passing a ball to a space, leading a teammate |
| | Cutting to a space, asking for a pass |
| | Marking a designated player |
| Equipment: | Ball of appropriate weight and size for children |
| Goal of Game: | Three children are passing the ball between them while two others are trying to intercept it before it is caught in the end zone. |
| Initial Rules: | Play starts with one offensive player behind restraining line with the ball, other four in the field |
| | Play ends when offense successfully catches ball in their end zone at the other end of the field |
| | Player with the ball may not travel |
| | No contact between players |
| | Only offensive team allowed in end zone |
| | Whenever ball is intercepted or goes out of bounds, play starts over behind the restraining line |
| Rules Still to Be Decided: | How to change from defense to offense |
| | When to change from defense to offense |
| | Scoring if desired |
| Rules That Might Need Modification as Play Progresses: | Boundaries |
| | Other ways to restart play when ball is intercepted or goes out of bounds |

| Discussion: | Much the same process can be followed as was described for the previous game-like task. This game, however, is more complicated because you now have a total of five players, three offense and two defense, along with challenging boundaries. We encourage you, whether you choose to involve the children or not, to try to work individually with each game going on in your class. Individual differences become increasingly dramatic when children play a game of this nature. Be reminded that the purpose of the game is to learn and be able to use selected basic strategies/tactics. If these strategies/tactics are not being used, you will have to figure out why this is occurring. One technique used successfully to help children help themselves is to videotape their games and then lead an observation/discussion session with them before they try to improve their games. |
|---|---|

## *Tag Games*

Tag games are invasion games, made simpler by the fact that neither objects or implements are usually involved. They can be particularly helpful as part of a games lesson, because they require the agile footwork so much a part of most games. Equally important, however, tag games offer a good opportunity to introduce the idea of basic strategies/tactics with a child-centered orientation. Bandhauer and Rovegno (1992) developed a tag unit and it is included at the end of the chapter. (For the follow-up on this unit see Rovegno & Bandhauer, 1998.)

### BIOMECHANICAL PRINCIPLES AFFECTING QUALITY OF PERFORMANCE

When guiding children into game-like tasks and game play, we encourage you to emphasize the decisions they need to make so the strategies/tactics work for them. Biomechanical principles do not apply here. They do apply, however, when the emphasis is on the effectiveness of the skills used to implement these strategies/tactics. The same principles apply as presented in Core Content 1, 2, and 3. These principles include concepts related to the production and reduction of force and the use of center of gravity. What should be stressed here is that maximum force will rarely, if ever, be required in either the game-like tasks or the games themselves. The stress is on the effectiveness of the movement pattern in the given situation, and this requires players to use the right amount of force, not maximum force, applied in the optimal direction.

### MOTOR DEVELOPMENT PRINCIPLES AFFECTING QUALITY OF PERFORMANCE

Because the context for both game-like tasks and actual games is dynamic and complex, Newell's (1986) three-factor constraint theory needs to be kept in mind at all times when observing game play. It helps you to interpret why the children are or are not being successful. Whenever you or the children decide to make a change in a game-like task or game, this decision will have a pronounced effect on the children's performance. That is why it is so important that you can observe what occurs when any change is made.

## PROGRESSION

As before, progression is based on your observations and your interpretations of the observations. Game-like tasks are generally less complex than actual games, because they are not always bound by rules. With these tasks and games, the change of the object or implement can make them easier or more difficult depending upon the rules and conditions of the task or game in question. To give children optimal opportunity to learn strategies/tactics, it is critical that children get a chance to participate on a continuous basis. Between one and five per side in cooperative games and between one and four per side in competitive games are good guidelines to follow. Games that use implements such as field/ice hockey and lacrosse sticks are quite challenging, but when scaled to fit the children can be used with upper grades quite well.

In terms of the strategies/tactics, those associated with wall/net games appear the easiest, followed by striking/fielding games, and then invasion games. In terms of the nature of the game, we support the use of both cooperative and competitive experiences, as long as they are conducted in relation to the developmental levels of the children.

It is important to design your games curriculum to include learning experiences in all game categories, so that all the basic strategies/tactics identified can be learned. While they are being introduced and initially developed in the elementary school, especially in the 4th and 5th grades, it is expected that the learning of these strategies/tactics will continue throughout middle and high school.

## EXPERIENCES FOR REFLECTION

1. Interview experienced coaches from different sports and ask them to tell you all the changes that have occurred in the sports they coach since they began coaching. Discuss with them the reasons for these changes and what effects they had on their coaching and their players. Compare your notes with some of the modifications recommended and discussed in this chapter. What are the most important ideas that you have gained from these interviews in relation to your understanding game structure, and how might it influence your games teaching program?

2. Ask permission to observe on an elementary school playground during a recess period. Find a group of children who are playing a game and observe them over a 10–15 minute time period. Identify the strategies/tactics that are needed to make their game work. Describe how the children use them in the game. If the children are handling the strategies/tactics well, how are they able to do this? If not, why are they having difficulty? If this game were going on in your class, what might you do next and why? If you have time, compare two or three groups of children representing different ages and genders. Keep the following story in mind as you observe the children's game play.

When reflecting on content progression across all the grade levels of my program, I have always felt that the transition between 2nd grade content units and 3rd grade content units was the biggest jump; bigger than the transition between any other two grade levels. The complexity of movement skills needed for participation is greater and the cognitive requirements of increasingly complex movement environments demand much more from 3rd graders, it seems, than the other year-to-year content transitions between grade levels. This idea was reinforced in the third grade games unit that I just finished teaching.

I was working on a unit that dealt with beginning offensive and defensive strategies in soccer. At a very simple level, we were trying to deal with marking the player with the ball and taking action to evade a defender. I thought the class was really grasping the concepts of offensive and defensive strategies as I observed them playing their small-sided soccer games and I was feeling pretty good about successfully making one of those big 2nd grade–3rd grade content leaps. That is until Benita came running up to me with tears streaming down her cheeks. "Mrs. Waddail. Mrs. Waddail. Cheryle's trying to steal the ball from me. I have the ball and she is trying to take it away. Make her stop. Make her stop, please." Benita's concept of how offensive strategy worked was that she was suppose to dribble the ball down the field, take an unencumbered shot on goal, and have no one try to steal the ball away from her. Come to think of it, I guess that would be a pretty good offensive strategy!

3. Select the sport that you play the best. Change one of its basic rules (e.g., offsides to no offsides), boundaries (e.g., small area to larger area), or equipment (e.g., high net to lower net). How will this change affect the playing of the sport? Do you think you would like the change?

# *core content*

## Game Forms

### FOCUS OF CONTENT

Two game forms: conventional and original

In one sense, game forms are not content, rather they are a vehicle through which much of the content in core units 1–5 can be taught. Conventional games are those games that are already made up and original games are those you and the children make up yourselves. Both types of games, after initially played, usually require some modification if they are to meet the needs of all children. We encourage the modification process to be child-centered so they can learn through their own participation what modifications are needed and why. This way the children have a greater opportunity to discover for themselves how rules, equipment, and boundaries affect the nature and structure of games. It also helps them see what skills they might need to work on and for what purposes if they are to successfully play the game.

Try to envision a game, conventional or original, as a vehicle through which both the movement skills and strategies/tactics are given meaning. Or think of a game as a crossroads or intersection where movement skills and strategies/tactics meet, interact, and become one. Games are like dances in dance lessons and movement sequences in gymnastic lessons. They bring together and unify movement skills performed in a specific context that gives them unique structure and meaning. When children's movement skills are effective in the context of a game and when children's use of strategies/tactics are effective in the context of their movement skills, this is the moment that movement skills and strategies/tactics are interrelated, playing off one another. It is also the moment that playing a game can be great fun.

### APPROPRIATENESS OF CONTENT

The material and ideas presented and discussed are most suited for children in 2nd through 5th grades always keeping in mind three requirements:

1. The game is designed as an integral part of the lesson.
2. The game is selected to help meet your lesson objectives, in particular those related to strategies/tactics.
3. The game meets the criteria designed to assess its educational value (see Core Content 6).

**IDEAS FROM WHICH MOVEMENT TASKS ARE DESIGNED**

A different format will be used to present this core content as in Core Content 4, Basic Strategies/Tactics. New ideas related to game forms are introduced and others revisited. Biomechanical principles and motor development principles will not be addressed as they have already been discussed in the previous units of work.

## Conventional Games

Core Content 4 includes a number of conventional games specifically selected to support the learning of basic strategies/tactics common to three categories of games—wall/net, striking/fielding, and invasion. Taken together, these games and their basic strategies/tactics form an introduction to games playing and to game structure designed especially for young children participating in school physical education programs. The games included in Core Content Unit 4, along with game-like tasks and original games, are more than enough for a well-rounded program that gives equal time to educational gymnastics and educational dance.

With each year of experience as a licensed professional, you will find additional conventional games that meet your objectives through contact with other specialists, as well as personal reading and continuing professional development experiences such as workshops, mini-courses, conventions, and graduate work. Many professional textbooks are excellent resources as they often have rich sections devoted to conventional games. When seeking and finding new games to integrate into your program, take care in selecting them so that they meet the three criteria listed under the section, Appropriateness of Content.

As a summary statement regarding conventional games, the following story about a student teaching experience centered around "Snowball," a conventional game (Nichols, 1994, p. 491), is presented. It is shared here because it highlights a number of issues regarding the use and misuse of conventional games.

Mr. Ross, the university supervisor, arrived halfway through the third-period class. When he walked into the gym, he was greeted with shouts and yells from twenty-five 4th-grade children all throwing yarn balls seemingly wherever they wanted—behind and under the bleachers, against the back walls, and along the floor. Some children were simply holding on to them. It looked as though there were two equal teams, one on each side of a center line. Children were retrieving the yarn balls by sliding and running while others were standing along the sides just watching. The noise was such that Mr. Ross could hardly be heard when he greeted Mr. Kimbol, the cooperating teacher. Mr. Paulin, the intern teacher, was standing on one side of the gym, at the center line with his back against the bleachers. He was energetically encouraging the children to use overarm throws when they threw the yarn balls and shouting, "Throw quicker, you're taking too long. And don't forget to use opposition when you throw."

The game continued until five minutes were left in the lesson, at which time Mr. Paulin asked the children to leave the yarn balls on the floor and come sit down in the center of the gym. They came to the center, some running and sliding, some walking and kicking the yarn balls and others walking quietly, not touching anyone. Mr. Paulin commented, "You played that game very well. Did you like it?" Many of the children shouted "Yes!" Others could be heard saying, "I liked it because I hit Chris and Jean." Others did not respond or were unable to be heard.

Time permitted a follow-up conference with both the intern and his cooperating teacher. Mr. Ross was obviously quite upset with what he had just observed and asked Mr. Paulin immediately, and somewhat aggressively, "Why are you playing this game?" He answered quickly by saying, "You gave us this game in our games class." Mr. Ross, taken aback, realizing the truth in that statement, but unable to hide his frustration from spilling over after what he had just seen, said, "Yes, you're right, I did. But I gave it to you as an example of a conventional game NOT to be used in its originally presented form. We did play it just like the way you did in your lesson, but then went on to identify and try out changes that could be made so children had to use the basic strategy of the game to be successful. We used the game to learn principles of game modification based on strategy. It was not a game that you were to use as initially presented in class." The intern just looked at Mr. Ross and was silent.

Gathering his wits and some composure because he was acutely aware of the defensive position in which he had just placed Mr. Paulin, Mr. Ross said, "All right, if you really want to play this game, of course you can. But some major changes must be made, because the way it is being played is both uneducational and unsafe. What changes do you think should be made?" Mr. Ross waited a reasonable length of time, but the intern still remained silent. "I know what we'll do," said Mr. Ross. "Let me give you several rules within which you must work and let's see what happens. What do you think?" "O.K." was the reply.

"Here are the rules. You may not let the children run or slide at any time, and you must only coach them to throw the yarn ball into empty spaces. You may not coach the skill of throwing in any way. If you stray from these rules, either Mr. Kimbol or I will slip up behind you and remind you of them. Fair enough?" Mr. Paulin agreed, beginning to show some interest along with a certain degree of hesitancy. "I can't coach the skill, only where the yarn ball is to land?" "That's right," said Mr. Ross.

The next class came in and when it became time to play Snowball, Mr. Paulin split the class into two equal teams, explained the game, and got them into play. Noise erupted, and yarn balls went all over the gym as before. The children began to run and slide. Mr. Paulin stopped the game and made it very clear that there was to be no running and sliding, as he had told them earlier in the lesson. He asked the children why he was making this rule and they said that it was for their safety. He also told them, "When you are throwing the yarn ball, be sure to use opposition. Does everyone know what that means?" A loud chorus of "Yes" was heard. Where upon, Mr. Kimbol quickly slipped up behind Mr. Paulin and said, "Remember, you can only coach the strategy, not the skill. You can only point out where the yarn ball is thrown, not the technique!" He held the children for a moment longer and added, "I also want you to look for empty spaces and then throw the yarn ball into them." With this addition, Mr. Paulin let play resume.

As the game proceeded, running and sliding gradually disappeared, but Mr. Paulin could see that something was still wrong with the game. He motioned Mr. Ross over and said, "It still isn't working, I can't seem to get the children to throw into empty spaces, what should I do?" "Why do you think they can't do this?" asked Mr. Ross. After a moment, Mr. Paulin said "Oh! I see, there are no spaces in which to throw the yarn ball!" "Right!" said Mr. Ross. "Now, what can you do to change this situation?" It did not take long for Mr. Paulin to realize that he had to reduce the number of players per side and figure out a rotation system. He simply had too many children on the floor at one time. Because the class was due to end in three minutes, he decided not to make the changes right then, but would do so with the next classes. Before Mr. Ross left to go back to the University, he encouraged Mr. Paulin to explore with him and Mr. Kimbol what options he had relevant to what he now knew to be causing the game not to work. He told Mr. Paulin that he would be back to see this class the next time they played Snowball.

The next time Mr. Paulin taught Snowball, he made a number of changes. He divided the class into four teams of six to seven each, two teams playing the game while two teams waited for their turns each standing quietly with their backs against an end wall, ready to rotate in when their turn came. Teams exchanged places after a minute of play.

Prior to their playing the game, Mr. Paulin had reviewed by way of a demonstration what it meant to throw a yarn ball into an empty space. He also began to stop the game whenever the children threw a yarn ball where someone was positioned, instead of into space. At these times, he would recreate what he had just seen and ask the children if this were what throwing to a space looked like? He began to ask different children to show him and the class what they should be trying to do. In subsequent discussions, he asked them what sports did they know that required passing or throwing to empty spaces and why this was needed in those games? He also gave them opportunities to change the type of ball they used and to modify any rule that they thought needed it.

It was evident from watching the class play the "modified" game of Snowball that things were different from before. The children were beginning to throw yarn balls (and other types of balls) to empty spaces. They also learned what other sports, and under what conditions this strategy/tactic can be used. The children had stopped shouting and yelling and were spaced apart from each other. The only noise heard was the hustle to collect a ball off the floor, the move into position to catch one, or the "Oh!" that escaped from children who missed the yarn ball because it had been thrown into a space they had not been able to cover. The teams switched places easily and each time got the game underway quickly. Everyone participated. Children got antsy if Mr. Paulin let the game go too long before switching teams. Because the children did not ask for it, Mr. Paulin did not keep score and was too busy keeping the flow of the game going and helping the children implement "throwing to a space," that he forgot to keep it.

### QUESTIONS FOR REFLECTION RELATED TO THE SNOWBALL STORY

1. What issues in Snowball have been discussed earlier in this chapter?
2. Do you think Mr. Paulin's solution and the subsequent manner in which the children played the game meet the criteria for a game having educational value?
3. How were the decisions reached for modifying Snowball? Do you agree with how they were decided?
4. Why did the children stop shouting and yelling?
5. Did it bother you that at no time did Mr. Ross or Mr. Kimbol encourage Mr. Paulin to improve the throwing skill of the children, in particular, their use of opposition?

## *Original Games*

Original games are just that, original. That is why it is difficult to present any in this chapter, for once they are written down, they become conventional games. The invasion game, 3 versus 2 Alamance End Ball in Core Content 4 is a good example. That game was made up by a group of preservice teachers as part of a class experience and then field tested with 5th-grade students.

Original games can be made up by the teacher, the children, or both working together. While teachers will always need to make up games to use in their classes, we support a child-designed orientation as well. By participating in their own game designs, children are encouraged to develop problem solving and critical thinking skills and to gain a deeper understanding and appreciation about games and the relationship between game structure and game skills.

When do you use original games? How often? Can children really design them or do teachers end up doing most of the work? All very important questions, but ones that cannot be answered specifically because the concept of original games has a streak of creativity and spontaneity in it that should not be suppressed. You have to believe in the concept philosophically, for original games are not neat and your original games lessons will not always be tidy! Our profession has been advocating them for quite some time and over the years we have gained valuable insight into the process of making up games. Rovegno and Bandhauer (1994), drawing on their experiences teaching original games with children, shared how their understanding of the process changed over time. Their insights are valuable and are summarized here for your reflection. When children design their own games, they need:

**1.** *More structure than has been advocated in the past.* For example, Rovegno and Bandhauer (1994) used to say "Make up a dribbling game," but now say "Make up a game working on dribbling to avoid having the ball taken away from you" (p. 61). Through experience and their research, they began to realize that while giving children initial structure was still important, it was equally important to give them additional structure highlighting both skills and basic strategies/tactics.

**2.** *To be made aware of why games have rules, penalties, and boundaries.* Not knowing, for example, why a rule exists or how to alter a rule to make the game fairer, often gives rise to arguments and negative social behaviors. Recognizing this as reality, points to the rich content inherent in games and how this content can be the center piece when children are designing their own.

**3. Help in understanding the meaning of cooperation and competition.** Children will design games that are both cooperative and competitive but often seem to have difficulty understanding the processes behind both. They need more assistance in understanding the meaning of cooperation as well as the meaning of competition.

**4. More guidance to understand even the most basic of the strategies/tactics used in many games.** For some reason, this has been thought to be unnecessary, especially if children make up their own games. They need help, however, in grasping the basic concepts of offense and defense as they operate in different types of games. Once children understand strategies/tactics, they can design and play their own games remarkably well.

**5. Active help from the teacher.** For years the myth existed that when children design their own games, the teacher should not tell them what to do. As Rovegno and Bandhauer (1994) pointed out, "to facilitate active knowledge construction in children requires an active teacher" (p. 62). Successful teachers know when to help children with the design of their game and when to stay back and observe. This teaching skill becomes easier with experience.

**6. Support of the teacher that designing games is, in fact, a relevant activity and related to playing sports.** In the past it has been said that teachers who support child-designed games are "anti-competition, anti-sport, and anti skill-development" (Rovegno and Bandhauer, 1994, p. 63). There is nothing further from the truth. Child-designed games are consistent with the constructivist approach and with teaching from a developmental perspective. They foster equal opportunity for all involved. The material, as has been pointed out, is closely linked with basic strategies/tactics common to all games.

**7. To realize that many of their games will (naturally) resemble adult sports (e.g., soccer, football, tennis).** Teachers used to worry about this, but for reasons that were unclear. More often than not, either the equipment, the structure teachers give children, or the children's past experiences will be sufficient influence to have many of their games resemble some aspect of an adult sport. The main difference is that the game they design usually accommodates their developmental needs.

**8. Not to scream, laugh, or cheer to indicate they are having a good time.** Experience has demonstrated consistently that when children are actively involved in learning and working hard, noise is at a minimum. Working quietly, however, takes a teacher committed to helping children become involved with their work at such a level.

**9. Assistance in handling personal, disruptive social behavior.** Child-designed games are not argument-free nor do they eliminate embarrassing moments from occurring. Because children make up their own rules, boundaries, etc., less of this type of behavior seems to occur. Children are children and teachers must be ready to see them through these difficult moments. Most likely, many children will have seen adult performers on television losing control or being embarrassed by something they did. We must not relinquish our responsibility to help them understand why certain behaviors are not acceptable. Helping children understand what having respect for individual differences means must guide our actions when situations of this nature confront us.

**10. Constant support and encouragement when trying to use problem solving and critical thinking skills.** To help all children increase their abilities to problem solve and to think critically are two central goals in education today. It is not enough to be "captured by the idea of having children design games" (Rovegno & Bandhauer, 1994, p. 63), you have to work to make it work.

## PROGRESSION

Progression was addressed in Core Content 4—Strategies/Tactics as it relates to both game forms. But which of these two forms should come first, conventional or original? Should you begin by taking most of the responsibility for the game, or should you involve the children right from the start? These questions are not going to be answered for you, for the answers must be generated by you.

## EXPERIENCES FOR REFLECTION

1. With a partner, find at least two specialists who work with both conventional and original games, and who believe that children should be actively involved in making decisions about how their games are played. Ask to observe their classes. Take notes independently and then discuss together what you have observed, focusing on sharing objective observations. This means that you are not going to evaluate what you saw, just describe it. To complete this experience, discuss with the teachers what they were trying to do and how well they thought they had accomplished it. What insight did you gain from this experience related to children's involvement in both game forms?

2. With the help of a practicing teacher, work with a small group of children (3–5) in helping them design a game. Ask the teacher to help you decide the initial structure of the game, being sure that it relates to their class work and has enough structure to get them started. Before working with the children directly, make a list of decisions that you think the children will have to make in designing their games to make them work. With this list in your head give the children the initial structure, then guide them through the rest of the process. After the experience is over, write out or discuss with another classmate, all that you learned from this experience. If you were to repeat the process again, would you change what you did? In what way?

3. Take one of the conventional games described in Core Content 4, and with another classmate, present it to two different small groups of children. With the first group, take all the responsibility for modifying and coaching the game. With the second group, have the children involved in assessing their progress and making the decisions about modifications and what they need to work on. With your partner, compare what happened between the two groups. Reflect on your results. What did you learn?

*core content*

## Criteria for Assessing the Educational Value of a Game*

FOCUS OF CONTENT

Six criteria, in the form of questions, to use when assessing the educational value of a game:

Does the game allow for active participation by all children?
Does the game work? Does it challenge children to be successful?

---

*The ideas expressed in Core Content 6 are based on a working paper written in 1987 by Marie Riley, *Emerita Professor,* the University of North Carolina at Greensboro, and on the way in which our students have interpreted it for their personal use. The paper is titled "Games Teaching in Elementary School Physical Education—Is It Really Educational?"

Does the game promote positive social behaviors?

Does the game flow?

Is the game safe for all children?

Is learning occurring?

## APPROPRIATENESS OF CONTENT

Whenever a game is part of a lesson, these educational criteria are to be applied. Their use needs to become second nature for both teachers and children. As a teacher, whenever you set a task for children that is game-like, or an actual game, these criteria form the basis of your observations and follow up teaching. In fact, all but the criterion related to the flow of a game could be used to assess the educational value of an entire lesson.

## *The Assessment Criteria*

**1. *Does the game allow for active participation by all children?*** Children should have adequate and reasonable opportunity to be involved in the game, to run, dodge, back up a teammate, handle the ball, or make a score. In other words, they need to feel that they have made a contribution to the game. Small-sided games contribute greatly to meeting this criterion.

**2. *Does the game work? Does it challenge children to be successful?*** Do the children use the basic strategies/tactics required for the game? Can they make the decision to pass the ball ahead of a teammate or to cut into an empty space and then actually do it? Are their movement skills (e.g., running changing directions, passing ahead, catching tossed balls quickly) holding up in the context of the game or are they regressing? If it is the latter, is it because they cannot perform the skill as a single skill at an appropriate level, or is it because the game context is too complex for them?

Meeting this criterion often implies that children are toward the more mature end of the continuum of basic locomotor and manipulative skills associated with games, and can use them as combination skills in relation to basic offensive and defensive strategies/tactics. Again, the use of small-sided games and appropriate equipment and implements contribute greatly to meeting this criterion.

**3. *Does the game promote positive social behaviors?*** Do children support each other's efforts? Can their playing be described as unselfish? Are they comfortable playing with the group or do they hang out on the fringes? Are there no demonstrations of pouting, throwing or kicking equipment, shouting, impatience with mistakes, either their own or their classmates? Does anyone quit the game? Does everyone respect and recognize individual differences?

If any of the negative side of these behaviors are demonstrated, then probably the children are not ready for the game in question. Maybe the rules are too difficult, or the equipment too long, too hard, or too heavy. Perhaps the strategies/tactics that are needed are too advanced for the children's physical, cognitive, or social readiness.

**4. *Does the game flow?*** When playing the game, does it seem to be continuous? If the game has to stop often, for any reason, the game is not flowing. A way to assess this criterion is to ask yourself if the game is pleasing to watch. If it is, then it is most likely flowing; if is not, then it most likely is not flowing. In a game that is flowing, children hustle to get balls that get away from them. They encourage their classmates to get back in the game quickly if, for example, they had to go outside the boundaries to fetch the ball. These actions indicate the children's interest in and focus on the game and they contribute to keeping the game flowing.

PHOTO 4-17
The social behaviors demonstrated here indicate that the educational value of this game experience is in question.

- - - - - - - - - - - - - - - - - - - - - - - - - - - - - - - - - - - - - - - - - - - - - - - - - - - - - - - - -

**5.  *Is the game safe for all children?***   At no time should children worry or fear that they could get hurt if they played the game. Do all children treat each other with dignity and respect? Is there adequate space for the game to be played? Is the equipment modified so it can be handled safely by children (e.g., soft balls, shortened handles on striking implements)? If balls are being thrown at targets on the wall or at plastic pins on the floor, is it safe *after* the ball hits the target? Is the game too confusing for some of the children that they might bump into each other or not be able to participate fully? If a soft type of dodgeball is being played for the purpose of learning how to dodge, is the ball *soft* and is it being thrown *softly?* Is it thrown underarm and aimed so that it touches the dodgers *below the knees?* Are children given a choice whether or not they would like to play? If any unsafe condition exists during the playing of a game, or if children appear concerned for their safety or the safety of others, the game should be stopped and modified immediately to eliminate the situation or taken in a different direction to dissipate the unsafe condition.

**6.  *Is learning occurring?***   As part of a physical education lesson, and because the game being played supports specific objectives, it is important that you see *learning occur during* game play.  Meeting this criterion implies that you continually observe the children to see if the changes in their game playing abilities are becoming permanent and that these changes are consistent with your objectives. Help children realize that playing the game means to learn to play the game better each time.

### LISTENING TO CHILDREN'S VOICES

These six criteria can guide your observations and actions at all times but particularly when you have children in a game-playing situation. While this assessment will often be done by you, we want to encourage you to do some of it with the children. Take time to teach the children these criteria so that they can use them to assess their own playing of games. This type of discussion helps children learn about the nature of games, an important objective that we have linked with the core content focused on strategies and tactics.

### IDEAS FROM WHICH TASKS ARE DESIGNED

- In groups of three to six, study the criteria and explanations and rewrite them into your own words to fit on one sheet of paper. You can add other criteria or express these differently. This document, then, becomes your working version of the criteria used to assess the educational value of a game. The next step is to find out if they can be used. Try applying them first to a videotape and then to a live situation.
- Use a video tape of a group of children playing a small-sided game (four to six maximum). With the same group who developed the above document, view the tape and assess the educational value of the game using your document. Write out your assessment. Based on your group's assessment, decide whether or not for these children, the game should be modified in any way. If yes, what modification(s) would you suggest and why? If no, support your judgment.
- If the opportunity can be arranged, teach your document to the children in the video. Guide them in assessing their own game using these criteria. Compare their assessment with your group's assessment.
- Use your framework and observe live one group of children playing a small-sided game (two to four) from a position of a non-participant, that is, someone else is responsible for the children. Observe more than one group, until you are observing an entire class, subdivided into small-sided games (two to four), but still from a position of a non-participant. When ready, shift your role from being a non-participant to being a full participant as the teacher. As you work with the children, try to observe their game play and assess it against your criteria. Start working with one group of children progressing slowly to the entire class.

### PROGRESSION

There is no set order in which these criteria should be used or when they should be used, except perhaps, the criterion of safety, "Are the children safe?" Behaviors and situations that relate to this criterion should always be observed first.

Decisions as to the order and emphasis of these criteria are important for you to make in relation to your own situation. From experience, we have found that once you become committed to these criteria, you will be using them simultaneously, for they relate to each other. They can also guide the development of a positive learning climate for each lesson that you teach.

When you are first learning to apply these criteria in the reality of school settings, begin by observing one group of children playing a small-sided game on video. Watching a video allows you to replay it as often as you wish and is a great stimulus for discussion. Once you are comfortable using these criteria watching a video, try using them in a live situation, but still with only one group of children. Work your way up until you are teaching a full class with a number of games going on simultaneously.

## EXPERIENCES FOR REFLECTION

1. Discuss with a classmate how these criteria might relate to objectives of a physical education program, or more specifically, to a lesson in that program.

2. What were some of the challenges that you faced when using these criteria in field experiences or student teaching? Write them down. Then, opposite each one, note how you could meet these challenges the next time you are in a similar situation.

3. Write out for yourself, how you think these criteria are related. Are there some criteria that you think are more important than others? Are there others you think should be included?

4. Interview practicing specialists as to how they evaluate the educational value of a game. How are their criteria different or similar to those that we have suggested? Did any of these specialists suggest a criterion that you would like to add?

Putting this particular core content last was done on purpose. Taken together, these criteria represent a games teaching philosophy expressed in a succinct and holistic manner. When studying and critiquing them, you will be revisiting all the material presented in this chapter, as well as challenging your own position as to what is of educational value to learn in games.

## References and Reading List

Bandhauer, D., & Rovegno, I. (1992). Teaching game structure and strategy. *Teaching Elementary Physical Education, 3* (6), 7–9.

Barrett, K. R., Williams, K., & Whitall, J. (1992). What does it mean to have a "developmentally appropriate physical education program?" *The Physical Educator, 49,* 114–118.

Bunker, D., & Thorpe, R. (1986). The curriculum model. In R. Thorpe, D. Bunker, & L. Almond (Eds.), *Rethinking games teaching* (pp. 7–10). Loughborough, England: Loughborough University of Technology.

Doolittle, S. A., & Girard, K. T. (1991). A dynamic approach to teaching games in elementary pe. *Journal of Physical Education, Recreation and Dance, 62* (4), 57–62.

Griffin, L. L., Mitchell, S. A., & Oslin, J. L. (1997). *Teaching sport concepts and skills: A tactical games approach.* Champaign, IL: Human Kinetics.

Haywood, K. M. (1993). *Life span motor development* (2nd ed.). Champaign, IL: Human Kinetics.

Kareen, B., & Clayton, B. L. (1993). *Making sense of competition. Teaching Elementary Physical Education, 4* (6), 1, 4–7.

Lawther, J. D. (1951). *Psychology of coaching.* Englewood Cliffs, NJ: Prentice-Hall.

Lenel, R. M. (1969). *Games in the primary school.* London: University of London Press.

Newell, K. M. (1986). Constraints on the development of coordination. In M. G. Wade & H. T. A. Whiting (Eds.), *Motor development in children: Aspects of coordination and control* (pp. 341-360). Dordrecht: Martinus Nijhoff.

Nichols, B. (1994). *Moving and learning: The elementary school physical education experience* (3rd ed.). St. Louis, MO: Mosby.

Roberton, M. A., & Halverson, L. E. (1984). *Developing children—Their changing movement: A guide for teachers.* Philadelphia: Lea & Febiger.

Rovegno, I., & Bandhauer, D. (1994). Child-designed games—Experiences change teachers' conceptions. *Journal of Physical Education, Recreation and Dance, 65* (6), 60–63.

Rovegno, I., & Bandhauer, D. (1998). Teaching game strategy: Building on the basics. *Teaching Elementary Physical Education, 9* (1), 19–23.

Rovegno, I., Skonie, R., Charpenel, T., & Sieving, J. (1995). Learning to teach critical thinking through child-designed games. *Teaching Elementary Physical Education, 6* (1), 1, 6, 7, 15.

Thorpe, R., Bunker, D., & Almond, L. (Eds.). (1986). *Rethinking games teaching.* Loughborough, England: Loughborough University of Technology.

Turner, A., & Martinek, T. (1995). Teaching for understanding: A model for improving decision making during game play. *Quest, 47,* 44–63.

Weinberg, R. S., & Gould, D. (1995). *Foundations of sport and exercise psychology*. Champaign, IL: Human Kinetics.

Werner, P. (1989). Teaching games: A tactical perspective. *Journal of Physical Education, Recreation and Dance, 60 (*3), 98–101.

Wessinger, N. P. (1994). "I hit a home run!" The lived meaning of scoring in games in physical education. *Quest, 46,* 425–439.

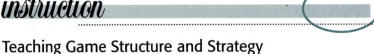

## *instruction*

## Teaching Game Structure and Strategy

*by DIANNA BANDHAUER AND INEZ ROVEGNO*

All games have strategy. If children play even the most basic game in physical education they will need to understand its strategy to be successful. Just because children "do" an activity does not mean that they understand the content.

The strategy of a children's game may seem so obvious to adults that they don't recognize the need to teach it. Likewise, physical education lessons include games for which teachers teach the skills but not the strategy. We contend that children need to be taught game strategy with as much care as we give to teaching skills.

We also think instruction should go well beyond telling children the rules of games to helping them acquire a deep understanding of game structure. Game structure is the meaning of rules, boundaries, equipment, and players in relation to the strategy of the game. One cannot assume that children understand concepts as seemingly simple as a boundary or the need for rules.

Children need to be taught about game structure before they can understand the games they play or create games that are anything more than extended drills. Helping children understand the structure of games insures that they have a sound basis for designing, modifying and playing their own games both in physical education and outside of school.

We describe here the initial game strategy/structure unit taught at Lecanto (FL) Primary School. This 3rd-grade unit forms the basis for our later, more in-depth instruction on game structure and strategy, and it begins to teach children the process of creating and modifying their own games–the central component of the 4th- and 5th-grade games program.

At Lecanto Primary the focus is on game structure and strategy concepts (in addition to the skills) that cross the four game forms: invasion, wall/net, field, target. These game forms were first described by Mauldon and Redfern (1969) but have since been elaborated in ways we find helpful by Almond (1986), Ellis (cited in Almond, 1986), and Werner (1989).

### UNIT CONTENT

The game we use to introduce basic structure and strategy is tag–an invasion game–is both age- and ability-appropriate for 3rd-graders. The skills (running on different pathways, changing directions quickly, dodging) are not cognitively complex for this age, and children can perform these skills well enough to focus on the main unit objectives of strategy, game structure, and learning how to create and modify games.

The lesson structure of the unit alternates game play with large or small group discussions aimed at identifying problems, modifying the game, and clarifying strategy. These discussions enable all children (not just the ones who figure it out on their own) to better understand game structure and strategy.

Our primary methods are to ask questions and set tasks in which children design and modify their own games. Posing problems and asking questions rather than telling information enables children to actively construct a deep understanding of games content. It is important to let children try out their ideas even if you anticipate problems with the structure they devise. The unit takes four to six lessons and is divided into four segments.

## *Segment I: Boundaries and Basic Strategy*

### OBJECTIVES

1. To identify and make explicit what worked or did not work to avoid being tagged and to tag a runner (i.e., the strategy).
2. To recognize how lack of boundaries or boundaries that are too large is one reason a game is not working; to understand that boundaries that are too large favor the runners (offense); and boundaries that are too small favor the taggers (defense).
3. To understand that rules are not sacrosanct and that children can change rules to make games better.
4. To learn that for a game to work it must provide reasonably even opportunities for defense and offense. If the offense gets out immediately or if the defense rarely thwarts the offense, the game has no suspense or excitement and is not at the appropriate level of challenge to foster learning for both teams.

We begin the unit by having the children play tag with one chaser, no boundaries, and small groups of any size. Make sure you have a lot of space. This game will not work very well because the defense (chaser) will have a very difficult time catching the offense (runners). After the children have all been chasers, have a group discussion to identify and solve problems that were discovered.

By focusing on problems, children come to understand the need for boundaries. Strategies children discussed at Lecanto Primary were running in zig zag pathways, running behind another player, running fast, "faking out" the chaser, and pretending not to be chasing a certain runner.

Have the children make their own boundaries (experimenting with the size) and play the game again. While they play they should consciously use and practice the strategies discussed.

## *Segment II: Rules and Consequences*

### OBJECTIVES

1. To learn that games have rules that make them fun and fair.
2. To begin to understand how to make rules to solve problems.
3. To learn that if you break rules there will be consequences that give the advantage to the opponents.

Have the children make their own boundaries and play tag with a minimum of one chaser, small groups, and flag football flags. Before starting have the children decide what to do when someone is tagged or when you lose all of your flags.

You may need to set some guidelines for the penalties children select. At times, children will decide that the penalty will be to sit out. However, children readily agree that it is no fun to sit out and that the goal of physical education is for all children to practice and learn—something that cannot occur when you are sitting out.

At Lecanto Primary the guidelines are that the penalties must:

- give the advantage to the opposite team.
- not force anyone to sit out, and
- be game-skill related (e.g., no laps, jumping jacks, push-ups).

Some of the penalties children designed were to lose a flag, join the chasers, give the chaser a flag so when teams rotate some chasers will have extra flags, have the tagged child become "it," and have tagged children become blockers for teammates.

Have children play their game. These games will work, but inevitably some children will intentionally and unintentionally step out of bounds. If the boundaries are not clearly marked, some children will argue whether they indeed stepped out of bounds. Hold a group discussion about consequences for breaking rules. Have children modify and clarify their rules, boundaries, and penalties and test their modified game.

In the beginning just make sure the children's penalties meet the teacher's guidelines. With older children or in future lessons you can also help children understand common consequences for breaking rules across the four game forms:

- awarding points (like in table tennis, tennis, squash),
- losing tries (football),
- losing the serve or ball (basketball, soccer, field hockey, volleyball),
- losing a player (like in ice hockey; this is modified to having a player join the other team), and
- awarding penalty shots or plays (field hockey, soccer).

## *Segment III: Rules and Srategy Surrounding a Base*

### OBJECTIVES

1. To design rules about bases that keep the game fun and fair.
2. To learn how bases or safety zones add options for the offense to outmaneuver the defense and responsibilities for the defense.
3. To understand that offensive and defense players can work together to outmaneuver the other team.
4. To begin to learn about offensive strategies related to creating space through the use of pathways, decoys, blockers, boundaries, bases, and safety zones.
5. To begin to learn about defensive strategies related to denying space through the use of boundaries, double-teaming to trap the offense, zone defense, person-to-person defense, and guarding bases and end zones.

Start with a group discussion, asking children to predict how their tag games will change if a base is added on which the runners can be safe. Do they foresee any problems? If they do not expect problems, have them add a base and try the game. Often children predict that too many players will get on base at once or that players will stay on the base too long or hover nearby. Have them devise rules they think might solve their anticipated problems and play the game. Continue the pattern of play, discuss, revise, play, and so on.

Frequently children put the base in the corner, giving the advantage to the chasers. This problem leads to a discussion about the strategy of using boundaries to trap the offense and further modifying the game to give more balance opportunities for offense and defense. Other modifications can be adding bases and having different rules for different bases.

At Lecanto Primary children typically design the following rules:

- You can only touch the base once per round.
- You can only have one person on the base at a time.
- Defenders (chasers) have to stand beyond a boundary surrounding the base.
- Captured flags are put on the base and can be recaptured by the offense (the defenders see this as a lure to bring the offense to a particular place).

In discussing what strategies were central to the game, defenders spoke of learning they had to assign some children to guard the base and some to chase in general space. Offensive players learned to turn their flagless side to the defender to protect the flag with the body, to use players with no flags as blockers, and to have players with two flags try to entice the defense away from the base.

## *Segment IV: Goal-Oriented Tag*

### OBJECTIVES

1. To work on offensive strategies related to creating space through the use of pathways, decoys, blockers, boundaries, and bases; to devise ways to beat a zone defense and ways to beat a person-to-person defense.
2. To work on defensive strategies related to denying space through the use of boundaries, double-teaming to trap offense, zone defense, person-to-person defense, and guarding bases and end zones.
3. To understand the importance of planning a team strategy and how to plan specific strategy related to a particular defense or offense.
4. To understand how the strategies and game structure of goal-oriented tag (with two side boundaries and a starting and ending zone) differ from tag games with no directional goal. This is similar to the change children will experience from in-place keep-away to goal-oriented keep-away with manipulative skills.

In this segment children are organized in groups of four to eight and play goal-oriented tag in which the runners have to cross from one end line to the other without getting tagged. Using the play-discuss-revise lesson structure, children explore the same rules and strategy of tag as in earlier segments but with the restriction of having a directional goal.

This new game structure mirrors the structure of major invasion games. Thus, the strategy concepts introduced in previous segments are revisited at more sophisticated levels, and children begin to work in basic invasion strategies. These strategies will be revisited in later units with the skills of throwing, catching, kicking, and striking.

Children at Lecanto developed the following game structures:

- Each team passes through one time and you count the number of flags pulled.
- When you lose your flags you become a blocker for your teammates.
- Start with one or two taggers, and when you lose your flags you become a tagger too.

Defense strategies the children identified included:

- a layered zone defense in which you back up the defender in front of you.
- planning who to chase with person to person defense, and
- using two defenders and the sidelines to cut off the offense running angles.

Offense strategies discussed were:

- sending a fast decoy to one side, with most players then running to the other side.
- picking a starting place in relation to where the defense was not standing.
- running all at the same time (a blitz) to counteract a zone defense, and
- running on zigzag pathways and crossing pathways to counteract a person-to-person defense.

### DEVELOPMENTAL APPROPRIATENESS

We think that teaching children about the strategy and structure of games should be part of a developmentally appropriate physical education program. To accommodate the developmental levels (ages and abilities) of all children, a games curriculum must

- provide chances for children to design and modify their own games in relation to their particular developmental levels and to break down the complexity of games, and
- provide sound progressive instruction about all aspects of games, giving all children an opportunity to succeed.

Teaching skills without teaching game structure and strategy privileges those children who pick up the strategy on their own. We do not think that simply playing games will make children more skillful or teach them about game strategy and structure. We think game strategy and structure needs to be taught.

## *References*

Almond, L. (1986) Reflecting on themes: A games classification. In R. Thorpe, D. Bunker, & L. Almond (Eds.), *Rethinking games teaching* (pp. 71–72). Loughborough, England: Department of Physical Education and Sports Science, University of Technology, Loughborough.

Mauldon, E., & Redfern, H.B. (1969). *Games teaching: A new approach for the primary schools*. London: MacDonald & Evans.

Werner, P. (1989). Teaching games: A tactical perspective. *Journal of Physical Education, Recreation and Dance, 60* (3), 98–101.

(Reprinted by permission from D. Bandhauer and I. Rovegno, 1992, "Teaching Game Structure and Strategy," *Teaching Elementary Physical Eduaction,* 3 (6): 7–9.)

# CHAPTER 5

# *Teaching Educational Gymnastics*

**O**ur approach to teaching gymnastics, as with games and dance, is guided by a commitment to and respect for the individual nature of children. Gymnastics-type movement is especially pleasing for children as they enjoy the challenge of running, jumping, leaping, spinning, rolling, balancing, and climbing. Educational gymnastics capitalizes on what children can learn through movement while at the same time expanding their skill in movement. *Children learning to move and moving to learn* (American Association for Health, Physical Education and Recreation, 1965) is a phrase from our past that captures perfectly the philosophy of educational gymnastics with its interactive view of content and method situated within a developmental framework as children construct personal meaning for what it is to move in gymnastic-like ways.

## Content Organization

The content for educational gymnastics is conceptually based and organized around four categories of movement:

- locomotion and stillness
- weight bearing/balancing
- weight transference
- gymnastics sequences (see Figure 5–1)

The classic skills often associated with gymnastics, such as handstands, headstands, cartwheels, forward rolls, and backward rolls, are not listed specifically. The absence of these skills does not mean that they are eliminated from the content. In fact, these skills play a very important role in this approach to gymnastics.

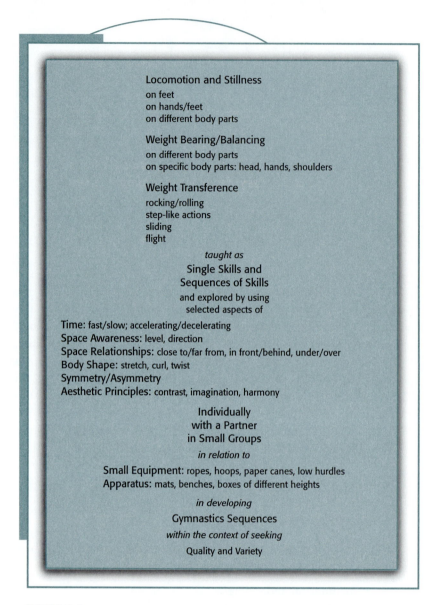

Locomotion and Stillness
on feet
on hands/feet
on different body parts

Weight Bearing/Balancing
on different body parts
on specific body parts: head, hands, shoulders

Weight Transference
rocking/rolling
step-like actions
sliding
flight

*taught as*

**Single Skills and
Sequences of Skills**

and explored by using
selected aspects of

**Time:** fast/slow; accelerating/decelerating
**Space Awareness:** level, direction
**Space Relationships:** close to/far from, in front/behind, under/over
**Body Shape:** stretch, curl, twist
**Symmetry/Asymmetry**
**Aesthetic Principles:** contrast, imagination, harmony

**Individually
with a Partner
in Small Groups**

*in relation to*

**Small Equipment:** ropes, hoops, paper canes, low hurdles
**Apparatus:** mats, benches, boxes of different heights

*in developing*

**Gymnastics Sequences**

*within the context of seeking*

**Quality and Variety**

FIGURE 5–1
Gymnastics core content framework for beginning teachers.

From the classic skills, eleven have been identified as a "critical set" of skills that we think are essential for all children to perform competently and confidently. They include:

1. five basic jumps
2. sideways (safety) roll

3. hand balance/body curled
4. shoulder balance
5. head/hand balance
6. jump/land/roll basic sequence
7. forward roll/shoulder roll
8. backward roll/shoulder roll
9. hand balance/body extended
10. cartwheel
11. jump for height

While many of these skills are identified by their familiar names, they are not to be viewed as the familiar "stunts" or "tricks" to be performed by the children and then checked off by the teacher. They are not ends in themselves; they are vehicles through which advanced gymnastics skills continue to develop.

Figure 5–2 illustrates the integration of these eleven critical skills with the four categories of movement. Together, they comprise the content of educational gymnastics.

Within each of the first three major categories, the critical skills that are best introduced during work with that particular content are listed. For example, when working with material from locomotion and stillness, introduce and integrate into your lessons the critical skills of the five basic jumps and the sideways (safety) roll. The skills to introduce and integrate with material from the weight bearing/balancing category are the hand balance/body curled, the shoulder balance, and the head/hand balance (headstand). The basic jump/land/roll sequence, forward roll/shoulder roll, backward roll/shoulder roll, hand balance/body extended (handstand), cartwheel, and jump for height have been suggested as skills to introduce and integrate under the third major category, weight transference.

By using the terms introduce and integrate, we want to convey that reaching a mature level in performing gymnastics movement is an ongoing process rather than one that can be accomplished in one or two lessons. We suggest when to introduce the skills either to the entire class or to individual children who show a readiness for them. Once introduced and brought into the lessons, they will be revisited often, for only with much practice will children's skills develop toward the more advanced levels of performance. Figure 5–2 suggests when these skills might first be introduced and how long they might need to be integrated throughout the program. With experience you will discover what progression works best with your children. Once you are confident with teaching and integrating these skills into your lessons, it will be easier for you to include other skills that you think are equally important.

Additional materials have been designed to help you with introducing and integrating these skills into your lessons. For each of the eleven critical skills,

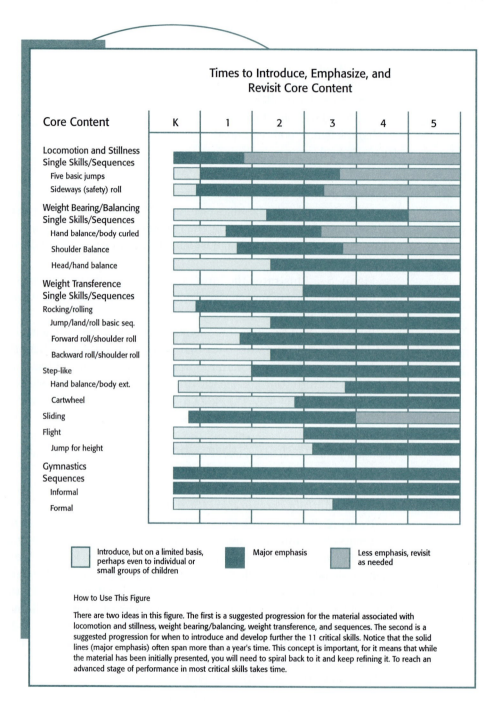

**Times to Introduce, Emphasize, and Revisit Core Content**

| Core Content | K | 1 | 2 | 3 | 4 | 5 |
|---|---|---|---|---|---|---|

**Locomotion and Stillness**
Single Skills/Sequences
  Five basic jumps
  Sideways (safety) roll

**Weight Bearing/Balancing**
Single Skills/Sequences
  Hand balance/body curled
  Shoulder Balance
  Head/hand balance

**Weight Transference**
Single Skills/Sequences
Rocking/rolling
  Jump/land/roll basic seq.
  Forward roll/shoulder roll
  Backward roll/shoulder roll
Step-like
  Hand balance/body ext.
  Cartwheel
Sliding
Flight
  Jump for height

**Gymnastics**
Sequences
  Informal
  Formal

Legend:
■ Introduce, but on a limited basis, perhaps even to individual or small groups of children
■ Major emphasis
■ Less emphasis, revisit as needed

**How to Use This Figure**

There are two ideas in this figure. The first is a suggested progression for the material associated with locomotion and stillness, weight bearing/balancing, weight transference, and sequences. The second is a suggested progression for when to introduce and develop further the 11 critical skills. Notice that the solid lines (major emphasis) often span more than a year's time. This concept is important, for it means that while the material has been initially presented, you will need to spiral back to it and keep refining it. To reach an advanced stage of performance in most critical skills takes time.

FIGURE 5–2
Suggested gymnastics content emphasis by grade level.

a section titled "Integration of Skills and Focused Teaching" has been developed. These materials follow the Core Content material.

## Why Educational Gymnastics?

Educational gymnastics is guided by a clear aim that impacts the learning environment and thus the way learners learn and teachers teach. The basic aim of educational gymnastics is the development of individuality and versatility in gymnastics movement through improving children's:

- quality or skillfulness of their gymnastics movement through body alignment, tension, and control
- range and variety of gymnastics movements performed with a skillful quality to them
- appreciation, understanding, and experience of the aesthetic dimension of gymnastics movement

The broader educational goal is for children to develop movement skills while learning to become responsibly independent by improving their ability to make informed decisions and becoming more competent and confident as active learners.

To achieve these goals both children and teachers take active roles in the learning process. Children become increasingly in charge of their destinations, while the teacher is actively engaged in facilitating the children's journeys. This process emphasizes all the areas of children's lives from which they construct meaning as they participate in different gymnastics movement situations. For some of you this approach to gymnastics will be different from what you experienced as a student in school. You will see that it places a lot of responsibility on children to think through what they might do and how they might do it under the direction and thoughtful guidance of a knowledgeable teacher (that's you!). Because children are developing gymnastics skill at their own rates and levels of development, and because you, as the teacher, are guiding them to learn to make appropriate decisions for their levels of skill, safety becomes an inherent characteristic of the approach.

To be competent and confident in gymnastics-type movement, children need a rich and strong experiential base to build on. This gymnastics base builds from within so that the individual becomes increasingly knowledgeable about what her own body can do. The development of this broad and rich base is the responsibility of the K–5 program. The material selected for this chapter forms a core of educational gymnastics content. It contains essential movement skills and knowledge to help beginning teachers to teach and to give children the opportunity to learn. Children need to feel competent and confident in the ways they handle their bodies and they trust you to guide them through this process. This is not to say that all children will be able to perform skills consistently at the most mature level or even reach that level in all skills, however, we should set high expectations for children because they are generally more capable than we think. Perhaps you remember how you felt the first time you were finally able to balance on your head without tipping over when you thought that you would never be able to do it?

I was teaching a gymnastics unit on jumping, landing, and rolling to a mainstreamed third grade class. I was using apparatus of different heights for jumping to accommodate for individual differences in skill levels. Jamal, who has spina bifida and wears braces on both his legs, came to physical education with his class. There were two of us teaching the class that day. About halfway through the period I turned around and saw Jamal standing on top of a gymnastics stool. The stool was about four feet high. I realized that he was about to fly off the stool and land with his braced legs taking the full force of his body. I quickly walked over and asked Jamal what he was planning on doing and he confirmed that jumping high off the stool was exactly what he had in mind to do. Obviously, I was concerned for his safety. I didn't know if he was making a good choice or not. I knew the school's physical therapist was just in the next room, so I told Jamal to wait while I consulted with the therapist on whether or not this was an appropriate task for him to attempt at that height. The other teacher took over the class and I dashed next door to check with the therapist. As I was coming back in the gymnasium door a minute later, Jamal was climbing back up on the stool. He looked at me and said, "Well, Mr. Sayrs, do you want to see me do it for my fourth time now?"

To be true to the essence of educational gymnastics, you will have to become skilled in teaching children to become active participants in their own learning. This is not a tell-the-children-what-to-do approach to teaching gymnastics. It is an approach that actively guides them to understand their own abilities, what they can do with those abilities, and to what heights they can take them.

# THE CORE CONTENT FOR TEACHING EDUCATIONAL GYMNASTICS TO CHILDREN

The content of gymnastics is structured around the four broad interrelated movement ideas of locomotion and stillness, weight bearing/balancing, weight transference, and gymnastics sequences (see Figure 5–1). The first category includes emphasis on traveling and stopping, first using feet and then using different body parts. Weight bearing/balancing, the second category, focuses on holding or balancing the body's weight on different body parts. The third category, weight transference, extends and formalizes weight bearing by exploring the specific types of weight transference called rocking/rolling, step-like actions, sliding, and flight. The fourth category focuses on the development of both informal and formal gymnastics sequences.

The material is taught both as single skills and sequences of skills and explored further through the use of time, space awareness, space relationships, body shape, symmetry/asymmetry, and selected aesthetic principles. Work in educational gymnastics can be done individually, with partners, and in small groups. All of this material is made more meaningful and powerful as it is developed in relation to small equipment and apparatus clearly guided by the two overarching goals of variety and quality in the context of the gymnastic sequence.

The development of the content in this chapter has been influenced by two texts in particular—*Teaching Gymnastics* (Mauldon & Layson, 1979) and *Themes for Educational Gymnastics* (Williams, 1992). The progressions and teaching suggestions shared are a result of much practical application of this material in public schools with children and in universities with preservice physical education teachers.

We think that the material selected will serve as a strong foundation for children prior to their middle school physical education gymnastics experiences as well as being personally meaningful and challenging for them as elementary-aged children. This content is by no means all the gymnastics content that there is to be taught. It has been carefully selected as appropriate for students in grades K–5 and for beginning teachers to teach. As a result of your continued professional development, it is expected that you will expand your knowledge and teaching of gymnastics beyond this core material.

## The Gymnastics Core Content Framework

### Locomotion and Stillness

The material in locomotion and stillness focuses on simple means of traveling (e.g., running, skipping, sliding, hopping) throughout space on feet, hands and feet, and on different body parts. Additional focus is placed on ways of stopping or actively pausing. Further focus is achieved when this material is developed both as single skills and then as short sequences. Two critical skills are highlighted within this material—the five basic jumps and the sideways (safety) roll. (See Integration of Skills and Focused Teaching 1 and 2.) The five basic jumps refer to the five different combinations of footwork that can be used for traveling and arriving on and dismounting from apparatus. The sideways (safety) roll is included here to give children a safe way to regain body control and come to a moment of stillness.

The material of locomotion and stillness is expanded by encouraging changes in speed, direction, and performance in relation to equipment (ropes, hoops, paper canes, low hurdles) and apparatus (mats, benches, boxes). Children need to learn how to vary the speed of their movements, as well as be able to move forward, backward, and sideward without bumping into anyone or falling over. How to stop and start on their own, as well as how to quickly adjust to a potentially dangerous situation, are important for children to learn. By adding equipment and apparatus to the environment, children are challenged to expand their basic locomotor and stillness skills to a greater level of complexity and body control.

## Weight Bearing/Balance

The focus of this material is on the different body parts that can support your weight. It is related to locomotion and stillness in that when you are traveling using feet, hands/feet, and other body parts, you are momentarily taking your weight on different body parts. The emphasis in this category, however, is on developing body control through balance using different body parts with different surfaces ranging from large body parts (e.g., back, hip, shoulder) to small body parts (e.g., one foot, two hands). When working with this material, the basic patterns of hand balance/body curled, the shoulder balance, and the head/hand balance are integrated and carefully developed. (See Integration of Skills and Focused Teaching 3, 4, and 5.) These critical skills are essential for more complex work as they invert the body, thus opening up more potential for increased variety and skill in movement. Weight bearing/balancing material also can be developed both as single skills and as sequences of different lengths.

Changes in level of the body and of individual body parts are included in this material. In addition, an introduction to body shape (curl, stretch, twist) is placed here because it brings a certain quality and aesthetic dimension to the children's work. This often is the first time they begin to "feel and look like gymnasts." When beginning to combine balances into a short sequence, use of direction (forward, sideward, backward) offers important opportunities for variations, as do using the ideas of symmetry and asymmetry. Working with a partner or in a small group opens up another dimension and further challenges the children. By using selected small equipment and apparatus, an even more challenging environment is developed, once again adding complexity to the material.

## Weight Transference

Weight transference is a logical extension of weight bearing, formalizing and advancing much of the previous material. With the previous material, the emphasis has been on the body part or parts that have taken the weight and the rest of the body as it achieves a balanced position. The shift in emphasis for weight transference is explained by Mauldon and Layson (1979):

> In transference of weight the stress is on what happens between weight being removed from one part and arriving on another; in other words, how the body moves between two points of support. Whereas weight bearing is concerned with relative stillness, transference of weight involves locomotion (pp. 76–77).

They identify four methods of weight transference that serve to focus the material in this category: rocking/rolling, step-like actions, sliding, and flight.

*Rocking/rolling.* These two forms of transferring one's weight involve transferring weight along adjacent body parts. There is continuous contact with the supporting surface as in forward, backward, and sideward rolls. Rocking results when the body moves back and forth along the same adjacent parts. The difference between rocking and rolling is that in the former, weight is transferred onto adjacent parts and then is brought back again. In the latter, the weight is transferred onto the next adjacent part. Rocking and rolling lead very easily into each other. The jump/land/roll basic sequence, forward roll/shoulder roll, and backward roll/shoulder roll can be formally integrated as a major means for developing smooth transitions within sequences (see Integration of Skills and Focused Teaching 6, 7, and 8).

*Step-like actions.* Walking is one of the first step-like actions that comes to mind when weight transference is defined. As weight is taken on one foot, the other one is preparing to receive the weight. As the weight is shifted from one foot to the other, there is a brief moment when both feet are in contact with the supporting surface with the weight distributed evenly. This type of weight transference can occur using many different body parts. Familiar examples include a handstand in which weight is transferred from one foot to two hands and back to one foot, and a cartwheel in which weight is transferred from one foot to one hand, to the other hand and then to the other foot. In both examples, the body is being supported alternately by the hands and feet. As these step-like patterns become familiar to children, they are more formally integrated and developed in the overall content progression. You may wish to integrate the hand balance/body extended and the cartwheel with this material (see Integration of Skills and Focused Teaching 9 and 10).

*Sliding.*    In sliding, the body is transferred from one place to another while the parts supporting it are in constant contact with the surface. Sliding does not require shifting weight from one body part to another. Most often the opportunity to slide is made possible in gymnastics by creating an inclined surface down which children can slide, supporting their weight on different body parts (e.g., hips, backs, fronts) while maintaining different body shapes. Children can slide along the top of a smooth bench, parallel to the floor, by means of pulling and pushing themselves. Sliding is a bit more difficult when going up an inclined surface, but children enjoy finding various ways that it can be done.

*Flight.*    In all the preceding methods of weight transference, contact with the supporting surface has been a constant factor. In flight, loss of contact with the floor or supporting surface occurs, sometimes momentarily, other times for longer periods of time. In the locomotion and stillness category, the five basic jumps are examples of weight transference through flight. When material from this third category is being developed, these jumps are brought back and used again, but at a higher level of difficulty. Most methods of flight use some combination of feet to feet, feet to hands, and hands to feet, and will most often be over a brief period of time. The time in the air will increase as the skill of the children increases and as they use apparatus of higher heights. Integrated with this material is the jump for height (see Integration of Skills and Focused Teaching 11).

## Using Aspects of Time, Space Awareness, Space Relationships, Body Shape, Symmetry/Asymmetry, and Aesthetic Principles

Changes in speed, level, and direction of movement as well as body shape give added depth and breadth to children's movement responses.

Incorporating changes of speed is most relevant for rocking, rolling, and step-like actions and creates very different sensations and outcomes. Using space in imaginative ways, such as changing level (high, medium, low) or changing the shape of the body or body parts (curl, stretch, twist), helps children find greater variety in their movement. Symmetrical shapes result when both sides of the body or body parts are identical to each other and asymmetrical shapes result when they are different. In addition, focus can be placed on different space relationships that can occur (close to/far from, in front/behind, under/over) between body parts, individuals, and groups.

Throughout the teaching of gymnastics, encourage children to make obvious their use of different speeds or levels through contrast, to imagine original and different ways to perform familiar skills, and to give their sequences harmony by showing a sense of balance and logic in them. All these efforts help children with the aesthetic dimension of their work, how their work might feel to them, and how others might see it. Aesthetics focuses on appreciating the beauty and style of the work. Although opinions will differ as to what children like, find interesting to do themselves, or see in their classmates' work, it is important to help them become aware of what visually appeals to them and why it is appealing.

## Working Individually, with a Partner, and in Small Groups

Cooperative work, sometimes with a partner and other times in small groups (3 to 5 individuals), plays a special role in meeting the goals of educational gymnastics. The collaborative problem-solving strategies and social skills that cooperation requires give children a real sense of challenge and accomplishment. Through working with a partner or small group, opportunities for new ideas associated with all methods of locomotion and stillness, weight bearing/balancing, and weight transference open up to greater possibilities.

One such possibility is exploration of the relationship of partners' positions and the timing of partners' movements. Partners doing the same movements simultaneously, while facing one another, creates a mirroring effect for their actions. Changing to face the same direction, while doing the same movements, at the same time, allows partners to match one another's movements. Matching movements, not simultaneously but done one after the other, is called copying. Children enjoy the challenges associated with sequence development that include mirroring, matching, and copying in relation to a partner or small group. These three partner-relationship ideas add another dimension of variety to children's gymnastics work.

## Relationship to Small Equipment and Apparatus

The use of equipment (e.g., ropes, hoops, paper canes, low hurdles) and apparatus (e.g., mats, benches, boxes of different heights) gives tremendous meaning to children's gymnastics work. They get excited when equipment and apparatus are brought into the lesson. Their inclusion clearly influences the range of movement possibilities. All material from all categories is "transformed" into different and more challenging movement skills when used in relation to small equipment and apparatus. Apparatus, with its ability to be arranged in various patterns and heights, becomes a central vehicle through which teachers can guide children toward their most challenging gymnastics work.

## Gymnastics Sequences

Two types of sequences, informal and formal, are used to further develop the core content. Linking movements together helps children learn about how movement skills are related, as well as challenging them to perform at a higher level of complexity. While the difference between these types of sequences is slight, we have found it to be a useful distinction.

In informal sequences, children are not expected to perfect skills to the same level as they are in formal sequences. In fact, these sequences often remain in an early stage of development. They rarely get to the selection and refinement stages. They are used to help children learn to link skills recently experienced as a means to achieve greater body control and to create a short piece of work that is one's own. Informal sequences are particularly useful when new material is being introduced or when first beginning to expand familiar material. Informal sequences may be shared with the class, but sharing should be kept to a minimum, for their real purpose is as a means of content development. Sharing of informal sequences is more for the purpose of clarification of the task than anything else, to be sure that the children know what is being asked of them. When it seems appropriate, sharing can also be used to help children get ideas from each other.

With formal sequences, children experience a more complete process of creating sequences and thus more time is given. This process includes defining a focus, exploring/improvising, selecting/organizing/refining, and sharing/evaluating. These latter two processes can occur individually, in small groups, or with the class as a whole. How, when, and for what purposes sequences are developed varies and is dependent upon the context in which the sequences are being created.

---

**Quality and Variety**

---

Educational gymnastics focuses on improving the quality and variety of children's gymnastics movement. This means that throughout every lesson these two concepts should always be in the forefront of teachers' minds when they are teaching. They help create the context for each class. Variety helps children increase their body awareness and develop a broad range of skills, whereas quality improves efficiency of movement, as well as its aesthetic dimension. Children who manage their bodies skillfully effectively use such mechanical principles as center of gravity and force production/absorption. Visual appeal is brought about by their ability to clarify their body shapes through appropriate body tension, as well as use aesthetic principles such as contrast, imagination, and harmony. As concepts, quality, and variety should be appreciated as partners—children should be focused on them together.

# UNDERSTANDING THE CONTENT FROM A TEACHING PERSPECTIVE

Because the relationship between content and method are so interactive, teaching suggestions are integrated throughout the chapter in the Core Content units and in the material focused on the eleven critical skills. To help you reflect on the material from a teacher's perspective, the Core Content is presented as the four major movement categories previously described. These units of work should not be confused with unit plans that you will be developing for teaching, as they have not been constructed for the same purpose.

The order for the first three content units—locomotion and stillness, weight bearing/balancing, and weight transference—is a suggested progression. There is much flexibility within each unit, but the idea that basic body control through locomotion and stillness precedes the idea of weight bearing/balancing is important. Once general body control is achieved, children can focus on what it means to take their weight on different body parts necessitating a higher level of body control. When they can travel, stop, and balance, focusing on specific forms of weight transference becomes the next step (Mauldon & Layson, 1979). The four content units are:

## CORE CONTENT 1. LOCOMOTION AND STILLNESS AS SINGLE SKILLS AND IN SEQUENCES

Locomotion and stillness on feet, hands/feet, and different body parts taught as single skills and sequences of skills individually and with a partner explored by using selected aspects of:

time
space awareness

in relation to:

small equipment
apparatus

and integrating from the critical skills set:

five basic jumps
sideways (safety) roll

## CORE CONTENT 2. WEIGHT BEARING/BALANCING AS SINGLE SKILLS AND IN SEQUENCES

Weight bearing/balancing on different body parts, on specific body parts (head, hands, shoulders) taught as single skills and sequences of skills, individually, with a partner, and in small groups explored by using selected aspects of:

time
space awareness
space relationships
body shape
symmetry/asymmetry

in relation to:

small equipment
apparatus

and integrating from the critical skills set:

hand balance/body curled
shoulder balance
head/hand balance

## CORE CONTENT 3. WEIGHT TRANSFERENCE AS SINGLE SKILLS AND IN SEQUENCES

Methods of weight transference to include rocking/rolling, step-like actions, sliding, and flight taught as single skills and sequences of skills, individually, with a partner, and in small groups explored by using selected aspects of:

time

space awareness

space relationships

body shape

symmetry/asymmetry

in relation to:

small equipment

apparatus

and integrating from the critical  skills set:

jump/land/roll basic sequence

forward roll/shoulder roll

backward roll/shoulder roll

hand balance/body extended

cartwheel

jump for height

## CORE CONTENT 4. GYMNASTICS SEQUENCES

Forms of gymnastics sequences: informal and formal

## K–5 Progression

Figure 5–2 gives the overall picture of how the content might be emphasized and organized for a K–5 program. It suggests times to introduce, emphasize, and revisit this material. It also suggests when to introduce and integrate the skills that have been defined as the critical set.

The dark gray segments represent when this material might be used as the major emphasis in designing lessons. The medium gray segments suggest that for some children you may have to revisit material previously taught. The light gray segments suggest when material could be used to design a task for an individual or small group of children to make it more challenging for them.

## Remainder of the Chapter

The four core content units of locomotion and stillness, weight bearing/balancing, weight transference, and gymnastics sequences are presented and developed first. Following the core content material, some brief comments about arranging equipment and apparatus in support of content and skill development are given. These comments relate to material across all four core units. The chapter concludes with a section entitled Integration of Skills and Focused Teaching for each of the eleven critical skills identified as essential for children in becoming competent and confident movers in the context of educational gymnastics.

## *core content*

## Locomotion and Stillness as Single Skills and in Sequences

### FOCUS OF CONTENT

Locomotion and stillness on feet, hands/feet, and different body parts taught as single skills and sequences of skills individually and with a partner explored by using selected aspects of:

> time
> space awareness

in relation to:

> small equipment
> apparatus

and integrating from the critical skills set:

> five basic jumps
> sideways (safety) roll

### APPROPRIATENESS OF CONTENT

This material is needed when you first introduce educational gymnastics to children, no matter the grade. Its purpose is to give the children a feel for what "basic body control" means and to be introduced to a learning environment that emphasizes decision-making and problem-solving. The teacher needs to be sure that children can demonstrate the basic body control needed for safety and the social and cognitive skills necessary to create a positive learning environment.

**IDEAS FROM WHICH MOVEMENT TASKS ARE DESIGNED**

*Locomotion and Stillness—Part A: Introduction*

- Traveling on feet (i.e., easy running) throughout the general space

> travel at different levels
> change direction
> vary the speed
> add turns

- Traveling on feet (i.e., easy running) and stopping

> decrease speed by decelerating
> pause or stop in an active pause
> come to a sudden, abrupt stop in a small space
> come to a stop from a jump

(See Integration of Skills and Focused Teaching 1: Five Basic Jumps)

- Traveling on feet using the five basic jumps

    jump from one foot to the other (a leap)
    jump from one foot to the same foot (a hop)
    jump from one foot to two feet
    jump from two feet to one foot
    jump from two feet to two feet (a double-footed jump)

- Traveling on hands and feet

    travel on two hands and two feet
    travel on two hands and one foot

- Traveling on other body parts

(See Integration of Skills and Focused Teaching 2: Sideways (safety) Roll)

- Traveling by rolling
- Traveling on hands alone, feet low
- Traveling on feet, hands and feet, or other body parts with changes in level and direction

    alternate high with low
    vary the direction of travel

- Traveling on the feet, hands and feet, or other body parts with changes in speed

    vary the speed
    alternate slow with quick
    accelerate and decelerate

## Locomotion and Stillness—Part B: Continued Development

- Creating informal sequences

    link the five basic jumps with changes of direction
    link travel on feet with travel on other body parts showing changes of direction
    link traveling actions together showing change of speed and direction

- Using tasks from ideas in Parts A and B redesigned to include ropes and hoops placed on the floor

    travel in, out, and around one's own rope or hoop
    travel in, out, and around all ropes and hoops

- Using tasks from ideas in Parts A and B redesigned to include benches and boxes of low heights. (Sliding by pushing/pulling can be introduced here.)

    travel on, over, along bench or box using feet only, feet and hands, or
    different body parts
    change direction
    alternate slow with quick

PHOTO 5–1
Traveling by rolling.

PHOTO 5–2
Traveling on hands and feet in, out, and around ropes, hoops, and blocks and canes placed on the floor.

PHOTO 5-3
Traveling on different body parts on, over, and along benches and boxes.

● ● ● ● ● ● ● ● ● ● ● ● ● ● ● ● ● ● ● ● ● ● ● ● ● ● ● ● ● ● ● ● ● ● ● ● ● ● ● ● ● ● ● ● ● ● ● ● ● ● ● ● ● ● ● ● ● ● ● ● ●

### BIOMECHANICAL PRINCIPLES AFFECTING QUALITY OF PERFORMANCE

*Center of gravity and balance.*    When traveling forward and controlling one's body by quickly stopping, the body must be low with the feet in a fairly wide forward/backward stride position or loss of balance will result. These actions lower the body's center of gravity and keep it from going outside its base. Encourage children to "grip" the floor with their feet. This action also brings a firmness to the whole body. This concept is important because children are constantly managing their centers of gravity as much of their work is related to balance—whether keeping it, losing it, and moving it about.

When children begin to experiment with traveling by taking weight on their hands, it is important for safety considerations to have them keep their bodies curled, their hands shoulder width apart, their feet relatively low, and heads up. The head-up position in this situation will assist children from going over.

*Production/absorption of force.*    Not much height is stressed with this material, only normal range of motion is needed from the arms and legs when jumping. If, when teaching the five basic jumps, for example, you want children to gain additional height, the backward thrust of the arms and the downward flexion of the body must be such that when the legs push off and the arms thrust forward/upward, both are timed so more height is achieved.

If children's jumping is to be controlled and basic body management achieved, a constant resilient action is needed in the ankles, knees, and hips. When children take weight on their hands, as well as other body parts, they should be encouraged to place them on the floor gently, not slap or throw them down. It is a form of "giving," but because the floor cannot give, children must do it for themselves. It can be pointed out to the children that skilled body control starts with their ability to take care of their own weight when using the floor and apparatus as support surfaces. Heavy landings and different body parts making noise when they touch the floor or apparatus demonstrate a lack of body control and, consequently, are unsafe.

When rolling sideways, children need to be reminded to round out the body parts on which they are rolling to achieve a smooth roll. Rolling is a very important skill that is used to absorb force over a distance and to protect the body from potential injury. To do this, body parts must be rounded and held in toward the center of the body.

In these introductory lessons, there is much opportunity to let children figure out for themselves how to keep their centers of gravity from not falling outside their bases, how to put weight on hands without any noise, how to land quietly from a jump, and how to roll sideways smoothly. The main goal here is for children to have a heightened awareness of their bodies and what they can do, and for children to demonstrate that they can control their bodies in a gymnastics environment.

## MOTOR DEVELOPMENT PRINCIPLES AFFECTING QUALITY OF PERFORMANCE

Of Newell's three factors affecting motor development, the environment is key in locomotion and stillness. Think of the gym as a special environment, a gymnastics environment, that is being constantly negotiated safely and skillfully by children. They will sometimes be moving slowly and at other times more quickly. They will sometimes be moving alone and at other times with a partner or with a small group. There will be lots going on. Children must be able to move in the space safely without harming themselves or others.

This environment changes by the way teachers structure it; that is, the spatial arrangement of the equipment and apparatus as well as their texture and height can be structured in a number of different ways. Tasks are created specifically in relation to the way equipment and apparatus are placed and designed. The material in the category of locomotion and stillness is developed with fairly simple equipment and low apparatus, arranged as single pieces (one per child), and well spaced out.

We have very few hypothesized sequences for gymnastics skills and must rely heavily on what has been learned through observation and experience. From their work with children, Roberton and Halverson (1984) have observed the following:

1. Children's ability to move slowly develops after their ability to move quickly.
2. It is easier for children to slowly increase their speed than it is to slowly decrease it.
3. When traveling on the feet, forward movement develops before backward movement, which develops before sideward movement.

In relation to traveling, experience has shown that when children first try to land softly or place their hands or other body parts on the floor or apparatus gently, they tend to do it abruptly. Sometimes there is even an audible "thud" or "slap." The control needed for this particular movement quality takes awhile to develop and, consequently, needs to be a lesson focus for a long time.

When children first try to do a sideways roll, they tend to roll across their seats and knees rather than the broad surface of their backs and shins. This seems to be caused by their inability to stay tucked as they begin to roll sideways or, perhaps, by an uneven push from their hands. Children often place their hands toward their faces (actually over their eyes!) rather than gently pressing them into the floor as they begin their rolls. If they do manage to start with their palms against the mat, sometimes they then press the backs of their hands against their faces, rather than letting them relax and go along for the ride. It takes a lot of time and body awareness for children to learn how to use their hands to protect their heads and faces and to help initiate the roll.

## PROGRESSION

When thinking about progression, there are three aspects of it that constantly interrelate to achieve an interesting and challenging lesson. One is progression related to the movement content. Another is progression related to the equipment and apparatus that will be used. And the third is progression related to the amount of choices or decisions given the children within the movement environment.

For example, in working with the five basic jumps, teachers could present these jumps first as single skills and then in different combinations as informal sequences using no equipment—content progression. The next step might be to continue the linking of two or more jumps, but in relation to hoops placed on the floor, first just in and out of the hoops, then with turning added, and finally developing a short informal sequence including two basic jumps with two changes of direction—content progression; equipment progression. Finally, with benches placed throughout the space with mats at the ends and to one side, children could be first asked to go on, off, over, or along the benches using as many of the five basic jumps as they could; then, changing directions when and as often as they choose and adding a turn where appropriate. A further progression would be to use other body parts on which to travel—content progression; apparatus progression; decision-making progression.

The progression related to content and equipment/apparatus is fairly standard in educational gymnastics, and most beginning teachers find it useful when they first start teaching. It keeps the interest of the children and moves nicely from the simple to the complex. We like to think that the climax of a lesson centers around the use of apparatus. This aspect of each lesson is the most challenging for children and does much to enhance their skill development and peak their interest.

The third type of progression is related to the types and amounts of decisions that you, the teacher, will build into your instructional tasks. Drawing children into the learning process and giving them responsibility over some of their own learning is not an approach to teaching that just happens. You have to learn how to share different aspects of the learning environment with children if you are to reach the educational gymnastics goal of helping children improve their ability to make informed decisions and become competent and confident learners.

For beginning teachers and teachers inexperienced with educational gymnastics, it is helpful to start with tasks designed with a more narrow focus, then, gradually design tasks with broader ones. In other words, at the beginning the teacher makes more of the decisions. Having children travel using just their feet, then feet and hands, then suggesting they use other body parts is an example of starting with a narrow focus and gradually broadening it. As children become more familiar with the learning environment and their roles in it, and teachers become more familiar with how children respond, more decisions can be given to the children.

Whenever you begin educational gymnastics for the first time, be it with a K or fifth-grade class, the material associated with locomotion and stillness should be taught first. This content is very important to include. With younger children, you can stay with this material longer than with older children, especially if you are fortunate enough to have boxes and benches. With older children (grades 3–5), you will have to move on more quickly, for this material is not challenging enough once they have experienced it and can demonstrate the basic control for which you are looking. It helps orient children to the gymnastics learning environment, and gives you an indication of how well they can control their bodies and follow directions.

## EXPERIENCES FOR REFLECTION

1. With a classmate visit playgrounds where children are playing and also visit a children's gymnastics lesson at either a YMCA, YWCA, or similar organization, or a private club. Try to observe children

from 5–12 years of age. Describe the two types of environments. What are their similarities and differences? Observe the children and describe what they do. Write an essay or journal entry related to children's movement capabilities within these movement environments. At the end, complete the following sentences to reflect on what you wrote:

I learned. . .
I'm beginning to wonder. . .
I was surprised. . .

2. Of all the ideas outlined in this chapter, identify which of them you think would be the most difficult to teach children and which of them would be the easiest? With a small group of classmates, share what makes an idea hard or easy to teach.

## *core content*

## Weight Bearing/Balancing as Single Skills and in Sequences

### FOCUS OF CONTENT

Weight bearing/balancing on different body parts, on specific body parts (head, hands, shoulders) taught as single skills and sequences of skills, individually, with a partner, and in small groups explored by using selected aspects of:

> time
> space awareness
> space relationships
> body shape
> symmetry/asymmetry

in relation to:

> small equipment
> apparatus

and integrating from the critical skills set:

> hand balance/body curled
> shoulder balance
> head/hand balance

### APPROPRIATENESS OF CONTENT

This material should come right after the work focused on locomotion and stillness. The ability to take weight on different body parts is fundamental to the successful performance of most gymnastics skills. This content remains important across all grade levels and will be revisited and expanded throughout the six-year program. This material includes the skill of balance, or maintaining stillness, over different body parts, as well as the body's weight moving over different body parts.

**IDEAS FROM WHICH MOVEMENT TASKS ARE DESIGNED\***

## *Weight Bearing/Balancing—Part A: Introduction*

- Finding different body parts on which weight can be balanced

    balance on feet, hands, head, knees, shins, sides, stomach, back, shoulders
    use alone and in combinations

(See Integration of Skills and Focused Teaching 3: Hand Balance/Body Curled)

- Traveling by taking weight on hands alone, feet low

    use foot patterns of five basic jumps for pushing off and landing
    come down in different places by means of a twist

(See Integration of Skills and Focused Teaching 4: Shoulder Balance)
(See Integration of Skills and Focused Teaching 5: Head/Hand Balance)

- Experimenting with taking weight on matching parts (e.g., shins, knees, forearms)
- Experimenting with placing body parts in different relationships to each other

    place close together, far apart, side by side, one in front of the other

- Balancing, taking weight on dissimilar parts; isolated parts

PHOTO 5–4
Finding different body parts on which weight can be balanced.

• • • • • • • • • • • • • • • • • • • • • • • • • • • • • • • • • • • • • • • • • • • • •

\*Arranged in a suggested progression adapted from Mauldon & Layson (1979).

- Adding the idea of body shape

    focus on body part(s) taking the weight
    focus on body part(s) not taking the weight
    use symmetry and asymmetry

- Adding the idea of body tension so children can sense "a liveliness within the body, alert to any action which might follow" (Mauldon & Layson, 1979, p. 72), as opposed to "resting" on different body parts

## *Weight Bearing/Balancing—Part B: Continued Development*

- Creating informal sequences that link two or more balanced positions

    work alone, with a partner
    show a clear stillness in the balances
    let positions move easily into one another
    link balancing with rolling

- Using task ideas in Parts A and B redesigned with ropes and hoops placed on the floor

    travel into and out of a hoop taking weight on different body parts
    travel back and forth over a rope taking weight on different body parts
    change direction
    vary the speed

PHOTO 5–5
Balancing taking weight on similar or dissimilar parts.

change level

use the five basic jumps, but now with more height

- Using task ideas in Parts A and B redesigned for partner work

  vary position of facing like back to back, side to side, behind/in front
  match movements like balances, body shapes, sequences
  contrast movements with high/low, curled/stretched, fast/slow

- Using task ideas in Parts A and B redesigned with benches and boxes of low heights, find different combinations of body parts on which weight can be taken and balanced

  supported by apparatus only
  supported by the apparatus and mat together
  vary the body shape

PHOTO 5–6
Balancing tasks redesigned for partner work.

PHOTO 5-7
Balancing tasks redesigned for partner work.

vary space relationships of body parts to apparatus

work alone, with a partner

• Using task ideas in Parts A and B redesigned with benches and boxes of low heights, find different body parts that can support your weight while traveling

vary the space relationships of body to apparatus

vary the shape of the body

use 1–2, 2–2 basic jumps to mount and dismount the apparatus

increase gradually the height of the jump used in the dismount

recover from the jump with sideways and forward rolls

### BIOMECHANICAL PRINCIPLES AFFECTING QUALITY OF PERFORMANCE

*Center of gravity and balance.*   As mentioned earlier, children need to understand the center of gravity concept and how it relates, in this case, to balancing on different body parts. The larger the body surface (back, shoulders, hips) and the larger the base of support (two hands and two feet, head and two hands placed in a triangle) the more stable the balance.  Children can "feel" this principle by teachers giving them very specific balances to perform.

*Absorption of force.*   Now that the children will be jumping higher, they will have to learn how to dissipate the force of their bodies by landing with increased control. Broer (1984) described it well:

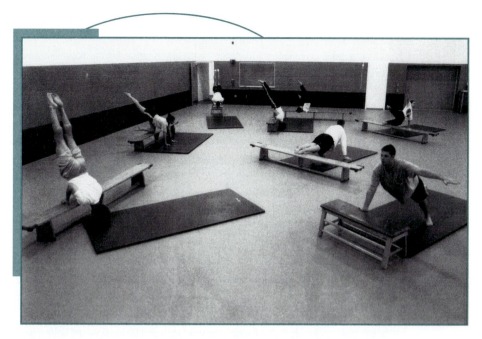

PHOTO 5–8
Balancing/weight bearing tasks developed further by adding benches and boxes of low heights.

A controlled bending of the joints of the legs allows the body to keep moving and gradually slows it. This controlled bending is commonly called "giving," and the gradual force dissipation is called "force absorption" (p. 119).

As their jumps increase in height, the ability to give will have to keep improving as more force will have to be absorbed. To dissipate the force of their bodies even more, the downward direction of the landings can be redirected into a roll after the landing on the feet is completed. Following a give with the hands and arms, the body weight is taken onto the shoulders and along the spine (or across the back in a sideways roll) and onto the feet. Distributing the absorption of force over such a large area clearly slows down the momentum. Besides being mechanically efficient, children enjoy linking jumping with rolling and balancing with rolling. The more proficient they become, the greater the chances of transfer to other situations that call for force absorption (e.g., tripping, catching a ball off balance).

*Force production.* When jumping, there is a coordinated pattern between the use of the arms and legs, especially when height is desired. For low jumps or low jumps and turns, the arms are used primarily for balance. For jumps for height, the arms and legs clearly must work together with considerable force. The bending of the hips, knees, and ankles and the backward/upward swing of the arms in preparation for the jump are followed by a pushing of the legs against the floor with an upward/forward thrust of the arms to full extension. The greater the range of motion through which the arms and legs move, the higher the jump. The timing needed for this skill is not present in many children, especially younger ones. It takes time to develop to the advanced level.

## MOTOR DEVELOPMENT PRINCIPLES AFFECTING QUALITY OF PERFORMANCE

Of Newell's three factors affecting motor development, the environment is still key and for the same reasons as stated in Core Content 1. The environment here is similar, but the movement skills being attempted are quite different, thus, everything is new again.  Balancing implies stillness, and as body parts reach farther away from more narrow bases of support, the centers of gravity rise and children become less stable.

Raising box heights creates a change in task requirements. This change is enough for some children to regress momentarily in their skill levels as they try the task for the first time. Regression in the use of the arms and legs in jumping for height is often seen when children move from jumping off of the floor to jumping off of a bench or box. After a few practices, however, the coordinated use of the arms and legs usually returns, unless the height of the box is too much.

When first learning to balance on different body parts, Mauldon and Layson (1979) observed that children look like they are "resting" on them, rather than "holding" the body in a position over a base of support ready to move in a new direction. When children are skilled in using the right amount of tension in their bodies, they can "feel" a held position.

Of the motor skills for which we have developmental sequences, two have been hypothesized that are helpful with teaching and assessing children's progress with the material in this category—the standing long jump and the forward roll (Roberton & Halverson, 1984). (See Tables 5–1 through 5–4.)

While the standing long jump is not the same skill as the jump for height, all components for the preparation phase can be adapted very easily. The arm component for the flight and landing phase is also useful. Instead of the legs "tucking" and the trunk "leaning," as they do in the standing long jump, the trunk and legs in the jump for height should be fully extended at the peak of the jump. Less mature children will demonstrate varying degrees of flexion in their legs and trunks before they can fully extend. Additional developmental information related to the movement skills emerging from this material are included in Integration of Skills and Focused Teaching 3, 4, and 5.

### PROGRESSION

The comments about progression written with Core Content 1 Locomotion and Stillness apply here as they do throughout all the Core Content units. To give added guidance regarding progression, we have listed the ideas in the section "Ideas from Which Movement Tasks Are Designed" in a suggested progression. The fact that we have done this should not discourage you from creating your own progression. Usually, however, working alone is considered by most to be less challenging than working with a partner, no equipment simpler than small equipment, and apparatus work to be the most challenging.

Included in the material is the suggestion of working with a partner. For very young children this may be too early, but for the older ones it is quite appropriate. When asking children to work with a partner in gymnastics, recognize that this is an entirely new movement situation for them. Up to this time, the children's main responsibility has been to avoid each other and focus their attention on themselves while they work. Working with a partner shifts this orientation toward cooperation in which both children work as a unit.  Mauldon and Layson (1979) suggested a useful progression when thinking how to integrate partner work into lessons. Four types of partner work are suggested: copying part or the whole of a partner's sequence, making and negotiating obstacles without contact, matching actions, and taking all or part of each other's weight.

In the first type, children could begin by copying each other's pathway, then the main actions (e.g., jumping, turning, rolling), and lastly, a short sequence. The second type, that of using each other as obstacles,

TABLE 5–1

## Developmental Sequences for the Standing Long Jump Takeoff Phase

### LEG ACTION COMPONENT

*Step 1*  **Fall and catch.** The weight is shifted forward. The knee and ankle are held in flexion or extend slightly as gravity rotates the body over the balls of the feet. Takeoff occurs when the toes are pulled from the surface in preparation for the landing "catch."

*Step 2*  **Two-foot takeoff; Partial extension.** Both feet leave the ground symmetrically, but the hips, knees and/or ankles do not reach full extension by takeoff.

*Step 3*  **Two-foot takeoff; Full extension.** Both feet leave the ground symmetrically with hips, knees, and ankles fully extended by takeoff.

### TRUNK ACTION COMPONENT

*Step 1*  **Slight lean; Head back.** The trunk leans forward less than 30° from the vertical. The neck is hyperextended.

*Step 2*  **Slight lean; Head aligned.** The trunk leans forward less than 30°, with the neck flexed or aligned with the trunk at takeoff.

*Step 3*  **Forward lean; Chin tucked.** The trunk is inclined forward 30° or more (with the vertical) at takeoff, with the neck flexed.

*Step 4*  **Forward lean; Head aligned.** The trunk is inclined forward 30° or more. The neck is aligned with the trunk or slightly extended.

### ARM ACTION COMPONENT

*Step 1*  **Arms inactive.** The arms are held at the side with the elbows flexed. Arm movement, if any, is inconsistent and random.

*Step 2*  **Winging arms.** The arms extend backward in a "winging" posture at takeoff.

*Step 3*  **Arms abducted.** The arms are abducted about 90°, with the elbows often flexed, in a high or middle guard position.

*Step 4*  **Arms forward; Partial stretch.** The arms flex forward and upward with minimal abduction, reaching incomplete extension overhead by takeoff.

*Step 5*  **Arms forward; Full stretch.** The arms flex forward, reaching full extension overhead by takeoff.

*Note:* These developmental sequences have not been validated. They are modified by Halverson from the work of Van Sant.[73, 69]

Reprinted by permission from Roberton & Halverson, 1984.

should be kept simple and guided tightly by the teacher. It probably should be held for older children and only after they are familiar with the material in Core Content 3. For example, one child could lie in a fully stretched position along the edge of a mat and the other jump over "the obstacle" completing the sequence with a roll.

**TABLE 5-2**

*Developmental Sequences for the Standing Long Jump Flight and Landing Phase*

LEG ACTION COMPONENT

*Step 1*   **Minimal "tuck."** The thigh is carried in flight more than 45° below the horizontal. The legs may assume either symmetrical or asymmetrical configurations during flight, resulting in one- or two-footed landings.

*Step 2*   **Partial "tuck."** During flight, the hips and knees flex synchronously. The thigh approaches a 20 to 35° angle below the horizontal. The knees then extend for a two-footed landing.

*Step 3*   **Full "tuck."** During flight, flexion of both knees precedes hip flexion. The hips then flex, bringing the thighs to the horizontal. The knees then extend, reaching forward to a two-foot landing.

TRUNK ACTION COMPONENT

*Step 1*   **Slight lean.** During flight, the trunk maintains its forward inclination of less than 30°, then flexes for landing.

*Step 2*   **Corrected lean.** The trunk corrects its forward lean of 30° or more by hyperextending. It then flexes forward for landing.

*Step 3*   **Maintained lean.** The trunk maintains the forward lean of 30° or more from takeoff to midflight, then flexes forward for landing.

ARM ACTION COMPONENT

*Step 1*   **Arms "winging."** In two-footed takeoff jumps, the shoulders may retract while the arms extend backward (winging)[56] during flight. They move forward (parachuting) during landing.

*Step 2*   **Arms abducted; Lateral rotation.** During flight, the arms hold a high guard position and continue lateral rotation. They parachute for landing.

*Step 3*   **Arms abducted; Medial rotation.** During flight, the arms assume high or middle guard positions, but medially rotate early in the flight. They parachute for landing.

*Step 4*   **Arms overhead.** During flight, the arms are held overhead. In middle flight, the arms lower (extend) from their overhead flexed position, reaching forward at landing.

*Note:* These developmental steps have not been validated. They have been modified by Halverson from the work of Van Sant.[73, 69]

Reprinted by permission from Roberton & Halverson, 1984.

More competent children might be asked to take weight on their hands as they go over their partners, who are close to the floor and in an extended position.

Matching or copying a part or the whole of a partner's movement is fun for children and they take to it quickly. Tasks must be simple at first, because children are not used to timing their movements to anyone else. It requires using each other's capabilities to the best advantage.

TABLE 5–3

*Developmental Sequences for the Forward Roll Initial Phase*

**HEAD AND ARM ACTION COMPONENT**

*Step 1*  **Head support.** Little weight is taken on the arms and hands. The hands are often placed on the surface even with the line of the head. The angle at the elbow is approximately 45°. The child may be unable to hold the weight evenly, so the body collapses to one side.

*Step 2*  **Head and arm support.** The arms and hands partially accept the body weight. The base of support of the hands tends to be wide from side to side and behind the head toward the feet. The angle at the elbow is greater than 90°.

*Step 3*  **Arm support.** The arms and hands now accept the weight as the roll begins, permitting the head, with the chin tucked, to slide through the arms.

**LEG ACTION COMPONENT**

*Step 1*  **One-leg push.** One leg leads in leaving the surface, then the knee and hip of the lead leg flex while the other leg extends on the push-off.

*Step 2*  **Two-leg push.** Both legs push off equally. The knees flex to about 90° as the balance is lost.

*Note:* These sequences have been modified from Williams[80] and Roberton & Halverson.[79]
Reprinted by permission from Roberton & Halverson, 1984.

Finally, using each other's weight in some way is the fourth type of task that can be used. Taking balanced positions in which both partners either pull away from each other and maintain the position or lean in and push toward their partners are appropriate experiences for older children. Just the process of trying to find these moments of "counter tension or counter resistance" (Mauldon & Layson, 1979) using different body parts and different balanced positions is exciting in and of itself.

*Quality and variety.*    Up to this point the concepts of quality and variety have not been mentioned. Nowchildren should be ready to deal with these concepts and teachers should begin to incorporate them into lessons. Variety and quality should come together eventually for one is not sought at the expense of the other, except perhaps at the very beginning when variety may take a slight edge.

Many tasks in this form of gymnastics are structured to encourage children to find different ways to move. That is the variety part. Finding different ways to move is very difficult at first, and most children find one or two responses and stop. Since the purpose of gymnastics is to increase body awareness and develop a broad range of skills, children's ability to seek alternate responses to a task becomes important. It is a skill in and of itself, and you will need to figure out ways to help them learn how to respond appropriately. At first, it is helpful to specify how many different ways they might try a movement. Their ability to seek variety without the teacher's constant support develops gradually over time and is how you hope the children eventually come to respond.

## TABLE 5-4

*Developmental Sequences for the Forward Roll Completion Phase*

ARM ACTION COMPONENT

*Step 1*  **Little assistance.** The arms may remain back by the head until pulled off by the forward motion of the body.

*Step 2*  **Incomplete assist.** The arms swing forward to assist in the completion of the roll when the shoulders and/or middle of the back have touched the surface. The elbows are extended during the assist. The hands may be used to push the body to the feet at the end of the roll.

*Step 3*  **Continual arm assist.** The arms swing forward to assist in continuation of the momentum of the roll, as soon as the weight has transferred to the shoulders. The arms continue to assist in a forward-upward direction until the weight is over the feet.

HEAD AND TRUNK COMPONENT

*Step 1*  **Head and trunk lag.** As the hips begin forward-downward movement, the child abandons the body to gravity. The upper trunk and hips land on the surface almost simultaneously. As the middle of the back and hips land, the head and upper back lag behind, often remaining close to or just off the surface, even when the lower back has made contact.

*Step 2*  **Partial head and trunk lag.** The shoulders touch the surface before the middle of the back and hips, but the head and shoulders do not then leave the surface again until the middle of the back has touched. The body usually continues the roll in a semipiked position over the pelvis.

*Step 3*  **No head and trunk lag.** The head leaves the support surface just after the shoulders touch. Both the head and trunk continue moving forward and upward throughout the roll. By the time the lower back contacts the surface, the head and shoulders are well off the mat.

LEG ACTION COMPONENT

*Step 1*  **Knees extend; hips extend.** The legs tend to hold their push-off position until the lower back or pelvis touches the support surface. At this point, extension in the hip increases, contributing to the loss of curl in the roll. The knees either increase in extension or continue in an extended position. The angle at the hip may reach approximately 120° and is then held if the body continues rotating over the pelvis.

*Step 2*  **Knees flex; hips extend.** Leg action begins as in Step 1. When the middle of the back touches the support surface, extension at the hips increases also as in Step 1, but the knees flex rather than continuing in an extended position. The roll may continue with the body in this position or the hips may flex.

*Step 3*  **Knees flex; hips flex.** The knees begin flexion just after the hips begin the forward-downward movement in the roll and maintain that flexion throughout the roll. The hips continue flexion throughout the roll.

Note: These sequences have been hypothesized from Williams,[80] and Roberton and Halverson.[79]

Reprinted by permission from Roberton & Halverson, 1984.

With the material in this core unit, the concept of body shape and body tension have been introduced. These two concepts are the beginning of the quality part. Also, much stress has been placed on force absorption, another aspect of quality. Quality refers to the efficiency of the movement as well as its aesthetic aspects. Good body management requires effective use of mechanical principles. Clarity of body shape and body tension create a visual appeal in movement very similar to the visual images that skilled dancers are able to create.

As children become more skilled in their ability to balance on different body parts and change their body shapes, it is time to ask them to make these shapes clear through proper body alignment and appropriate tension, tightness, and control. These criteria should be consistently woven throughout all lessons from now on.

### EXPERIENCES FOR REFLECTION

1. Children often are challenged in seeking alternate responses when asked to experiment with, explore, or find different ways to move. Discuss in your class why you think this is so, "exploring" a number of different reasons yourself. Think about children's current experiences in schools, home, and in society at large. Reflect on how these experiences may encourage limitations in responding. Complete your discussion by identifying at least three different strategies that you think you could use to help children learn to seek variety more easily.

2. For those interested in the history of educational gymnastics read Ruth Morison's first booklets, *Educational Gymnastics* (1956) and *Educational Gymnastics for Secondary Schools* (1960) for a glimpse of the concept of educational gymnastics when it first emerged in the professional literature. What ideas of Morison's captured your interest particularly? Do you see those ideas in the approach taken in this chapter?

## *core content*   3

### Weight Transference as Single Skills and in Sequences

#### FOCUS OF CONTENT

Methods of weight transference to include rocking/rolling, step-like actions, sliding, and flight taught as single skills and sequences of skills, individually, with a partner, and in small groups explored by using selected aspects of:

> time
> space awareness
> space relationships
> body shape
> symmetry/asymmetry

in relation to:

> small equipment
> apparatus

and integrating from the critical skills set:

> jump/land/roll basic sequence
> forward roll/shoulder roll
> backward roll/shoulder roll
> hand balance/body extended
> cartwheel
> jump for height

## APPROPRIATENESS OF CONTENT

The purpose of this material is for children to continue the refinement and further development of the different ways they have been balancing and transferring their weight in previous lessons. The material in this category follows logically from the material in the previous two. By refinement we mean continuous development of the children's skills and skill combinations toward their most advanced patterns.

In addition, lessons focused on this material seek to elicit a more mature level of variety and quality. The critical skills should now become a strong foundation and true vehicle for the discovery of more skills and skill combinations. Further, they act as threads that bind together informal and formal gymnastics sequences.

New movement skills and skill combinations are continuously elicited from the children as they work with this material. And most important, the formal gymnastics sequence takes on a prominent role here (see Core Content 4–Gymnastics Sequences).

### IDEAS FROM WHICH MOVEMENT TASKS ARE DESIGNED

## *Transference of Weight—Part A: Introduction*

- Rocking from shoulders to feet and back again

> begin by sitting with rounded back, head and legs tucked and hands gently placed on knees
> rock with changes in speed
> return from shoulders with increased speed, reach forward to stand or jump up
> repeat rocking until weight is transferred to shoulders, twist right/left and rock back to feet
> rock until weight is transferred to shoulders, extend body into air just before coming back into a curled position
> vary the shape of the body once timing has been established (e.g., legs apart, legs separated, legs partially bent/stretched)
> develop quick informal partner or group sequences experimenting with where members face at the beginning and where they face at the end

- Rocking sideways on feet

> rock with feet together, feet apart

- Rocking forward and backward on feet

> rock with feet together, feet apart

(See Integration of Skills and Focused Teaching 6: Jump/Land/Roll Basic Sequence)

(See Integration of Skills and Focused Teaching 7: Forward Roll/Shoulder Roll)
(See Integration of Skills and Focused Teaching 8: Backward Roll/Shoulder Roll)
(See Integration of Skills and Focused Teaching 9: Hand Balance/Body Extended)
(See Integration of Skills and Focused Teaching 10: Cartwheel)

- Rolling in different ways

    vary the direction of the roll
    roll from standing, walking, jumping (1–2, 2–2)

- Rolling with a partner

    experiment with different relationships to each other such as facing, side by side, back to back, one in
        front of the other
    experiment with different timing such as at the same time, one after the other

- Finding different ways to get from feet to shoulders using rocking/rolling
- Finding different ways to shift weight using step-like actions

    shift weight from one foot to the other foot
    shift weight from one foot to two hands
    shift weight from two hands to two feet, one foot
    shift weight from knees to shoulders

PHOTO 5–9
Jump/land/roll basic sequence.

PHOTO 5–10
Jump/land/roll basic sequence.

shift weight from feet to shoulders
shift weight from knees to head and hands
shift weight from feet to head and hands
encourage the use of rolling for transition

(See Integration of Skills and Focused Teaching 11: Jump for Height)

- Jumping using the five basic jumps

  emphasize height and landing
  emphasize body shape while in the air
  emphasize turns while in the air

- Create informal (or formal) sequences that link two or more methods of weight transference

  link rocking, rolling
  link rocking, rolling, flight
  link step-like, rolling
  link step-like, rolling, flight

## Transference of Weight—Part B: Continued Development

- Using task ideas in Part A redesigned with mats, ropes, and hoops placed on the floor in different arrangements, travel in, out, over, and along using different methods of transferring weight

PHOTO 5–11
Continued development of jumping using the five basic jumps traveling in, out, and over ropes, hoops, and blocks and canes placed on the floor.

· · · · · · · · · · · · · · · · · · · · · · · · · · · · · · · · · · · · · · · · · · · · · · · · · · · · · · · · · · ·

     change speed
     change direction

- Matching partner's movements using at least two different methods of transferring weight

     change speed
     change direction

- Using task ideas in Parts A and B redesigned with benches and boxes of low heights, alternate between step-like actions to get on the bench and flight (2–2 feet jump) to come off the bench

     change speed
     change direction
     land and roll in same direction
     land and rock
     land, control weight, and redirect it
     change body shape

- Combining sliding with step-like actions and rolling, traveling along, on, off, back and forth the length of a bench

     change speed
     change direction
     land and roll in same direction

**PHOTO 5–12**
Using flight (2-2 feet jump) to come off benches and boxes of varying heights showing changes in body shape while in the air.

• • • • • • • • • • • • • • • • • • • • • • • • • • • • • • • • • • • • • • • • • • • • • • • • • • • • • • •

> land and rock
> land, control weight, and redirect it
> change body shape

- Mounting the box using step-like actions, dismounting by means of flight (2–2 feet jump), followed by a roll and recovery to feet

> change speed
> change direction
> land and roll in same direction
> land and rock
> land, control weight, and redirect it
> change body shape

- Rolling across the top of a box, dismounting by placing hands on floor, lowering body into a roll, and coming to feet (stand or jump)

> vary body shape
> add a step-like action following the roll

Remember that step-like actions are not only with the feet. Encourage use of many different body parts as well as inverted positions. By now children have the confidence to take their weight on their head, for example, on the top of a box (low height) and convert that into a roll. Likewise, those who have gained skill in balancing on their hands, or shifting their weight from one hand to the other in a cartwheel, should be further developing these skills with boxes and benches.

## BIOMECHANICAL PRINCIPLES AFFECTING QUALITY OF PERFORMANCE

The same biomechanical principles—center of gravity, force absorption, and force production—continue to apply to all material represented by this category of weight transference. Specific applications are addressed when the skills from the critical set are discussed.

## MOTOR DEVELOPMENT PRINCIPLES AFFECTING QUALITY OF PERFORMANCE

Of person-environment-task constraints, the environment is still most important and must be observed continuously for its effect on children's motor responses. It is during this work that children will become increasingly advanced (i.e., more mature) with the critical skills in all environments (no equipment, small equipment, apparatus). As they begin to use these skills on benches and boxes and as part of their sequences, expect regression to less mature movement patterns. This will occur because the situation in which these skills and skill combinations are being performed has changed.

In addition, options for the design and redesign of tasks are now vast. And that is what is so much fun about being a teacher of and a child in educational gymnastics. There are lots of options, and the work can take many directions. Children, however, do not cope well with too many choices built into the tasks, especially in the beginning, so carefully think through the specific content on which you want to focus. Experience has demonstrated that beginning teachers have difficulty eliciting quality movement responses with tasks that are designed for multiple responses or that have problem solving as an inherent part of them. It is not enough that children respond in multiple ways. Their multiple responses still need to be quality ones.

Of the critical skills placed in this category of content, Roberton and Halverson (1984) have hypothesized developmental sequences for the forward roll (see Tables 5–3 and 5–4). Studying these sequences will help you interpret individual children's progress in this skill. For specific information on how to use this knowledge when working with less mature rollers see Integration of Skills and Focused Teaching 7. Where we have developmental information related to the other skills, it is included in the sections Integration of Skills and Focused Teaching 8, 9, 10, and 11.

### PROGRESSION

The basic concepts regarding progression that have already been discussed apply to this material as well. In addition, we suggest that you keep two things in mind.

1. Keep revisiting the critical skills so the children can become increasingly more advanced and varied in the way they perform them and in the way they use them on apparatus and in sequences. A lot of practice is needed for advanced work to emerge. A suggested order of these skills has been given throughout the chapter, but once they have all been introduced the order and when you revisit them is up to you. These skills are never really finished as they are viewed more as vehicles for more skills and skill combinations than as end products themselves. The more responsible children can be for their own learning, the easier it will be to bring back these skills and have children work on them at their individual levels of development.

2.  Do not forget the dual concept of variety and quality. Review what was suggested in Core Content 2—weight bearing/balancing as it applies here as well. There is a tendency to forget the quality part for the variety part. They need to be built together.

**EXPERIENCES FOR REFLECTION**

1.  Obtain permission to videotape 8–10 children from the same classroom responding to a task of your choice, but one in which they have been asked to seek variety and include movement patterns consistent with rolling and balancing. Include in your group of children various heights, weights, genders, races, and motor-ability levels. By yourself or with a partner, view the tape of these children working on this task and record observations of their ability to seek variety, demonstrate clear body shapes, and absorb and produce appropriate amounts of force in relation to task requirements. Based on these written observations, place these children along a developmental continuum for each of the above criteria. If this were your class, based on your observations, in what directions could you go next with their gymnastics work? Decide first which category of content (1, 2, 3, or 4) should be the focus and then the material within that category that might be appropriate. There is no one answer, but be able to justify your answer on the basis of your observations.

2.  Select one of the critical skills included in this material and read as much as you can about it. Include in your reading at least one text from each of these categories: formal or Olympic gymnastics texts, educational gymnastics texts (especially those written by Mauldon & Layson in 1979, Williams in 1992, and Morison in 1969), and elementary, middle, and high school curriculum texts. Synthesize the information and insight gained from all these authors about your skill. Finally, think through how this insight can be blended into your teaching, specifically when you incorporate this critical skill into your lessons.

## *core content*      4

## Gymnastics Sequences

### FOCUS OF CONTENT

Forms of gymnastics sequences: informal and formal

The content of locomotion and stillness, weight bearing/balancing, and weight transference are taught both as single skills and as sequences of skills. Throughout this chapter, we have been calling these skill combinations, gymnastics sequences. Because gymnastics sequences play such an important and continuous role throughout the K–5 gymnastics program, they are presented as Core Content 4.

Sequences are defined as a series of actions that are so skillfully linked together that all movements within the sequence fit together logically (Mauldon & Layson, 1979). Two types are being suggested: informal and formal. In informal sequences, children are not expected to perfect movements at the same level as in formal sequences; in fact, informal sequences generally remain in the early stages of development. Nor are the children expected to share the results of their informal sequence work with others to the same degree that they may share their formal sequences. In formal sequences, children experience the more complete process of sequence development and thus more time is spent on them. Formal sequences are also shared with individual class members or the class as a whole in some way. How, when, and for what purposes vary and are dependent upon the context in which they are being developed.

Educational gymnastics is more than just doing a single action, such as balancing on your head and hands keeping the body extended, or taking weight on hands keeping the body curled as you go over the top of a bench, or doing a forward roll along the top of a box. It is the blending of these actions in personal and creative ways and through this blending process inventing other ways to move that is the essence of skillfulness in educational gymnastics. Further, the act of exploring and discovering how movements truly fit together affords a rare and unique opportunity to develop a deeper understanding of movement; one that is more powerful than can be learned from performing movements only as single skills. Sequence development is a wonderful opportunity for physical educators to support and foster the creative spirit of children.

Central to the way educational gymnastics is taught is the belief that by becoming active participants in their own learning, children will learn how to move as well as move to learn. Moving to learn is a powerful outcome of creating sequences and gives children rare opportunities to realize more about themselves as developing, moving persons.

## APPROPRIATENESS OF CONTENT

Figure 5–2 shows that informal sequences can be used throughout all grades whereas formal sequences are suggested to begin close to the 3rd grade. Our rationale is to give children ample time to build a strong foundation upon which they can further advance their work throughout the 3rd, 4th, and 5th grades. If too much time is spent on sequences in K through 2nd grades, in the formal sense specifically, children's skills foundation could be too weak to support the more advanced work associated with the upper grades. Formal sequences take time to develop if children are to receive the educational value they offer. When and how often formal sequences are used are ultimately philosophical decisions. You will need to wait until you have had some experience in teaching educational gymnastics and you know your children before making those decisions. For now, however, your goal is to learn how to help children develop both kinds of sequences and to gain insight into the development process. The rest of this section focuses on information to help you as you begin to learn about teaching sequences and how best to develop them with children.

### DESIGNING A GYMNASTICS SEQUENCE

The development of sequences is like building sentences in language. Morison (1969) equates it to the sentence structure of language:

> Words are put together to form phrases, and one or more phrases form a sentence. The linking of words and phrases, and the placing of stress and pauses gives the sentence meaning, rhythm and flow. Similarly, phrases of movement may be joined together to form sentences (p. 119).

As a metaphor, sentence building is useful in helping children understand sequence development and it can be easily related to their work in the classroom. The process has a number of steps, each freely flowing in and out of each other, but each clearly possessing its own essential and meaningful function. Four steps are discussed here—define a focus, explore/improvise, select/organize/refine, and share/evaluate (Cheney, 1989; Hawkins, 1991; Mauldon & Layson, 1979; Rovegno, 1988).

*Define a focus.*   To get started designing either type of sequence, children need a focus. This can be determined by the teacher or the children themselves. When using informal sequences the focus is usually determined by the teacher as the sequences emerge naturally and quickly from the direction of the lesson and the tasks being used. For example, a focus could be selected such as the five basic jumps (Core Content 1), symmetrical balancing on different body parts (Core Content 2), or rocking and rolling (Core Content 3). A focus gives children something to concentrate on that will immediately stimulate them to move in new and interesting ways. If the focus does not function in that capacity, it is most likely too broad, too abstract, or too unrelated to what the children have been doing.

*Explore/improvise.*   Once children have a focus, they are encouraged to explore ways, as Cheney (1989) explained it, to do that which they have already decided to do! This is a great way to think about it because children have been developing a large repertoire of movement skills that are now available for a different purpose. True improvising, on the other hand, is more spontaneous. It is a process of "letting things happen, rather than intellectually predetermining what will occur" (Cheney, 1989, p. 82). With children, these two processes will most likely mingle, as the difference between them may be too subtle and not important. It is important that we help them catch the spirit of exploring so that new movements or new combinations of movements result. True exploration should lead to some improvising, certainly among the more confident children. Rovegno (1988) called this process "movement brainstorming." This is a good term to use at this stage of sequence building because children tend to talk about what they are going to do rather than doing it.

For example, if the sequence focus is on rocking, rolling, and balancing, the children would be given time to explore all possible ways they could think of to combine rocking, rolling, and balancing. As their teacher, you would encourage full exploration by encouraging use of different body parts, changes in level and speed, or any other aspects that appear to be missing. As a result of this "movement brainstorming," new ways to perform the actions of rocking, rolling, and balancing (i.e., new to the child) and new ways to combine them should result. This phase of developing sequences can be exciting and stimulating. From these explorations and improvisations, children should now have a substantial repertoire of movement skills and skill combinations from which to select, organize, and refine their ideas into a sequence. If the exploring/improvising phase of sequence building is cut short too soon, or if it is entered too early, children will not be ready for the next step.

*Select/organize/refine.*   Children must now select those skills and skill combinations they wish to keep and organize their selections into a logical sequence. Children will have to arrange and rearrange, combine and recombine their selections until the sequence feels right and is personally meaningful to them. This can take quite a bit of time. Within this three-part process of selection, organization, and refinement, there are certain elements that can be used as criteria to help you and the children step back, so to speak, to look at what is developing and assess its quality. Following is a list of questions that children can use to help them monitor themselves in the development of their sequences. Teachers need to carry these questions in their heads, as they can serve as a framework to guide children according to their individual needs.

1. Does my sequence reflect the focus with which I started? Does it need changing?
2. Does my sequence project a sense of the whole? Does it have a beginning? Does it develop and go somewhere? Does it have an ending?
3. Am I using a range of body parts on which to balance or transfer my weight?

4. Are the shapes of my body clear? Am I using the right amount of tension? Do I use both symmetrical and asymmetrical shapes? Am I using the space fully in terms of level and direction? Do my body shapes complement each other? Contrast with each other?
5. Am I using speed effectively for the situation?
6. Does my sequence demonstrate continuity of movement? Are the different movements logically related? Are my transitions smooth between individual skills and skill combinations?

For children just starting to design sequences, the concepts in these questions (e.g., different body parts, change of direction) give them a concrete way to begin. Even if you use some of the same movement concepts for the focus of a sequence as are included in the questions, the questions should act as a guide to assess sequence quality. The questions are comprehensive in nature and go beyond the content of any one child's individual sequence. Adapting these questions for assessing dance sequences builds a nice bridge between gymnastics and dance, the latter focusing more on the development of aesthetic principles, however, than is done in gymnastics.

*Share/evaluate.* Sequences can be shared for different reasons and at any stage of the process. We like to think of these sharing sessions more as observation and discussion sessions rather than of sharing in the

**PHOTO 5–13**
This gymnast is beginning the select/organize/refine step of sequence development. As the teacher, what would you do to help guide her through this step?

PHOTO 5-14

PHOTO 5-15

PHOTO 5–16

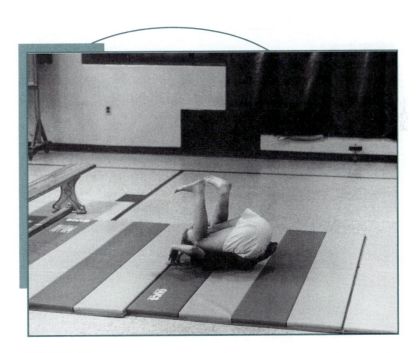

PHOTO 5–17

PHOTO 5–18

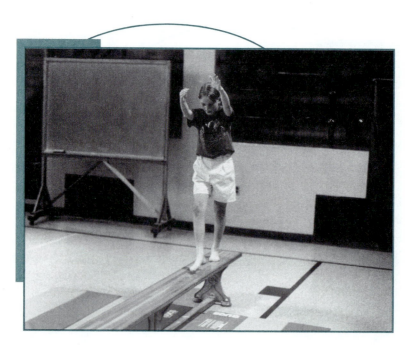

PHOTO 5–19

PHOTO 5–20

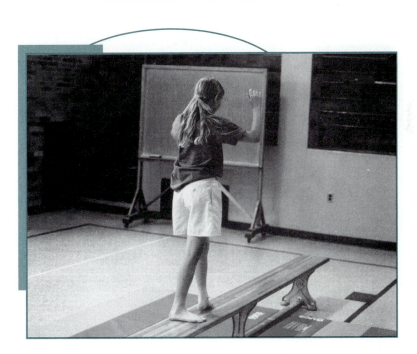

PHOTO 5–21

PHOTO 5–22

PHOTO 5–23

PHOTO 5-24

PHOTO 5-25

PHOTO 5–26

PHOTO 5–27

PHOTO 5-28

sense of "show and tell." Children can share their work to receive feedback on specific aspects of the sequence, or on the sequence as a whole, or they can share it for others to appreciate what they have accomplished and how they approached the task. Sharing can occur at any time when it is needed to advance progress. The effectiveness of sharing is strongly influenced by the way teachers guide these sessions and the preparation they do prior to conducting them. Following are three points to consider as you prepare to guide an observation session with children:

1. *The purpose for sharing the sequences.* Is it to give specific feedback in relation to selected criteria or is it to give groups an opportunity to enjoy and appreciate the work of others and perhaps get some new ideas for their own sequences?

2. *When and how it will be done.* Will you have two groups of children with each group sharing with the other, or half of the groups sharing with the other half, or each group sharing with the entire class?

3. *The questions you plan to use to guide the children's observations.* Will they be focused on the transitions between skills and skill combinations, or on the use of space in terms of direction and level, or on the part of the sequence that is the most interesting?

Children need to learn how to share and evaluate sequences in a supportive and focused environment. They also need to look at their classmates sequences to express what they like about them and what interests them and why. As future teachers, you are challenged to learn how to do this as it is a very important aspect of educational gymnastics. If done well, it helps children see and understand more clearly what they are doing while at the same time it raises their awareness of how to use criteria for assessing their own progress.

In terms of the teacher's role, sequence development is a time to use more indirect approaches to teaching; those that draw children into becoming active participants in their own learning. This can be done with carefully framed questions that focus children on specific criteria that give quality to body shapes such as clarity and symmetry/asymmetry, the use of space such as at different levels or directions, and continuity of logically linked skills and skill combinations. The teacher assists children in realizing what is actually happening within the sequence, helping them decide if that is really what they want, and gaining insight into how to do what they set out to do originally (Hawkins, 1991).

Throughout this process the teacher is helping the children become more independent in their learning through encouraging and developing their ability to self-evaluate and become more competent and confident in the performance of their sequences. In this environment, children clearly will be afforded the opportunity to learn to move as they move to learn.

### MOTOR DEVELOPMENT PRINCIPLES AFFECTING QUALITY OF PERFORMANCE

No formal research has been done examining the developmental stages of sequence building. We know that children enjoy doing them and get a true sense of accomplishment when they are completed. And they love to work with partners in gymnastics. From personal experience and from several authors of gymnastics and dance texts, here are some useful ideas that give insight into how the skill of sequence building develops over time. These ideas are organized within the frame of the four steps of sequence building.

1. *Define a focus.* At first children will have difficulty doing this as it is an abstract idea. After they have had some experience with building both informal and formal sequences where their teachers have identified a focus, children can more readily take on this responsibility.

2. *Explore/improvise.* When children begin to explore and improvise they are satisfied very quickly. They really do not delve deeply into these processes. They take one or two turns and stop. They seem to discover what they already know how to do and are unable to go beyond the obvious or comfortable. Because the concepts of exploring and improvising are major ways of learning in educational gymnastics, children will need to be introduced to this way of learning right from the first lesson. Do not be surprised, when they are asked to make their first formal sequence, however, if they go back to the less mature behavior of being satisfied quickly. Your role as a facilitator is critical at this stage. Using the questions suggested previously, or variations of them, can quickly help you extend children's ability to explore and improvise as well as temper the natural urge to give them the answer.

3. *Select/organize/refine.* Children often select movement skills or skill combinations they have just done without much thought as to how some other skills or skill combinations might fit better. Again, your role as facilitator is critical. It is during this step that sharing work in progress might be helpful so that others can give reactions and suggestions. Videotape is an excellent way to help children develop a discriminating mind. The more children get into the refinement aspect and observe others' work, the more their ability to select among alternative movements grows.

One of the most difficult qualities for children to achieve within sequences is to demonstrate continuity. Continuity occurs when movements flow into each other so easily that each new movement seems to naturally emerge or flow out of the preceding one. In their early attempts they simply string skills together without recognizing if they go together. To reach the mature level of continuity children must recognize how skills fit together. They must see relationships among skills, for example, when you land from a jump your body naturally goes down, which can easily be used as the preparation for a rolling action.

It helps children to understand that each skill has a preparation phase and a recovery phase. They tend to think of them as just one phase—the skill itself. For example, if they want to take weight on their heads and balance with legs in a wide stride position and then roll over to their feet, what they will do getting into that position is the preparation phase, and how they will roll out of it, is the recovery phase. Mature continuity emerges when the recovery phase of each skill is completely blended or fused with the preparatory phase of the next movement. Children at first do not understand this concept which naturally affects the flow of their sequences (Mauldon & Layson, 1979).

From the perspective of continuity, remember that children at first have difficulty linking dissimilar movements smoothly. Movements which involve weight transference using a number of different body parts are also more difficult, particularly when inversion and changes in direction and level are involved (Mauldon & Layson, 1979).

Further, variation of speed is another ingredient that assists in the continuity of movement sequences. To help create this feeling of continuity, it is an appropriate use of speed for the situation that children must accomplish. At first, when they try to show a change of speed it is hardly noticeable. Their speed is more at a constant rate; a rate that they can control and obviously feel comfortable with. Only after much practice and further exploration of changing speeds in different situations, can they begin to use speed appropriately for the sequence.

**4. *Share/evaluate.*** Children love to share their work. In a sharing situation, they often feel that they are going to be entertained by the performers. Consequently, when children begin to view their peers' work for the purpose of learning from it, they may laugh and, in their own ways, make fun of their classmates.

To use sharing and evaluating as a quality learning experience, the preceding behaviors cannot be allowed even though they are understandable. You will have to work through these behaviors using a supportive, but firm hand. When first observing each other's work, do not allow any laughing to occur, period. The potential effect that laughing can have on their feelings is explained to the children up front. Discuss with the children how personal feelings affect progress in gymnastics. Individual differences and how we can learn from them are important topics for discussion when sharing work.

Later, when sharing and evaluating are a strong and positive part of your gymnastics lessons, if something happens that is truly funny, and not related to a child's personal gymnastics ability, then laugh. Laughter is healthy. When this occurs, grab it as a teachable moment so that children learn the difference between laughing at someone's efforts and laughing together because of a truly funny experience. We need to laugh at ourselves, but not at someone else's expense. From our experience, establishing this kind of environment is not difficult as the children get the message very quickly and respond to it well.

Of the three patterns for sharing outlined earlier, we recommend the first two be used almost exclusively. That is, begin with individual sharing with others first, then in twos or small groups sharing with other twos or other small groups. Finally, there may be times when it is appropriate to have half of the class sharing with the other half. In the latter situation, suggest they only look at one sequence, two at the most, as it will be difficult for the children to look at so much at once. Reserve sharing sequences with the whole group for very special reasons, and then only when you know you and your children can create a positive, supportive environment in which it can occur.

### EXPERIENCES FOR REFLECTION

1. Observe with a partner an informal or formal gymnastics sequence performed by one of your class-mates. All three of you discuss in what ways the chosen movements logically or illogically fit to-gether. Your discussion can be both verbal and in movement. If movements do not fit together logically, then suggest possible changes and observe/discuss again. Keep observing/discussing until the movements in the sequence come together logically. If the sequence does fit together logically, then discuss how you could make it more difficult or aesthetically pleasing. Try out the suggestions and observe/discuss again.

2. Compare the four steps in designing and performing a formal sequence. The comparison could be done in small group discussion or in writing a reflection paper. Consider the following ques-tions in comparing the steps: Why is each step important? What is the relationship between defin-ing a focus and exploring/improvising? What is the relationship between exploring/improvising and selecting/organizing/refining? What happens to sequences when not enough time is planned for their development?

3. Think carefully about sequences and prepare a brief statement that could be included in a news-letter to parents explaining the role of gymnastics sequences in their children's physical education program.

# ARRANGING EQUIPMENT AND APPARATUS TO ENHANCE CONTENT AND CHILDREN'S SKILL DEVELOPMENT

Within all the core content sections titled Motor Development Principles Affecting Quality of Performance, Newell's constraint theory has been linked to the use of equipment and apparatus. Consistently it was pointed out that how equipment and apparatus are used will affect children's level of skill development. We want to return briefly to this concept and dis-cuss it a bit more.

## Type and Amount

It is acknowledged that many schools do not have the equipment and apparatus needed to design and implement an effective educational gym-nastics program. We have taken a conservative position regarding equip-ment and apparatus, selecting what is minimal to get started. For those fortunate enough to have more expensive and advanced apparatus, such as large and complex climbing equipment, hanging ropes, parallel bars, balance beams and horses, we encourage you to supplement this material with the Mauldon and Layson (1979) and Williams (1992) texts. We developed our core content material with the following basic set of equipment and apparatus in mind:

- Mats                  1 per child
- Ropes                 1 per child
- Hoops                 1 per child
- Paper canes           1 per child
- Low long benches      1 for every 4 children
                        (ideally 1 for every 2 children)
- Vaulting Boxes        1 for every 4 children
                        (ideally 1 for every 2 children)

If this number of mats is impossible, we suggest that you start with exercise mats or carpet rectangles, but with enough for children to have their own. You can gradually build up your regular gymnastics mat supply. It is not necessary to have all this small equipment, but children enjoy using different equipment even if the tasks are similar. One set of ropes, hoops, or paper canes can get you started nicely. You can even use bean bags as small gymnastics equipment. It would be helpful to have ways to raise the height of the ropes, hoops, and paper canes so that children have options as to the height at which they want to work. Traffic cones or plastic milk bottles placed on their sides or upright, for example, could be used to alter the height of small equipment.

Commercially bought benches usually have a balance beam on their underside so they can be used in two ways. They are expensive, but worth it. They can also be made. Bench tops need to be completely smooth and the bench itself wide enough so children can take weight on hands as well as jump from it without it tipping over.

Whether vaulting boxes are bought or made, be sure they are constructed to permit setting to at least three different heights. The tops should be soft, but durable. It is on these box tops that children become adept at rolling, balancing, and transferring their weight using different body parts.

It cannot be emphasized enough that the more children can work without waiting for turns, the more advanced they become and the safer the environment in which they are working. Bored children waiting for their turns find creative ways to get into trouble in class. It is particularly important that at the beginning children have the opportunity to work alone. They need to become focused and discover what it means to be active participants in their own learning and learn to take care of themselves in this setting. They need to be active right from the start and get into the habit of working continuously. Turn taking should be the exception rather than the rule. To create an environment that encourages such full participation takes careful planning and astute organizational skills on the part of the teacher.

## Equipment and Apparatus Arrangement

There are two basic patterns for the arrangement of equipment and apparatus. They can be arranged as single pieces or in combination with other pieces. In the latter pattern, two or more pieces of the same or different types can be used. When mats are used for safe landing areas, they are not considered to be a separate piece of equipment. The following arrangements demonstrate these patterns (see Figure 5–3).

1. A single rope or paper cane placed on the floor in a straight line (single).
2. A hoop placed on the floor with a rope leading up to it placed at right angles (combination, different types).
3. Three hoops placed on the floor, two in a straight line and one to the side (combination, same type).
4. A paper cane placed across two twelve-inch traffic cones, followed by a mat, followed by three paper canes placed parallel to the mat (combination, different types).
5. A bench placed on the floor (single).
6. Two benches (or boxes) placed parallel to each other ten feet apart (combination, same type).
7. Two boxes (or benches) placed at right angles to each other (combination, same type).
8. A bench placed at a right angle to a box (combination, different types).

When arranging equipment and apparatus attention must be paid to several safety principles:

1. *Spacing.* Equipment and apparatus must be spaced such that the traffic patterns created by their arrangement allow ample space for children to move through the pattern and back to its beginning. No child should come too close to a wall, another classmate, or an adjoining piece of equipment or apparatus at any time because of the way the equipment and apparatus are arranged. In particular, sufficient room for rolling and recovery should be planned for carefully.
2. *Security.* Equipment and apparatus must be arranged so that they are secure and will not slip or slide away from mats. Boxes and benches need to be secured to mats using the mat Velcro strip where possible. If there is no Velcro strip, the edge of the bench or box can be placed directly on the mat. If by doing this, however, the box or bench becomes unstable, remove it and place it directly on the floor.

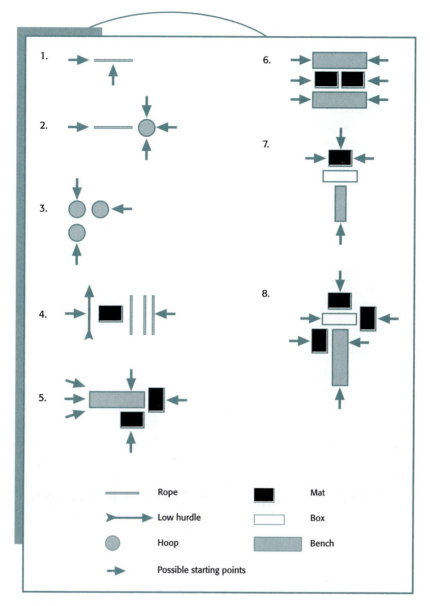

FIGURE 5–3
Basic apparatus patterns.

3.  *Safe working area.* If different pieces of equipment or apparatus are to be
    brought on and off the floor by the children during class, be sure that they
    are stored in a safe place when not in use. This applies to extra hoops,
    ropes, and canes, as well as extra pieces that raise and lower box heights.

4. *Carrying equipment/apparatus.* Children should walk slowly and quietly whenever they are carrying equipment and apparatus from one place to another. Talking, if allowed, should be held at a level that allows children to hear the teacher's voice easily. Moments arise when teachers need to get children's attention quickly, and they must be free to do this at all times. Children should walk forward whenever possible when carrying equipment and apparatus, and walk slowly enough to avoid coming too close to other children carrying other pieces.

Children should use good body mechanics when they carry boxes and benches, for these pieces are heavy and awkward. Two to four children per piece should be the rule, depending on the children's physical development. Equipment, apparatus, and mats should be placed on the floor, not dropped. When setting up the space for classes, if it is possible, place the apparatus and mats around the edges of the gym. It saves time in getting them out and they are easier to move during the lesson than if you have to get them out of an equipment storage area. It also shortens the distance children have to carry them.

## Enhancing Children's Motor Development

*Linear/nonlinear arrangements.* If you are trying to elicit the use of different directions, some of the equipment needs to be placed at different angles to each other. If not, the arrangement will be too linear and children will have difficulty changing their directions. Equipment and apparatus placed at different angles to each other elicit the use of different directions and different pathways.

Linear arrangements also entice children to build up speed and they end up going too fast. If linear arrangements are too long, then they will elicit running and hurrying movements, neither of which you want. This situation quickly becomes a safety problem. This is not to say that you must not use linear arrangements, rather it suggests that when you do, the shorter the better. An example of a linear arrangement that is too long is two hoops placed in a line on the floor, followed by a low hurdle, followed by a hoop raised on its edge next to a mat, followed by a long rope placed in a straight line.

*Height of apparatus.* The height at which a box or other piece of apparatus is placed is a very significant decision to be made. If it is too high, children become fearful and many regress to less mature patterns, or fail to try at all. While practice often returns them to a more advanced level of performance, it sometimes does not. Arranging the apparatus at different heights provides important options for children. Those of you fortunate enough to have large climbing apparatus that you can hook a bench on and raise it off

PHOTO 5–29

Gymnastics equipment arrangements elicit different types of movements. What movements might you expect from children using these three different arrangements?

the floor at an angle, must decide on a proper height and degree of slant. As previously mentioned, children need to work from different heights, but the option should be there for them to change it as their needs become known.

*Observing children's movement responses.* No matter whether you are a beginning teacher or an experienced one, the way your equipment and apparatus are arranged may not elicit from the children the desired motor behaviors. One of the most powerful tools that you have to help this situation, should it occur, is your own observation ability. If you can see clearly what the children are doing, then you have a strong base from which your teaching can evolve. As you gain experience teaching children educational gymnastics, your observation skills will improve. Do not underestimate their power for affecting your success as a teacher! Start right at the beginning learning how to observe children's movement patterns in relation to the equipment and apparatus they are using. Challenge yourself to steadily improve this skill throughout your teacher preparation. If you do, then you will have made a very important first step in becoming a skillful teacher of educational gymnastics. The more you learn how children develop their motor ability within this unique setting, the more you will be able to help children construct meaning in their experience of educational gymnastics.

## Integration of Skills and Focused Teaching 1
### Five Basic Jumps

**IMPORTANCE OF THE SKILL**

The five different foot combinations of jumping are considered very basic because they are used continuously throughout every lesson in gymnastics and form the basis for projecting the body into the air and securing its safe landing. The basic foot patterns are associated with all locomotor skills whether used in a games, gymnastics, or dance context.

**SKILL DESCRIPTION AND PROGRESSION**

There are five different ways to transfer weight using your feet. In educational gymnastics these ways are called the five basic jumps. Specifically, they refer to the different combinations in which the feet are used to travel. The five combinations are:

1. two feet to two feet (2–2)
2. two feet to one foot (2–1)

---

TABLE 5–5

*Developmental Sequence for Leg Action in Hopping*

*Step 1* **Momentary flight.** The support knee and hip quickly flex, pulling (instead of projecting) the foot from the floor. The flight is momentary. Only one or two hops can be achieved. The swing leg is lifted high and held in an inactive position to the side or in front of the body.

*Step 2* **Fall and catch; Swing leg inactive.** Body lean forward allows the minimal knee and ankle extension to help the body "fall" forward of the support foot and, then, quickly catch itself again. The swing leg is inactive. Repeat hops are now possible.

*Step 3* **Projected takeoff; Swing leg assists.** Perceptible pretakeoff extension occurs in the hip, knee, and ankle in the support leg. There is little or no delay in changing from knee and ankle flexion on landing to extension prior to takeoff. The swing leg now pumps up and down to assist in projection. The range of the swing is insufficient to carry it behind the support leg when viewed from the side.

*Step 4* **Projection delay; Swing leg leads.** The weight of the child on landing is now smoothly transferred along the foot to the ball before the knee and ankle extend to takeoff. The support leg nearly reaches full extension on the takeoff. The swing leg now leads the upward–forward movement of the takeoff phase, while the support leg is still rotating over the ball of the foot. The range of the pumping action in the swing leg increases so that it passes behind the support leg when viewed from the side.

*Note:* This sequence has been partially validated by Halverson and Williams.[70]

Reprinted by permission from Roberton & Halverson, 1984.

*Developmental Sequence for Arm Action in Hopping*

Step 1    **Bilateral inactive.** The arms are held bilaterally, usually high and out to the side, although other positions behind or in front of the body may occur. Any arm action is usually slight and not consistent.

Step 2    **Bilateral reactive.** Arms swing upward briefly, then are medially rotated at the shoulder in a winging movement prior to takeoff. It appears that this movement is in reaction to loss of balance.

Step 3    **Bilateral assist.** The arms pump up and down together, usually in front of the line of the trunk. Any downward and backward motion of the arms occurs after takeoff. The arms may move parallel to each other or be held at different levels as they move up and down.

Step 4    **Semi-opposition.** The arm on the side opposite the swing leg swings forward with that leg and back as the leg moves down. The position of the other arm is variable, often staying in front of the body or to the side.

Step 5    **Opposing-assist.** The arm opposite the swing leg moves forward and upward in synchrony with the forward and upward movement of that leg. The other arm moves in the direction opposite to the action of the swing leg. The range of movement in the arm action may be minimal unless the task requires speed or distance.

*Note:* This sequence has been partially validated by Halverson and Williams.[70]
Reprinted by permission from Roberton & Halverson, 1984.

3. one foot to two feet (1–2)
4. one foot to the other foot (1–other; a leap)
5. one foot to the same foot (1–same; a hop)

With older children who have both the strength and balance to do all these jumps, they can be taught in any order. With younger children, however, it is suggested that you present the 2–2 and 1–2 jumps first as they require the least strength and balance. Then, as these children can handle more speed and cover more distance, 1-other becomes possible. Lastly, and most challenging, are the 2–1 and 1-same combinations as they require considerable strength and balance (Roberton & Halverson, 1984). Keep in mind that these skills can be expanded by combining them with traveling, traveling and changing directions, traveling and turning, and traveling in relation to small equipment and apparatus.

### INTEGRATION AND TEACHING OF THE SKILL

These jumps can be presented initially in the first or second lesson on locomotion and stillness. They can be taught in different ways from direct to indirect approaches. A combined approach using some problem solving and some indirect teaching is a nice way to start. Linking jumps is not always easy and having children find the best combinations for linking is another good movement problem for them to solve. Developmentally, the K and 1st-grade children will be the most challenged by these and will more than likely have to revisit them often. To help you understand children's progress with the hop, developmental sequences are most helpful (Roberton & Halverson, 1984).

Right from the start, whenever children are using any of these basic patterns, insist on and elicit from them resilient and quiet landings. With this skill you will be setting the tone for all future jumping and landing tasks. When you first introduce the basic jumps do not stress too high of a height; rather one that is easy for children to manage and that keeps their bodies under control. Later on, height can be stressed as a way to develop the basic jumps to a more advanced level. Observe for and focus on the coordinated use of the arms with the legs, as this will be the children's main source of force to get higher height.

Besides thinking about these skills only as ways to jump, think about them as different combinations of the ways that feet can be used to mount and dismount apparatus and to increase variation in step-like actions (Core Content 3). For example:

- Mount a box by taking off with one foot and landing on two (1–2)
- Jump on and off a low bench from two feet to two feet (2–2). [It is recommended that unless the height is very low (twelve inches or lower), you should not let children land on one foot coming off a piece of apparatus. Landing on one leg from a height is taking an unnecessary risk.]
- Shift weight from hands to feet and feet to hands

## Integration of Skills and Focused Teaching 2
### Sideways (Safety) Roll

### IMPORTANCE OF THE SKILL

The sideways roll is the first roll that can be used easily and safely as a means for a smooth transition between different skills, such as between two different balanced positions. A sideways roll, even in the early stage of its development, can be linked with other traveling skills, especially some of the five basic jumps. As children refine this roll and can perform it under different conditions, it becomes a safety roll; a form of recovery if balance is lost unexpectedly. When more complex rolls are integrated in future lessons, such as forward and backward rolls, the sideways roll is a viable option for those children not ready for more complex ones.

This skill becomes very useful when introducing new ideas for linking in more advanced lessons. Using the sideways roll for a transitional skill lets children get the feel of "linking" immediately.

### SKILL DESCRIPTION AND PROGRESSION

Rolling is a locomotor skill that is performed along adjacent body parts and children enjoy doing it. In Core Content 1 locomotion and stillness, traveling by rolling is listed as an idea from which movement tasks can be designed. All children will have most likely experienced some version of this skill either on the grass, in the sand, or across a rug in their homes.

The sideways roll is a roll in which the body rolls over sideways in a curled position with the elbows, knees, and hips flexed throughout the roll. Weight is transferred over the shins/forearms/palms, then across the back and hips, and then the shins/forearms/palms again. The palms face outward toward the mat or other supporting surface to help protect the head. They are often used to help roll the body over, or in some cases, to initiate the rolling action. Below is a suggested progression for a sideways roll to the left adapted from Ryser and Brown (1990). The beginning position is with the weight on hands and knees:

1. Tip toward the left by bending the arm and bringing the elbow in towards the body
2. Twist head to the right, lower weight onto the shoulder and hip
3. As weight is being transferred over the back and hips, bring in both arms and legs to a curled position
4. continue the roll until weight is once again on the knees and hands

This skill can also be started from a curled position in which the weight is taken on the forearms/palms and the shins/tops of feet. In this position the body is already curled and all that needs to be done is for the children to push themselves over into the roll.

Once children roll over sideways smoothly while remaining in a curled position, they should explore how to accomplish the same thing from standing, walking, and a slight 2–2 foot jump. It is during these experiences that children become more aware of what their bodies can and cannot do.

### INTEGRATION AND TEACHING OF THE SKILL

The skill description gives specific information useful to help children who need assistance, especially when they first begin to learn how to do the skill. Many children can figure out how to roll sideways on their own, but there are some for whom this skill is a challenge. Because this skill contains little risk of injury, it is one that can be presented to the entire class at the same time, if you think the timing is right for most of the class. It can be presented either directly or with a task that gives them some options, such as "Find different ways that you can travel by rolling sideways, being sure to roll smoothly and slowly."

We encourage you to start teaching children to roll by first rolling sideways but aiming for a more natural roll than the one described above. When most of the children have enough body awareness and can take their weight on their hands with confidence (after or during the later part of material in Core Content 2), helping them learn how to roll forward and backward becomes appropriate.

## Integration of Skills and Focused Teaching 3
## Hand Balance/Body Curled

### IMPORTANCE OF THE SKILL

This skill is a prerequisite to all skills that require children to support their own weight on their hands/arms while in an inverted position. Its importance cannot be underestimated. Other skills from the critical set that depend on this skill are hand balance/body extended and the cartwheel. Much of what children will do when using apparatus requires taking full weight on their arms/hands at some point. Competency in controlling weight over one's hands becomes essential for continued development of this skill.

### SKILL DESCRIPTION AND PROGRESSION

A hand balance/body curled is achieved by placing the hands on the floor (mat, bench, box top) shoulder width apart and pushing off with two feet with enough force to lift the hips over the shoulders (back firm) and remain there for a brief moment. The body is curled (i.e., hips and knees flexed, ankles extended) and the head is up to keep the body from tipping over. A suggested progression for taking weight on hands adapted from Williams (1992) follows:

1. in a crouched position, spread fingers out wide and place hands on the floor; body is in a curled position
2. silently bounce feet up and down, keeping body curled and feet close to the floor
3. look at an imaginary spot in front of hands (to keep head up and the body from tipping over)

4. bounce feet up and down, with each bounce, try to keep feet off the floor for longer periods of time
5. bounce feet up and down, try to get hips over shoulders (head up, trunk straight and firm with hip and knee joints flexed)
6. once hips are over shoulders, twist in waist to return feet to a different place on the floor

The skill just described can be performed in relation to small equipment and apparatus. The different foot patterns associated with the five basic jumps can also be used. "As you bounce your feet up and down, sometimes push off with one and land on the other or push off with two and land on one." Developmentally, children have been observed to:

- Place hands wider than shoulder width apart before they can place them shoulder width apart
- Place their weight on their finger tips before they can place their hands flat on the supporting surface
- Tuck their chins before they can lift them and look at an imaginary spot in front of their hands
- Lift their feet high rather than their hips when pushing off the floor before they can lift their hips high

### INTEGRATION AND TEACHING OF THE SKILL

This skill is so basic to educational gymnastics that it should be started as soon as possible in the safest way possible. Beginning efforts will emerge as soon as the children try to travel on different body parts. You are encouraged, in either the first or second lesson, to introduce this skill to the entire class at the same time. The first objective is for all children to be able to silently bounce their feet up and down while looking at a spot in front of them and keeping their feet close to the floor. Once they can do this, you can introduce them to the idea of bouncing a bit higher, but still insist on silent landings. At this point options might be given as to how high their feet can go. For example, you could say, "Bring your feet up only as high as you can come down softly." This task shifts some of the responsibility for their own progress to the children.

Key points to remember when helping children progress toward the mature pattern of this skill are hands flat/shoulder width apart, head up, body curled, and soft landings. It takes most children a long time to accomplish the mature form of this skill (weight over shoulders, back firm/straight, body curled); you will need to revisit it often, each time encouraging the children to get just a bit higher.

## *Integration of Skills and Focused Teaching 4*
## *Shoulder Balance*

### IMPORTANCE OF THE SKILL

This skill is another inverted balance that children are able to do fairly easily, although to achieve a fully extended body shape with weight truly on the shoulders and not the neck takes time, strength, and flexibility to accomplish. Any of the many variations in between can still give children the feel of holding their weight on their shoulders and being upside down.

### SKILL DESCRIPTION AND PROGRESSION

Following is a suggested progression for the shoulder balance.

1. Seated on a mat with body curled, rock onto the shoulders and back to the seat; keep body curled
2. Rock back and forth, momentarily stopping the movement when weight is equally balanced on both shoulders and body is in a curled position (another form of shoulder balance and also important); hips might be slightly extended so knees are not in the child's face

3. Stop the rocking backwards when weight is on shoulders, slowly extend legs upward, and simultaneously extend hips, knees and ankles (hands can act as supports under the hips or arms outstretched with palms placed face down against the supporting surface; the latter being the more complex because of the strength and flexibility needed)

Observation of children working with taking their weight over their shoulders suggests that they have difficulty extending their hips at the beginning. This is an important action as it helps them to position their weight over their shoulders by raising the hips. There is so much flexion sometimes that children's hips become positioned so far from their shoulders (the intended base of support) that they cannot get their weight onto their shoulders. Gradually, through an increased awareness of where their shoulders are and what it feels like to have to support their weight, children begin to extend their hips. This change results in their bodies opening up and becoming fully extended. During children's initial attempts it is a good idea to show them how to place their hands under their hips for support and have them clearly demonstrate a shoulder stand with body curled before trying to extend.

### INTEGRATION AND TEACHING OF THE SKILL

First, think of the shoulder balance as two skills—shoulder balance with body curled and shoulder balance with body extended. Both are important and lead to other skills, for example, backward shoulder rolls. After children have had ample time to find different body parts on which they can balance, including their shoulders, it is appropriate to help all children more concretely grasp the components of this skill and assist them in performing this movement pattern at a more advanced level.

As before with the weight on hands/body curled pattern, guiding children to extend their hips, knees, and ankles only as far as they can remain balanced, encourages developmentally appropriate responses and again asks children to take some responsibility for their own learning. It also asks them to use their knowledge of center of gravity. As children begin to extend their legs, placing your hand gently on their "pointed" toes and asking them to push your hand up, will often elicit simultaneous hip and knee extension. If children try to go too fast and fall over backward, you need to stop them and discuss with them how their centers of gravity moved outside their bases of support and what can they do about it. When children are competent with this skill, a natural direction to take is to challenge the children to change the shape of their bodies as they balance on their shoulders.

That you do not expect all children to do the same thing, in the same way, and at the same time needs reinforcing often. Children generally are not used to working with physical skills from a developmental perspective. If other children can do it, they often think that means they should be able to do it too. Discussion of individual differences begins to be an important topic to integrate during lessons, since as your gymnastics lessons progress, individual differences will become even more pronounced.

## *Integration of Skills and Focused Teaching 5*
## *Head/Hand Balance*

### IMPORTANCE OF THE SKILL

The head/hand balance, or head stand, is very important because it frees the body in an inverted position that much more than the shoulder stand. It can be done on top of and along side of box and bench tops, adding challenge. In fact balancing on a box top is often easier as children can grip the sides stabilizing their bodies more easily. It is a skill that children want to learn and feel very accomplished when they do.

## SKILL DESCRIPTION AND PROGRESSION

For this skill progression to be used in a class with different levels of development, the children in your classes need to have sufficient body awareness that they can work by themselves carefully, making informed decisions as to what they can and cannot do. They know what they can do alone and when they need to ask for assistance (i.e., spotting by you or a classmate). If they do not yet have this ability, you must continue working with them to develop it before you continue in this progression. Likewise, you want to be alert to any peer pressure that individual children might be feeling. With your help everyone should feel free to work at their own levels and not to worry about what others can do in relation to themselves. You may have to discuss this important concept with children every now and then, as it is very natural for children to want to do what their friends can do.

Following is a suggested progression for taking weight on head and hands adapted from Williams (1992) and Ryser and Brown (1990):

1. Begin in a kneeling position
2. Place the head (at the hair line) on the mat
3. Place hands well back to form a stable triangular base of support (fingers pointing toward head; hands shoulder width apart or slightly wider)
4. Lift hips slightly by bringing feet closer to hands, push with hands and feet, slowly lift the legs until curled body is over base of support with back firm and straight, come back down softly
5. Repeat this last movement until it can be done easily and with confidence
6. When in a stable, balanced position, slowly extend hips/knees to straighten legs only going as high as you can maintain the balance

For Step 4: If you think you are about to lose your balance, then come back down, or, if you actually start going over, press with your hands to lessen the weight on your head, tuck your chin and roll out. It is often recommended that the knees be placed on the elbows in a tripod before having the legs extend. We prefer keeping the body curled with knees together right from the start. This option, however, may be useful for some children.

For Step 6 in the progression: If you begin to fall forward, quickly press with the hands to take some of the weight off of your head, then tuck head and hips and roll forward. If the balance is lost backwards, flex your hips and place feet on the floor.

Spotting for Step 4 in the progression: When needed, stand behind the mover with hands ready to support the hip area and keep the body from going over.

Spotting for Step 6 in the progression: As legs begin to extend up, place one hand behind the hips and follow the legs with the other; use just enough pressure to keep the body from going over. Watch for children who extend their hips before their knees.

Developmentally, children do one of two things when trying head/hand balances. First, for fear of going over, they will work too slowly or, second, they will work too fast and end up going over (Ryser & Brown, 1990). In addition, through observations of many children learning to balance on their heads, the following developmental trends are hypothesized as children try head/hand balances:

- Place the top of head on the mat before they can place it on the front (at the hairline)
- PLace their hands at either side of their heads before they can place them back toward their feet in a stable triangle

- When trying to extend the legs, extend first their hips, then their knees before they can do so simultaneously (this is the same action observed when children are learning to take their weight on their shoulders and extend their bodies)
- When trying to extend their legs, keep their ankles fixed in a flexed position, followed by extending their ankles after their hips and knees have extended, before timing ankle extension to coincide with the hips and knees
- When first rolling out of a balance that is lost, lift their chins and arch their backs rather than tuck their chins and round their backs

Once the head/hand balance is performed with confidence it can be used as a vehicle for many other interesting skills or parts of sequences. For example, let children find different ways to get onto their head and balance, for example, kicking one leg at a time or raising both legs in a wide straddle position or rolling forward and then directly into a head balance. Likewise, reverse the idea, and let the children find different ways to come out of a head balance.

Once this skill can be done competently and confidently, it becomes the means for additional skills to be invented, especially using apparatus. From using a mat, it is a natural progression to balance on the head on top of a box. But remember, getting to and dismounting from the head balance are movement skills in and of themselves and need careful guidance in their development. If you have worked sufficiently with your children on mats, and they are aware of their bodies, balances on apparatus will not be difficult for you or the children.

### INTEGRATION AND TEACHING OF THE SKILL

Once the children have had sufficient time to experience taking weight on different body parts, you can begin to encourage them to use their heads in their balances. At first, we suggest that you limit them to keeping at least one body part touching the floor. Remember what was said earlier—the children in your classes need to have sufficient body awareness so that they can work by themselves carefully, making informed decisions as to what they can and cannot do.

When children seem to have a broad range of body parts on which they can balance, the beginning parts of the head/hand balance can be done with everyone working individually. As children progress at their own rates and make their own decisions, the teacher can easily assist individuals or pair up children to help each other. Teaching them how to assist a partner with learning a skill could be introduced here as well.

Becoming skillful with this balance does not happen in one class period or a specified number of class periods. You will have to revisit it often over the years and provide many opportunities for children to practice all phases of the progression. It will not take long for dramatic individual differences to emerge if you are able to create a truly developmental environment. Some children will be finding different ways to get into a head balance, where others will still be working on a tucked balance. As long as the children are working at their own rate and showing progress, you are helping all of them learn.

### *Integration of Skills and Focused Teaching 6*
### *Jump/Land/Roll Basic Sequence*

### IMPORTANCE OF THE SKILL

We have included this sequence as a critical skill because it forms the basis for many short sequences or parts of longer ones. Many interesting variations can be structured within it. It is also a sequence that you can use to introduce children to how to explore and discover different ways to move, that is, to seek variety in their work. It gives both teachers and children a helpful structure with which to start.

### SKILL DESCRIPTION AND PROGRESSION

In its simplest form, this sequence includes a 2–2 jump, followed by a soft landing, and lowering of the body into a sideways roll. The sequence is completed with a recovery to the feet. Following is a suggested progression for the jump/land/roll sequence:

1. The five basic jumps
2. The five basic jumps with turns
3. A sideways roll
4. A sideways roll from standing and walking
5. Easy 2–2 jump, soft landing into a sideways roll, and recovery to the feet
6. Increased height of the 2–2 jump always going for the soft landing

Once the children can perform this sequence with competence and know how to land on their feet and change the direction of the downward movement to a forward one, some of these ideas can be tried:

- change the roll to a forward roll
- Change the shape of the body during the roll (e.g., piked position)
- Add an approach of the 2–2 jump and increase the height to include full body extension
- Change the body shape in the air or add turns prior to the landing
- Do a sequence with a partner facing each other, back to back, or side by side
- Instead of recovering to their feet, have children roll into a balanced position
- Change speeds during the sequence (e.g., quick jump, slow landing, quick roll and recovery; quick jump, quick roll, slow recovery to the feet)
- Change directions during the sequence
- Do a sequence in relation to small equipment and apparatus (e.g., jump from a box or bench, land, roll, and recover)

These ideas illustrate how this basic sequence can be redesigned to elicit a variety of movements from children. It is not being suggested, however, that you try them all; only those applicable to your situation. The ideas show you how a basic sequence can be used to create new and varied sequences. If you have carefully progressed through the work with your children, then the previous suggestions should be developmentally appropriate.

When children first begin to put this sequence of tasks together, which is basically the combination of a jump with a roll, they often forget to land on their feet first and let the downward flexion of hips/knees/ankles be the preparation for the roll. For this reason, this sequence is called the jump/land/roll sequence. Be alert to this developmental trend, because when children first jump from a box or bench it is important that they think "land on the feet, then go into the roll." Landing from a jump is excellent preparation for a roll. The body is flexed and its natural response is that it wants to extend. The body, however, will now be directed forward into a roll. A mature performance of this transition takes time and practice and is difficult for many of the very young children.

## INTEGRATION AND TEACHING OF THE SEQUENCE

When this sequence could be first introduced is difficult to say. We have had success with many children toward the end of 1st grade or the early part of the 2nd. It is so basic that it will be part of most sequences, informal and formal, in different variations throughout the K–5 program. More than likely, you will use it at different times during the same lesson, with and without equipment or apparatus. You will use it by itself and as a beginning point for bringing out more variation in and further development of children's movement. When children have developed some formal sequences of their own using this basic structure, they can perform these sequences as part of a personal warm-up to the lesson.

It is time to discuss a very important concept that is central to a successful educational gymnastics experience—that of children's natural tendency to learn from each other and want to copy what their friends are doing. The material in this category brings this desire of children to the forefront.

As children become more focused on their own work and more aware of what they can and cannot do, copying lessens, until then, you will have to be alert to it happening. When children first try to vary their movement responses, they run out of ideas quickly and start looking about for inspiration. That is why, from the very beginning, you must talk with the children about the purpose of educational gymnastics and how it is centered on them as individuals, and how you are interested in the progress of each of them in relation to individual development. It is here that you can talk again about individual differences and what they mean in this particular class.

Children learn from other children. This important way of learning must not be eliminated. What is different here is that children must learn how to assess their ability levels in relation to what they have seen others do and make judgments about whether or not they are ready to try what they have seen. Tell them that if they have seen some movement they would like to try, and they are unsure as to their readiness, to come ask you to help them make the decision.

If you see some movement skill being performed by a child and you would rather not have the other children be distracted by it, simply ask the child to stop doing it for now. When the children seem more focused on themselves, let that child work on the skill again. Following are three specific examples of distracting movement responses that you can count on happening. When they occur, we suggest that you stop the class momentarily and redirect its focus. Children will want to try to copy what they have seen and many will not be ready.

1. When first exploring balancing on body parts, children will try to balance on their heads with their feet extended into the air and some will fall over even though you have just said not to select parts on which you cannot hold your balance. Other children will be successful. When this happens, it is recommended that you ask all children to keep their feet close to the floor, one even touching, until you have the chance to work with all of them on balancing on their heads and hands. (See Integration of Skills and Focused Teaching 3.)

2. When first trying to jump from a bench or box and land and roll, some children lean down and reach toward the floor with their hands and try a mini dive roll. The dive roll is an advanced skill, especially from a height, that is placed in the content category of weight transference. It is an example of transferring weight by flight. At this point in our progression, we do not recommend children going from their feet directly onto their hands. It is too risky for many of the children—though some will want to try it. Once again, tell the children not to do this skill at this point and that you will bring it back at a later, more appropriate time.

3. When working with the head/hand balance, even if you have demonstrated and verbally stressed to children that they should keep their bodies curled during the first part of the progression, some will try to extend their legs. This usually causes a fall. As soon as you see one child do this, stop the class and carefully go over the task again, this time asking them not to raise their feet off of the floor more than six inches. Keep them on this task until they can all get that amount of body control before moving on.

The above strategy is important, even if you are holding some children back. For the brief moment that you are doing this, you have to be certain everyone can follow your directions. As soon as the children can do this part of the progression, encourage them to lift their legs slowly and only as high as they can without losing their balance. This task is now structured once again so that individual children can respond at their own rates and levels of development. Remember, that when the majority of children begin to balance on their head and hands confidently, it is time to teach them how to lose balance and roll over. Begin this with the body in a curled position until they can get the feel of pressing with their hands and tucking their chins. Be reminded that often when doing this skill for the first time, children lift their chins rather than tuck them.

## *Integration of Skills and Focused Teaching 7*
## *Forward Roll/Shoulder Roll*

### IMPORTANCE OF THE SKILL
The forward roll has a special place in educational gymnastics because it serves a number of important functions. First, it can be used to dissipate force over a distance at the end of skills such as jumping and cartwheeling. Second, it helps connect skills smoothly (e.g., head/hand balance with body extended, roll forward, to head/hand balance with body extended and legs apart) and thus helps make a sequence pleasing to the eye as well as logical in its design. With a quick turn on feet prior to rolling, a forward roll can take the sequence into new areas on the mat or within a group of apparatus. Lastly, forward rolls are "safety movements," because they can be used in situations where children fall or lose their balance and need a quick way to regain it without injury.

### SKILL DESCRIPTION AND PROGRESSION
Following is a suggested progression for the forward roll adapted from Roberton and Halverson (1984), Ryser and Brown (1990), and Turoff (1991):

1. Begin in a curled position with feet together (i.e., squat down) with hands placed on the mat shoulder width apart
2. With weight on both hands, bend arms slightly to allow back of neck to touch mat between hands; tuck head toward chest to "look at toes" and make neck and back rounded
3. Push body over head by extending both legs at the same time as arms lower and head tucks, barely touching the mat with the back of the head; head slides through arms and body remains curled throughout
4. Roll onto feet bringing arms forward and upward to assist in keeping the momentum going; finish with a small jump

## INTEGRATION AND TEACHING OF THE SKILL

At some point you are going to need to give some specific instruction related to the forward roll because you will observe that many of the children are ready for it and need it. Integration of this instruction can be done with the entire class or individual children.

To integrate instruction to the entire class, most of the children should have demonstrated sufficient arm strength and body awareness to perform weight-on-hands and sideways rolling tasks with competence. The timing of the integration is a delicate decision. If you bring this instruction in too early, a number of the children will not be ready developmentally. If you have timed it right, however, and children understand your instructions and how, through practice, they can improve their performance, they can continue to work at their own rates. The most important aspect of the forward roll is that children can support their weight as they tuck and slide their head between their arms and keep their body curled throughout the roll. Reviewing the developmental sequences for the forward roll is most helpful at this point (see Tables 5–3 and 5–4).

Giving the more formal instruction individually to those children who demonstrate a readiness for the skill, may be too difficult for beginning teachers to implement right away, but you want to learn how to do it as soon as you can. As children are working on tasks related to rolling, you can select those children you observe to be ready to roll forward, and individually suggest that they try rolling forward over their heads. At first you might simply ask whether or not they have ever done a forward roll and if the answer is yes, let them show you. Your follow-up instructions would be based on what you observe.

No matter which option you use, you may have to physically assist some children with their initial and subsequent attempts. This is best done by kneeling to one side and placing one hand on back of the head (not the neck) and other hand under the child's nearest thigh. Then lift with the "thigh" hand and tuck the child's head with the other hand.

You must be prepared for some children who can already do a forward roll. Some children will have had outside instruction in formal gymnastics so they will bring this skill into the class. When you are first working on different ways to roll, find those children quickly and recognize their skill level so they know you respect them for having it. Because there is so much to observe when an entire class is moving at once, you may want to ask them to do only a sideways roll until you tell them otherwise. Once you are comfortable observing the class and know more about the children you are observing, tell those children who can already do a forward roll that they may use it with the sideways roll as well.

As soon as all children can work alone demonstrating the ability to take responsibility for their own learning, you can design more complex tasks for the children who already can do a forward roll. For example, challenge them to link other movements that they have experienced either in front of or after the roll, or change their body shapes as they roll. They should be encouraged to use these skill combinations when working with apparatus.

## Integration of Skills and Focused Teaching 8
### Backward Roll/Shoulder Roll

### IMPORTANCE OF THE SKILL

These two rolls are important for the same reasons given previously for the forward roll.

### SKILL DESCRIPTION AND PROGRESSION

Because many children do not like doing a backward roll because of the pressure they feel on the backs of their necks, the backward shoulder roll is included. The backward shoulder roll is an excellent option and much easier to do than the backward roll. We use it with all children leaving the backward roll as a choice for those wishing to learn it. Below are suggested progressions for both. The first is a progression for the backward roll and is adapted from Ryser and Brown (1990) and Turoff (1991):

1. Weight on feet, body curled, back facing the direction of the roll, rock slightly forward and then backward onto the seat and roll backward (some teachers suggest that children place their hands by their ears, fingers pointing down and palms facing up)
2. As you roll, keep the head tucked, body curled (knees and hips flexed) throughout the roll ("keep looking at your toes")
3. Keep the momentum created by the rocking motion
4. When the hips take the weight, reach back with the hands close to the shoulders (elbows in close), palms down, and fingers pointing toward the shoulders
5. As feet pass over the shoulders, push hands against the mat (or supporting surface) to keep weight off of the head and to push to the feet
6. Place feet on the mat close to hands as they push up to relieve pressure on the head; return to standing or as your weight is taken fully on your feet, recover with a slight jump

Developmentally, children have been observed to:

- Open at the hip as they rock backwards before they can sustain a tight body curl throughout the entire rock onto their shoulders
- Slow the momentum created by rocking backwards, before they can keep it going and actually use it to their advantage
- Extend their hips when they feel the weight coming onto their shoulders resulting in additional pressure being placed on the head/neck area before they are able to sustain a curled body position throughout the roll
- Let their hands "go for a ride" before they can use them to actively push against the supporting surface and relieve pressure from the head/neck area

In addition to the trends identified above, studying the developmental sequences for the forward roll can give you additional insight as to what to expect. You may have to reverse everything, however, before deciding if it can be helpful.

The backward shoulder roll is an adaptation of the backward roll just described. The main difference is that the direction of the roll is along the back and over one shoulder, thus eliminating pressure on the back of the head and neck. Below is a suggested progression for this skill as outlined by Williams (1992, p. 91). It requires as a prerequisite the ability to take weight on the shoulders with the body extended, along with being able to feel a shift of weight from both shoulders to only one shoulder.

1. Take weight on shoulders, stretch legs in the air
2. Touch the floor with toes of one foot and return to balance on shoulders (e.g., right foot touches floor on right side of head)
3. Repeat, but tip and let toes take weight and return to balance on shoulders (weight is now shifting from being equally distributed on both shoulders to only one, the one over which the body will roll)

4. Repeat 2 and 3 on the other side
5. Repeat 3; when weight is on toes, bend the knee and take weight on it, continue the direction of the movement until the body weight is over the knee
6. Come up to the knees
7. Repeat 5 and 6 to the other side
8. Speed up the movement

A variation of the above progression follows:

1. Take weight on shoulders, keeping body curled (back straight, hips/knees flexed)
2. Slowly twist the trunk to one side while shifting weight onto that shoulder
3. Tip off balance reaching toward the floor with both knees
4. Come up to the knees
5. Repeat 1–4 to the other side
6. Speed up the movement

Children, when they first try this, are apt to move too quickly and their weight will not pass over their shoulders, but rather more over their heads (see 2). You want children to clearly "feel" their weight shift from both shoulders to one shoulder with the knees pointing over that same shoulder (results from a twist in the spine). Once they can achieve this position, all that is left is for them to tip over onto their knees.

### INTEGRATION AND TEACHING OF THE SKILL

As with the forward roll, at some point you will need to give specific instruction related to the backward roll and the backward shoulder roll. The two options previously mentioned are still pertinent. Specific instruction can be delivered to the entire class or to individual children.

To integrate instruction for the entire class, for either roll, most of the children should be comfortable taking weight on their hands while keeping their bodies curled, taking weight on their shoulders keeping their bodies curled, and rocking back and forth, momentarily balancing their weight on their shoulders at the peak of rocking backward. With practice, you will know when this type of instruction is best for you and your children.

From experience we have found that teaching the backward shoulder roll first is the best approach. Then, when all children are safe practicing this roll on their own, help children add the backward roll over their heads on an individual basis. This is quite easy to do and many children will seek your assistance and learn to perform the backward roll at a mature level. We do not recommend presenting the backward roll as a skill that all children must try at the same time. If, on the other hand, all the children in your class can do either a backward shoulder roll or a backward roll, then you could work with backward rolling with the entire class at the same time, being sure to give them a choice of using either roll.

When children are first discovering how the backward shoulder roll works, they do not seem interested in doing the backward roll. They like the shoulder roll. It is not until they need it in a sequence or want to use it with the apparatus, that they seek help. If they are ready for it, and the situation allows it, you could help them right then.

The most important aspect of the backward roll is to help children support their body weight by pushing their hands away from the mat thereby relieving pressure from their necks and heads. This is difficult to do and you will more than likely have to assist some children with their initial and subsequent attempts. Turoff (1991) suggested two approaches to help children learn to use their hands. The first approach is used with children who are not sure what it means to push down on the mat with their hands and the second is used with children who do know and can do it.

1. Kneeling next to a child, place one hand under (actually against) the child's neck and place the other hand under the lower back. As the child rolls, lift both hands, one to help keep the weight off the head and neck and the other to help the child turn over.
2. Stand next to a child and as the child becomes inverted, lift the child's hips (using both hands) to lessen the pressure on the neck and head.

## Integration of Skills and Focused Teaching 9
### Hand Balance/Body Extended

### IMPORTANCE OF THE SKILL

As an inverted balance, balancing on one's hands seems to open up a number of new possibilities and offers more of a challenge because of its narrow base. Being able to support your entire weight on your arms with the body extended takes considerable strength and balance. It is a great accomplishment when children achieve it, and clearly it affects their feelings of competence and confidence in gymnastics.

### SKILL DESCRIPTION AND PROGRESSION

Children should be competent in taking weight on their hands with the body curled before working toward weight on hands with body extended. Below is a suggested progression for taking weight on hands with the body extended leading to a handstand.

1. Place hands on floor, shoulder width apart, fingers out wide/flat, one leg forward and the other extended behind (this leg will become the swing leg)
2. Look at an imaginary cross in front of the hands (i.e., keep the head up)
3. Swing the back leg or free leg gently up and down while letting the other leg hang down (this leg helps to keep the children from going over)
4. Swing the free leg until it reaches the vertical, but remember to keep the other leg hanging down; swing the free leg gently at first, increasing height to the vertical
5. When able to swing the leg to the vertical, have a spotter catch the swing leg below the knee, then raise the other leg slowly to meet it

In using this progression, steps 1 through 4 can be done by the children themselves as long as they have the body awareness and arm strength. It is also helpful if you consider them as skills in and of themselves, because they are very useful in sequences and when using apparatus. Step 5 needs a spotter. This can be you or another child whom you have taught to spot properly. Both need to know how to catch and hold the swing leg when it reaches the vertical while the other leg comes up to meet it.

Developmentally, children have been observed:

- supporting their weight on their finger tips, before being able to place their palms flat on the floor
- letting the hang leg come up too high, before they can truly let it hang down while swinging the free leg up
- trying to bring the hang leg to the horizontal too quickly, before they time it to lift just after the swing leg has reached the horizontal (at this stage a spotter should be used)

## INTEGRATION AND TEACHING OF THE SKILL

We encourage you to hold off giving instruction to an entire class until you are certain the children have the necessary body awareness and arm strength to do the work, and thus have the necessary requirements to take responsibility for their own learning. Equally important, the teacher must be comfortable with having all the children upside down on their hands at the same time. With legs extended now, more momentum can be created and the likelihood of children losing their balance is greater. Helping children individually, with you or a class member as the spotter, should be integrated as needed.

This progression works well only if children can follow your directions and take responsibility for their own actions. If your children cannot follow what you ask them to do, for example, "keep one leg hanging down," having them all work at once may not be a good idea. Keeping one leg down is necessary for safety. It checks the momentum built up by the swing leg and helps keep the children from getting too far over their hands and losing their balance. How high they swing the free leg determines where the center of gravity will fall, and they are to be in control of this. Children need to take responsibility for taking care of themselves and this progression is a perfect example of one that relies on this behavior.

If, when you are working with the entire class, some children cannot or will not accept this responsibility, then we suggest that you stop, bring them to the center of the room, and discuss with them what you are seeing and why it is unsafe, and that it must stop. If after this discussion, they still have trouble following your directions, we suggest that you shift the lesson focus and design tasks with less responsibility for the children to assume. You can come back to the hand balance another time when they are more ready for it.

## *Integration of Skills and Focused Teaching 10*
## *Cartwheel*

### IMPORTANCE OF THE SKILL

The cartwheel is an example of a skill in which the body's weight is transferred over the base of support (one hand to one hand) rather than held stable like in the other inverted skills (e.g., shoulder balance, head/hand balance). When the cartwheel can be performed skillfully, it offers children another way to change the direction of their movement sequences as well as creating a number of new options when used in relation to small equipment and apparatus. Taking weight on two hands, as well as transferring weight from one hand to the other, is particularly challenging when used over a box or on, over, or along a bench. It is similar to hand balance/body extended in that it gives children a thrill when they can do it at a mature level. And doing a cartwheel is a great feeling!

### SKILL DESCRIPTION AND PROGRESSION

Following is a suggested progression for the cartwheel:

1. Face a paper cane placed on the floor
2. Place hands on either side of the cane; push off with both feet and land on both feet (2–2) on the other side of the cane; look at hands; keep body curled or semi-curled (this movement is similar to weight on hands/body curled except now the feet are being transferred from one side of a cane to the other)
3. Repeat Step 2, but kick legs over one at a time *(1-other)*
4. Repeat Step 3, but now beginning to place hands down one after the other (left then right, or right then left)
5. Keep working as in Step 4, getting feet higher and higher, eventually fully extending the legs

In situations 2–5 emphasize to the children to take their feet only as high as they can bring them down softly, and without losing their balance. The ability to transfer weight, going hand-hand-foot-foot with full body extension takes time to accomplish and a number of children will be working toward this mature pattern over a long period of time.

Developmentally, children have been observed:

- Placing hands directly in front of them, before they can twist their upper body and place their hands down (the paper cane helps to overcome this response)
- Placing both hands down together, before they can take weight on one hand followed by the other
- Quickly shifting their weight from one hand to the other, before they can sustain their body weight for any length of time over one hand
- Keeping their hips and knees flexed, before they can extend them while their weight is being transferred over their hands
- Landing heavily and off balance, before they can land softly and on balance
- One leg appears more extended than the other, before they can fully extended both at the same time

Some children might not want to include the cartwheel in sequences, because it takes a long time for most children to demonstrate this mature pattern. This decision limits their practice time of this skill and should be discouraged. Instead, encourage them to use it, but emphasizing flexed knees and hips instead of the fully extended shape. If they can extend their ankles during the time their bodies are passing over their hands, the clarity of their body shape will give their work a finished look. In effect, this modified cartwheel becomes a different skill.

### INTEGRATION AND TEACHING OF THE SKILL

A good time to integrate instruction related specifically to aspects of the cartwheel is after children have demonstrated sufficient arm strength and body awareness in weight-on-hands tasks. Also, we would wait until the children have had lots of experience with taking weight on their hands body curled on the floor, in relation to small equipment, and on, over, and along benches and boxes. The cartwheel takes considerable upper arm strength and body awareness and these tasks help to develop this. Integration of this instruction can be done, as we have previously discussed, with the entire class or individual children. If you have timed the instruction right, and the children understand the progression, they can practice it at their own rates when given the opportunity as part of their lesson.

And finally, prepare what you plan to do with the children who can already perform this skill at a mature level, for there will be several. We have found that as soon as the entire class can work alone demonstrating the ability to take responsibility for their own learning, more complex tasks can be designed for the children who can already do cartwheels. We often take this opportunity to challenge them to link other movements that they have experienced either before or following a cartwheel. Further, we encourage them to use these skill combinations when working with apparatus. The linking of movement skills, especially those that are familiar to them like a cartwheel, is new to most children. Their emphasis in gymnastics has usually stressed individual skills with little attention paid to understanding what their bodies can and cannot do. Linking skills is a wide open area for you to use with children and most helpful to their becoming competent and confident gymnasts.

## Integration of Skills and Focused Teaching 11
### Jump for Height

**IMPORTANCE OF THE SKILL**

To jump high and demonstrate clarity of body shape is dramatic both to the performer and the observer. When children can suspend their bodies momentarily in space, there is a "free" feeling that accompanies it only they can describe. This moment of freedom is a stimulating experience. To the observer, it is more of an aesthetic experience as they appreciate the beauty outlined by the body in space at its moment of suspension. Go to any dance concert and listen to the audience when dancers momentarily suspend their bodies in space either by projecting themselves into space or by being projected into space by others. You will often hear a collective, hushed gasp!

**SKILL DESCRIPTION AND PROGRESSION**

A jump for height can be described as a 2–2 take off and landing, with the goal being to jump as high as possible with the body fully extended at the peak of the jump. The arms and legs coordinate to help cushion the force of the body as it lands.

The first progression is obvious, keep increasing the height of the jump *always* accompanied by a soft landing. Begin on the floor, move to small equipment, and finally jumping off of apparatus set at different heights. Jumping for height takes time to develop to the advanced level, as there is an element of risk. Children will have to take this risk at their own rates.

As with the jump/land/roll basic sequence, once children are competent with the "basic" jump for height, it can be expanded when applied to small equipment and apparatus. For example, one can jump for height

- Using a 1–2 jump
- Turning while in the air
- Changing body shape (curl, twist, asymmetrical, symmetrical)
- Off of a box set at different heights (2–2, 1–2, turn, change body shape, turn)
- Off of a bench (2–2, 1–2, turn, change body shape, turn)
- Jumping with a partner at same time, at different times, facing, side by side and integrating ideas just mentioned
- Jumping with a small group at same time, at different times, facing, side by side and integrating ideas just mentioned

**INTEGRATION AND TEACHING OF THE SKILL**

This skill can be integrated throughout all lessons K–5 when appropriate. Remember, though, that the timing of the arms with legs to produce an efficient jump often needs instruction. With immature jumpers, usually children in K–2, you will often see

- Arms held high and in front of the body before take off
- Arms and legs working separately from each other
- Arms timed with the push off of the legs to help project the body into the air, only to see them drop immediately and spread out in anticipation of losing balance as they land
- Children fully extended in the air, but starting to bring their arms down before they have reached the peak of the jump

Whenever you see these and other less mature patterns, instruction is needed to help children progress in the skill. When working on the floor, and not off of a height, this can be done through questions on what needs to be done to improve their jumps for height. You can have children give answers and then select what to work on, or you can pose a question and let the children answer directly with movement. An example of the latter might be, "What do you need to do with your arms so that you can jump off of the floor higher?" When children are jumping for height off of a bench, another question might be, "I've noticed that when you are jumping from the benches, very few of you are able to show a fully extended body shape while in the air. What can you do to improve this? You may jump from the bench or from the floor to work this out."

As children work with jumping for height, watch carefully that they keep their heads up and are not looking down anticipating the next move. Be sure you have adequate mat protection where they are landing. Also, keep in mind that this skill is a jump *up,* not *out.*

## References and Reading List

American Association for Health, Physical Education, and Recreation (1965). *This is physical education.* Washington, DC: Author.

Broer, M. R. (1984). Basic mechanical principles governing body motion. In B. J. Logsdon, K. R. Barrett, M. Ammons, M. R. Broer, L. E. Halverson, R. McGee, & M. A. Roberton. *Physical education for children: A focus on the teaching process* (2nd ed.) (pp. 87–122). Philadelphia, PA: Lea & Febiger.

Cheney, G. (1989). *Basic concepts in modern dance: A creative approach* (3rd ed.). Pennington, NJ: Princeton Book.

Hawkins, A. M. (1991). *Moving from within: A new method for dance making.* Chicago, IL: a cappela books.

Mauldon, E. & Layson, J. (1979). *Teaching gymnastics* (2nd ed.). London: Macdonald and Evans.

Morison, R. (1956). *Educational gymnastics.* (Can be obtained through interlibrary loan from the Walter Clinton Jackson Library, University of North Carolina at Greensboro)

Morison, R. (1960). *Educational gymnastics for secondary schools.* (Can be obtained through interlibrary loan from the Walter Clinton Jackson Library, University of North Carolina at Greensboro)

Morison, R. (1969). *A movement approach to educational gymnastics.* London: J. M. Dent.

Roberton, M. A., & Halverson, L. E. (1984). *Developing children—Their changing movement: A guide for teachers.* Philadelphia: Lea & Febiger.

Rovegno, I. (1988). The art of gymnastics: Creating sequences. *Journal of Physical Education, Recreation and Dance, 59* (3), 66–69.

Ryser, O., & Brown, J. (1990). *A manual for tumbling and apparatus stunts* (8th ed.). Dubuque, IA: Brown.

Turoff, F. (1991). *Artistic gymnastics: A comprehensive guide to performing and teaching skills for beginners and advanced beginners.* Dubuque, IA: Brown.

Williams, J. (1992). *Themes for educational gymnastics* (3rd ed.). London: A & C Black.

# CHAPTER 6

# *Teaching Educational Dance*

*e*ducational dance is rooted in children's natural ways of moving. It gives expression to their natural movement and becomes the collective actions from which individuals can develop and come to know themselves within the aesthetic experience. Educational dance should be an integral part of the total physical education program so that children can be encouraged to nurture the aesthetic dimension in their lives. A physical education curriculum consisting only of games or of games and gymnastics denies children the chance to learn to move as dancers. Schools may very well be the only place where children have experience with dance, making its inclusion in the curriculum seem even more important. Without dance experiences, children would not have the opportunity for movement to be a means of aesthetic expression for themselves. Simply giving children the opportunity to dance while at school, however, does not explicitly define their dance experiences as educational dance. A curriculum that relies on children's experience of dance done to the music of the current popular culture is a curriculum that limits the range for constructing meaning within this aesthetic movement dimension. Educational dance and recreational dance have different purposes. The child's total experience of schooling is richer, more varied, and more broadly constructed and, therefore, more meaningful when it includes educational dance.

## *Unique Contributions of Educational Dance*

Dance movement is different from moving in games and gymnastics. You move in games to free yourself from an opponent to have a better shot at the basket or to smash the shuttlecock to the floor to keep your opponent from returning it. You move in gymnastics to travel from one part of the mat to another by transferring body weight from feet to hands to feet, as in a cart-wheel, or to dismount from a bench by jumping and landing with a roll. In dance, your focus is on the movement itself; on the internal kinesthetic awareness and feeling of your body's movement, the meaning that such movement has for you, and the meaning communicated to others as you move.

We usually communicate meaning in our lives through the spoken voice using words. We state an opinion, share information, and tell others what we think. There are times, however, when the spoken voice is not the "voice" to use and words are not the best medium of expression. Sometimes we need to speak with our inner voices and the way that we need to speak is through the expressive medium of movement. This is what dance is about. Dance is letting movement be the expression of your inner voice. It is the external expression of the internal voice. Dance is a deep sensing of self that permits connections to other parts of life that are personally meaningful. By repeatedly giving creative expression to your inner voice, you grow personally and make connections that otherwise would not be made. In this sense, dance can transform a person through the creation of new meanings in movement.

You might be uncomfortable with phrases like inner voice, deep sensing, creative expression, meaningful connections, transformation, and the aesthetic experience because you have not had many opportunities to say these phrases; to let dance speak as your inner voice. Your own discomfort should be the basis for recognizing that your students also may not have had many prior educational dance experiences and may be uncomfortable with the unfamiliar as well. You must help your students become comfortable with hearing their inner voices and expressing them through dance. You must create an environment where it is safe for them to move with expression, to explore aesthetic ideas kinesthetically, and to construct meaning from their dancing. A safe environment is a comfortable environment. The approach to teaching children's physical education presented in this book will help you construct such an environment.

The following story provides a brief glimpse into one teacher's struggle with creating meaningful aesthetic experiences with her students:

When I first started teaching, I knew that dance was important to include in my program. The kind of dance that I did, however, was very structured. I basically only taught folk dances because they come with very specific directions that were clearly written out by someone else who knew more about dance than I. When I did venture away from those, I still only taught dance units that I typically got from other teachers where the entire unit was a well-defined dance sequence itself. I realized that when I taught those units that I was "teaching the sequence" and not dance-like movement, organized in a sequence, as a means of expression and communication. As I got more experience teaching and gained more confidence in my own abilities, I began to have less need for every sequence to be so structured and for every child to be doing exactly the same movements in the sequence. I came to realize that I didn't need to rely on someone else providing me with a sequence to teach for my dance units. I found that I could give my students choices within certain constraints for developing dance-like ways of expressing their unique selves when creating their own sequences. Not everyone had to skip first. Not everyone had to rise in the same way. Not everyone had to work with the same number in their choreographic groups. I began to feel that my dance teaching was getting closer to helping my students construct meaningful dance experiences from my lessons than when I taught using other people's sequences and not giving the children any choices in what they did. I was beginning to build what I thought was an appropriate concept of educational dance, of children learning to be skillful at using their bodies as a means of expression and not simply mimicking the teacher's actions.

By chance, I discovered that my children's perceptions of this transformation that I was creating for the dance units in the curriculum were not the same as mine. On the last day of a unit, I like to tell the children what unit we will be working on next. I had just finished a games unit with this particular fourth-grade class and, as the children were lining up, I told them that our next unit would be in dance. It just so happened that there was a new student whose first day in our school was that day. He sort of gasped when he heard me say dance. I didn't yet know what type of physical education program he had experienced previously, although his gasp made me wonder. But I was excited for him that he would be experiencing one of my "transforming" educational dance units. My excitement was tempered though when the child next to him in line, a child whom I had taught since kindergarten, said, "Oh, don't worry. You just move into some empty spaces and stop in those shapes. It's not *really* dancing."

## The Educational Dance Teacher

Teaching educational dance is not easy. In games, a ball or some other piece of game equipment is often the central focus of the movement. In gymnastics, it is the apparatus or equipment that is integral to what the gymnast does. In dance, the movement itself is the main focus and, because the movement is the focus, the teacher has a more prominent role in the dance lesson than in a games or a gymnastics lesson. In one sense, the teacher has more responsibility for generating students' movement responses. In a class soccer game, it is the placement of a pass to a teammate that dictates the receiver's and defender's movement responses. In artistic gymnastics, it is the required elements for the floor exercise that dictate the gymnast's movements. In dance, what the teacher says and how it is said become the most important factors in how students express themselves and communicate through their movement responses.

When you, as the teacher, are helping students focus on movement as an expression or communication of their inner voices, recognize that your teacher voice is an outer voice for their inner experience. Your voice needs to portray confidence and strength but not be so "loud" that the children are unable to hear their own inner voices. Your voice needs to demonstrate knowledge and expectation of skill learning but not be so judgmental that they do not feel free to choose different ways to express themselves through movement. Your voice needs to convey natural excitement and love of dance but not be so overdone as to suggest false enthusiasm. Teaching moving from an inner perspective can be scary for both teacher and student. It is the teacher's responsibility to create a comfort zone for self and students that encourages responsiveness, permits choice, and generates excitement and enthusiasm.

Students overall responses to dance tasks can be viewed within a developmental perspective. Your first attempts at teaching educational dance content will probably be met with quick, one-time responses from your students. They will most probably do the movements you ask for but with minimum variation, inconsistent movement quality, and little or no expressiveness. Getting everyday movements to become dance-like movements requires expanding children's short responses, helping them practice those responses with increasing quality, and encouraging and clarifying the expression of their inner voices. As students develop in the ways that they respond to dance tasks, they learn to move in a variety of ways, move with more skill, and more clearly use movement as a means of expression and communication.

# THE CORE CONTENT FOR TEACHING EDUCATIONAL DANCE TO CHILDREN

Teaching toward the notion of getting ordinary, everyday movement to become dance movement requires the teacher to have an understanding of content for teaching in the context of educational dance. The nature of dance, that is, what makes dance dance, creates a different and unique context in which movement is taught. The unique contextual differences are emphasized in the content conceptualization for teaching educational dance as seen in Figure 6–1.

The Dance Core Content Framework is one adaptation of the Movement Framework (Chapter 3) for educational dance. To reflect its particular context, the Dance Core Content Framework is different from the core content frameworks for games and gymnastics even though all three are frameworks that depict movement.

This particular conceptualization is not meant to depict everything there is to know and to teach about educational dance content. Not every content category that could be included has been included nor has every included cat-

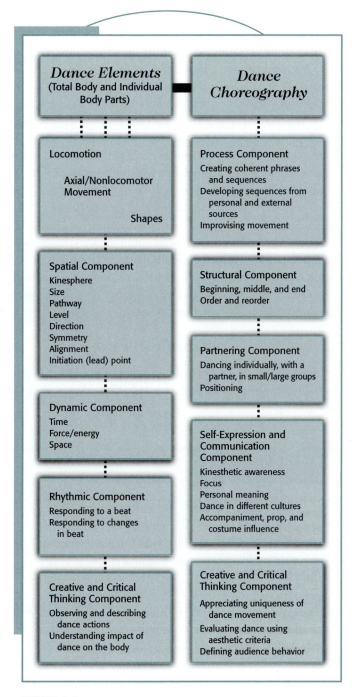

FIGURE 6–1
Dance core content framework for beginning teachers.

egory been expanded to its fullest. This is intentional. What has been included is what is thought to be essential for preservice physical education teachers both to know and to have teaching experience with as they prepare to begin their licensed teaching careers. A preservice teacher cannot be expected to know all there is to know about educational dance nor have experienced teaching every dance content concept during undergraduate preparation. It is assumed that preservice teachers will expand their knowledge and teaching of dance content beyond these core concepts as they continue to develop professionally beyond their initial licensure programs.

The Dance Core Content Framework with its various components will be discussed first. Then the core content will be organized around selected content ideas and presented in individual working units. The efforts of the National Dance Association of the American Alliance for Health, Physical Education, Recreation and Dance in developing dance standards for the National Standards in Arts Education publication (Consortium of National Arts Education Associations, 1994) and Laban's conceptualization of movement as presented in and interpreted by a number of sources, serve as the basis for the Dance Core Content Framework.

## The Dance Core Content Framework

Overall, the content for beginning teachers in teaching educational dance is viewed in two broad integrated categories—dance elements and dance choreography.

> ### Dance Elements
> *The rhythmic use of the body moving in space and time with force/energy including a critical and creative perspective. The body moving can be the entire body or individual body parts.*
>
> ### Dance Choreography
> *The combining of dance elements into a dance sequence that releases, follows through, and terminates kinesthetic energy.*

Dance elements can be performed by the whole body such as in running, rolling, or skipping, or by particular body parts such as the knees, legs, or head. Even when the element is being performed by an individual part, attention can still be paid to less active body parts to see how they are being used at the time. Such dance elements are seen as the dance actions from which sequences eventually will be constructed. Dance elements are the individual movements that are combined to create sequences. A sequence is a series of dance elements that is defined by a sense of rhythmic wholeness and completion. The act of combining dance elements into a unified sequence that has meaning for the dancer is the act of dance choreography.

## Dance Elements

Dance elements are grouped into three types: locomotion, axial/nonlocomotor movement, and shapes.

> ### Locomotion
> **Whole body transport from one spot to another with weight transference usually occurring on the feet. The eight basic locomotor actions in dance are:**
>
> | | |
> |------|--------|
> | walk | hop |
> | run | skip |
> | jump | slide |
> | leap | gallop |

In dance, locomotor movements permit dance actions to occur in different places and provide varied ways of getting to those places. They are the means by which dancers move about the dance space. Moving the entire body from place to place can be done displaying a number of expressive possibilities. Visualize three different dance phrases, for example, where dancers walk from one spot to another; one walking action is an ambling stroll; another has a lively, bouncy stepping action; and the third is a stiff awkward display of agony. Each dance walk expresses a different quality of this specific locomotor action.

Fundamental to dance are the eight basic locomotor actions. They each involve a transfer of weight on the feet. A walk is a transfer of weight from one foot to the other in a moderate tempo with at least some point of supporting contact with the ground at all times. A run is a walk in a fast tempo with a brief period of nonsupport. A jump is a transfer of weight with elevation from a two-foot take off to a two-foot landing. A leap requires elevation like a jump and is done by taking off on one foot and landing on the other foot. A hop also requires elevation from a one-foot take off but with the landing on the same foot. A skip is a step and hop on the same foot, alternating feet. A slide is a sideward step and quick leap that cuts one foot out from under the other. Similarly, a gallop is a forward step and quick cutting leap. Two additional locomotor actions are noted because of their use in dance: weight transference with elevation from a one-foot take off to a two-foot landing and from a two-foot take off to a one-foot landing.

Walk, run, jump, leap, and hop are even-rhythm movements with each transfer of weight taking the same amount of time. Skip, slide, and gallop are uneven rhythmic, two-action combinations with one action done quickly and the other more slowly. For example in the skip, the hop action is done quickly while the step takes comparatively longer to complete.

> *Axial/Nonlocomotor Movement*
> *Movement around an axis of the body while the body is anchored in one spot. Axial movements include:*
>
> curl, stretch, twist
> rising, sinking
> opening, closing
> spinning
> gesture
> fall and recovery

Axial movements do not involve body transport. They are done on the spot. They are movements around an axis that runs through the body. The body can become rounded and curl in, be stretched away from its center, or it can rotate or twist about a central axis without moving to another location. Rising and sinking move the body or a body part away from and toward the floor respectively, they are up and down actions. A rising movement can suggest reaching upwards, loftiness, beginnings, or potential as the body moves away from a deep level. Sinking could convey downwardness, endings, and lowliness. Opening and closing are similar to rising and sinking but the movement is away from and toward the torso and thus moves sideward instead of up or down. The expressive qualities of opening could suggest release, outwardness, an invitation, or a beginning while closing could suggest withdrawal, fear, tightness, or coming to an end. Spinning faces the entire body in new directions by turning on a central axis. One can spin to generate a feeling of vertigo, prepare to go off in another direction, or express the concept of whirling through the air. Gesture is a movement usually executed by one, or perhaps two, parts of the body like the arms, head, or shoulders. Gestures are meant to express a feeling, create a mood, or communicate an idea. Reaching toward someone is a way of expressing a caring feeling. A shrug of the shoulders could say, "I really don't care." And a slight toss of the head could communicate a *come-hither* look. A fall happens when the body weight goes off balance and gives in to gravity, while recovery occurs when balance is regained. While a deliberate fall and recovery are expressive dance elements, how to loose and regain balance as a safety precaution should be *taught* in dance as well. Non deliberate falls do occur in dance and children need to know how to safely absorb their body weight upon losing balance to reduce the risk of injury.

> ### Shapes
> *Spatial configuration of the body while moving and consciously held when pausing in a moment of stillness with more emphasis generally being given to the latter. Shapes can be described as:*
>
> narrow
>
> wide
>
> round
>
> twisted

While the body constantly has shape when it is moving, in educational dance the notion of shape crystallized in a moment of stillness is more pertinent in teaching children. The way in which the body is held in space expresses the dancer's inner voice and communicates meaning. A narrow, one-dimensional shape whose line is in one direction; a wide, two-dimensional shape that has both height and width; a round, three-dimensional shape that also has a curved line; and a twisted, three-dimensional shape that has a rotated, screw-like appearance each will express different feelings and ideas through the way the body is held in a moment of stillness.

**Components of Dance Elements.** Each of the three dance elements can be explored and studied more closely by examining the different components that go into making them what they are. The defining components for locomotor movements, axial/nonlocomotor movements, and shape-making movements are spatial, dynamic, rhythmic, and creative and critical thinking. It is the interaction of these components that permits a walk to be an ambling stroll or a bouncy jaunt or an awkward, stiff journey. In teaching educational dance, different components are emphasized at different times to fully explore all of the dance elements and, consequently, enrich the students experience of dance.

*Spatial Component*
*Describes where in space the body, both in stillness and in motion, is located. Descriptors for the spatial component are:*

*kinesphere*
*size*
*pathway*
*level*
*direction*
*symmetry*
*alignment*
*initiation (lead) point*

Kinesphere is the area surrounding the body that includes all the space into which the person can reach with torso and limbs. It is one's personal space. The image of a person inside a bubble is one way to visualize this concept. The bubble would be the person's kinesphere. In dance, the kinesphere is explored through a variety of movements and for a variety of reasons. For example, students could explore the concept of larger and smaller by being confronted with the problem of what they could do to make their kinespheres expand and contract. Kinespheres can also be used to address safety while moving in dance. As students come to know how far into space they can reach and how much space it takes to come to a stop when moving, they will know better how to avoid contact with others when that is the desired behavior.

Size is the spatial component that refers to how large or small a movement is. Most dance elements can be varied by size to change their look or their expressive qualities and to let students explore this dimension of the spatial component. A step so small that it almost cannot be seen requires a different way of moving and feels very different from a giant step that covers a lot of ground.

Movements made by the whole body or individual body parts etch a design or a pathway in space as an indication of where the movement is occurring. Pathways are either straight or curved or a variation of the two. Straight pathways could be used to get dancers from one spot to another quickly or to convey a feeling of directness. Curved pathways are created, for example, when the tension in a body part is released into a swinging motion or when the idea of coming-round-again-to-the-starting-point is what is to be communicated.

Changing levels within a dance element or between elements increases the variety of movement response and also opens up possibilities for other elements to be included. Rising and sinking result in change of level. The level (high, medium, deep) at which a dance element is done has expressive implications as well. A shape held at a deep level could express an identification with the earth while a high shape could express the idea of freedom in flight.

Similar to changes in levels, changes in direction increase variety in movement response, open the possibility for other dance elements to occur, and express feelings and communicate ideas. Running forward quickly toward another person then running backward away from him portrays the idea of meeting and parting. The change of direction made the occurrence of meeting and parting possible. Certain elements move the body in certain directions. Rising and sinking move the body in upward and downward directions; opening and closing in right and left sideward directions. Combining either a forward or backward direction with an upward or downward direction and a right or left sideward direction creates a diagonal direction.

Symmetry denotes whether the right and left halves of the body are located in space in identical, or similar, positions. If they are, then the body is said to be symmetrical. If they are not, then the body is said to be asymmetrical. Symmetry can suggest coherence, calmness, balance, or stability while asymmetry may suggest confusion, excitement, out-of-balance, or variation. Symmetry and asymmetry can be used to clarify expression and make dance elements more interesting.

Alignment in dance is the spatial relationship of parts of the body to each other and their relational position to the body's base of support and its line of gravity. Where in space body parts are located considering one's support base and line of gravity gives the dance element its form and shape. Some alignment relationships give the impression of smoothness and flow while others give an awkward and off balance impression. Alignment is also an important consideration in injury prevention in dance. For example, keeping the body aligned over its base of support, especially when the base is changing or moving, keeps the dancer on balance and not falling down.

Where within the body a dance element arises or begins its movement is another spatial consideration. The initiation of movement can come from the torso (central) or from the limbs (distal). Having movement originate in different places permits variety and, consequently, generates visual interest in the movement, as well as expanding the expressive qualities that can be demonstrated. A jump that "begins" in the torso and pushes down into the legs and through the feet into the floor and back through the legs and torso and continues through the arms to lift the body high into the air is visually quite different from a short, low jump that "begins" in the ankles and moves only to the toes.

> *Dynamic Component*
> *The effort qualities of movement that are revealed in*
> *the relationships among these three motion factors:*
>
> *time*
>
> *force/energy*
>
> *space*

Time, or the tempo in which a dance element is completed, is a dynamic component that helps characterize or define dance movement. Time refers to the duration or how long it takes to complete a movement. Sudden (very fast) and sustained (very slow) are the extremes of the time factor, which includes all differentiation of duration between the two extremes.

Force/energy describes the exertion or weight of movement. The extremes of the quality of force are strong and light. Strong movements require more energy or exertion than light movements. More muscle tension is needed for strong movements. Strong movements are weightier and more forceful and, therefore, express different aesthetic qualities from light movements.

Space, as a dynamic component, refers to the direct or flexible use of space. Less space is used with direct movements than with flexible movements as they are straight, undeviating types of movements. Walking from one place to another on the dance floor in a straight line would be an example of direct use of space. Flexible movements are bendable, pliant, or circuitous and, consequently, use more space. Walking between those same two places but going first to the left then to the right then to the left again is a flexible use of space. Directness and flexibility in movement communicate different ideas and feelings.

TABLE 6-1
*Eight Basic Effort Actions*

| TIME | FORCE/ENERGY | SPACE | | EFFORT ACTION |
|------|--------------|-------|---|---------------|
| Sudden | Strong | Direct | — | Thrust |
| Sustained | Strong | Direct | — | Press |
| Sudden | Light | Direct | — | Dab |
| Sustained | Light | Direct | — | Glide |
| Sudden | Strong | Flexible | — | Slash |
| Sustained | Strong | Flexible | — | Wring |
| Sudden | Light | Flexible | — | Flick |
| Sustained | Light | Flexible | — | Float |

Combining a time quality with one of force/energy and with one of space results in eight different combinations of the three motion factors. These dynamic combinations are shown in Table 6–1.

Each combination conveys a different dynamic quality and feels differently when performed. Children may like to feel the difference in taking sustained, strong, direct steps (a pressing action) compared to sudden, light, direct steps (a dabbing action) and may realize that they have a preference toward one or the other in everyday walking. Students may also use dynamic combinations to communicate ideas. For example, sustained, light, flexible arm movements communicate the floating quality of an autumn leaf falling to the ground. Effort combinations give students a wide range of possibilities on which to focus while exploring this important expressive component of dance content.

> ### *Rhythmic Component*
> *Moving in relation to metric components of accompaniment where sounds are divided into equal parts or beats, and in relation to organic components of accompaniment where natural characteristics are the rhythm. Moving here means both:*
>
> responding to a beat
>
> responding to changes in beat

Music, and other metric forms of accompaniment, have an underlying beat or rhythmic pulse. The beat can be either fast or slow and strong or light or some variation in between. Rhythmic patterns are created when different beats are put together in particular ways. Four strong beats could have the pattern of fast-fast-slow-fast or a different pattern such as fast-slow-fast-slow. Students' dance experience needs to include moving on or with a beat in a variety of patterns, as well as responding to changes in beat. From a developmental perspective, children will be able to respond to a beat before they are able to adapt their movement in response to changes in beat.

Organic rhythm is another form of rhythm to which dance movement can be connected. Organic rhythm evolves from natural occurrences and patterns such as a breeze gently rustling the leaves of a tree, the rapid fluttering of a hummingbird's wings, an ocean wave running up on the beach and quickly retreating again, and endless drops of water struggling to release themselves to gravity from their suspended state at the end of a faucet. Each of these examples has an organic rhythm that could serve as accompaniment to which students respond through movement.

*Creative and Critical Thinking Component*
*An integrative aspect to the performance of dance elements. This component includes:*

observing and describing dance actions
understanding the impact of dance on the body

Giving children opportunities to develop skill in observing and describing dance actions is a basic part of the teaching content for educational dance. Naming the shape that your body is in and recognizing that sinking changes the level of the body help students make wise choices in dancing, increase their ability to communicate about dance, and expand their ways of knowing the elements of dance. Being able to see and discuss their own and others dance actions will contribute to their overall constructions of the experience of dance.

Dance has an amazing impact on the body. Done appropriately, educational dance contributes to physical fitness components such as aerobic capacity, strength, flexibility, and muscular endurance. Dance can also have a negative impact on the body as in a dance injury. Preparing the body to dance by warming up and dancing safely by being in control of one's movements are as important in educational dance as they are in other forms of dance.

## Dance Choreography

Dance choreography is the construction of dance sequences. Five components of choreographic construction are described here: process, structural, partnering, self-expression and communication, and creative and critical thinking.

> ### *Process Component*
> ### *The means of composing dance sequences.*
> ### *The process includes:*
>
> creating coherent phrases and sequences
> developing sequences from personal and
> external sources
> improvising movement

A dance phrase is a short, simple sequence of related dance elements that has the feeling of a complete rhythmic thought. Sequences are phrases that have been linked together in a coherent fashion and that demonstrate a specific choreographic intention. The parts of a sequence have a shared characteristic or nature (e.g., a floating quality of dynamics, a contrast in tempo, an ebb and flow style) that gives them a sense of connectedness. The specific choreographic intention or purpose for a sequence can be developed from personal and external sources. Combining dance elements that represent a personal (internal) idea, or that are suggested by others or by an external object in the environment, is the basis of the choreographic process.

Improvising movement is the process of instant choreography and performance. Dance movement is created on the spot within the limitations of the dance environment. Improvising can be challenging because the dance environment is dynamic and also unpredictable. If you are improvising with other dancers, for example, you do not know what they are going to do next in response to the improvisation idea. You are unable to predict their movements adding to the challenge of your improvised movement. Dancers must respond quickly to an improvisation problem which is quite different from creating and repeatedly practicing a specific sequence.

> ## Structural Component
> ### The systematic arrangement, or syntax, of dance movement that has:
>
> *a beginning, a middle, and an end*
> *order and reorder*

Structuring a sequence so that it has a beginning, a middle, and an end contributes to the notion of rhythmic completion. The beginning is a release of kinesthetic energy. The middle is the continuation and follow through. And the end is the termination of that energy. The movements that are the release, follow through, and termination have an order or pattern for each sequence that gives the sequence its unique structure. By reordering or rearranging the parts of a sequence, a different pattern emerges with its own unique new structure.

> ## Partnering Component
> ### The number of individuals involved in the dance sequence and their expressive, communicative, and positional relationships in interacting with one another. This component includes:
>
> *dancing individually, with a partner, in small/large groups*
> *positioning*

Phrases or sequences can be composed for dancers dancing alone, with a partner, in small groups, or in large groups. The number of dancers dancing a phrase or sequence of movements has an impact on the expressive and communicative components of the choreography. Dancing alone, a child can become lost in his own movements. The inner voice that gets expressed is that of the individual child. Increasing the number of dancers dancing together expands the communicative possibilities by providing opportunities to create and express a shared meaning with other dancers. It also expands the choreographic complexity in certain ways as interactions between and among partners now must be considered in creating a dance sequence. Changing the partnering component during a sequence so that sometimes a dancer is dancing alone and sometimes with a partner or group is a possibility. The partnering component does not have to stay the same throughout a sequence.

In considering partner (two or more) interaction, the positional relationship of the partners is of importance. Where they are positioned and what kind of position they have in relation to one another is a critical part of choreography. Partners can be apart or together; they can be in front of or behind one another; they can be above or below each other; partners can support and be supported by one another; and they can be touching, facing, or enclosing others. These positional relationships can be shown by the whole body or by emphasizing individual body parts. Position has a communicative component in that partners could choose to express the ideas of meeting and parting (coming to and going away from); mingling and separating (like meeting and parting but done with a flexible space dynamic); leading and following (a leader shows the others how to move); mirroring, matching, and copying (doing identical simultaneous movements facing one another as if looking in a mirror, doing identical simultaneous movements facing the same way, and doing identical movements but not simultaneously); unison and successive (moving at the same time or one after the other); supported and being supported (held/lifted or being held/lifted by partners); and contrasting and complementing (moving in opposite or in similar ways) in constructing and performing dance sequences.

> *Self-Expression and Communication Component Understanding dance as a way of creating and expressing meaning in one's life. The components of this understanding are:*
>
> kinesthetic awareness
>
> focus
>
> personal meaning
>
> dance in different cultures
>
> accompaniment, prop, and costume influence

Expression and communication are enhanced by the ability of the body, through its sensory organs, to know what, where, and how it is moving as it dances. This is known as kinesthetic awareness. Being aware of the muscles and joints in the head, trunk, arms, and legs when moving to a high, stretched open shape helps you communicate more clearly what you are trying to say with your inner voice. A dancer's visual focus also adds to the aesthetic quality of movement by clarifying expression. Looking at the specific body part that initiates an action emphasizes the importance of that part and draws attention to it. Visual focus can also mean looking in lots of different places as may happen when traveling about to a new place.

Dance, as a way to speak with the inner voice, is a vehicle of expression of personal meaning. The body says what the voice does not. What is meaningful to the self can be expressed through movement and, thus, communicated to others. One's personal meaning can be shared through the moving body. Cultural meaning, as well as personal meaning, also can be communicated through dance. Different cultures have different dances known as folk dances that represent sources of understanding about those cultures. Folk dances are a unique way of getting to know various cultures.

There are a number of factors that can influence the expression and communication of meaning through movement. The form, style, and mood of the accompaniment selected for a sequence have an aesthetic impact on the dance elements of that sequence. Props, like a paper plate, a chair, or a "magic" stick, can suggest new expressive possibilities that are grounded in the properties of the prop itself. Making and wearing simple costumes adds to the aesthetic feeling of a dance and enhances the communication of meaning. For example, children could make and wear simple masks showing particular facial expressions that represent selected expressive qualities of their dance sequences. Accompaniment, props, and costumes are important considerations in dance choreography.

> *Creative and Critical Thinking Component*
> *An integrative aspect to choreographing dance*
> *sequences. This component includes:*
>
> appreciating uniqueness of dance movement
> evaluating dance using aesthetic criteria
> defining audience behavior

Appreciating dance as a unique form of movement is important for children to realize. Dance is different from games and gymnastics and aquatics and exercise. Its uniqueness should be both understood and experienced. A part of this understanding includes criteria for judging the aesthetic quality of dance movement. Students are encouraged to take the responsibility for constructively evaluating their own and their peers' work so that their dance can reflect continuing aesthetic development. Criteria could include, for example, skillfulness of dancers, variety in elements, interesting use of dynamic qualities, visual impact, and inclusion of original movements. When observing and applying these criteria, you become, in essence, a member of the audience. Demonstrating appropriate audience behavior, including constructively sharing evaluative opinions, is an important part of the experience of educational dance.

### Framework Summary

The Dance Core Content Framework for educational dance categorizes dance movement and other dance content appropriate for teaching dance to present an overall picture of what children's dance should be. It represents what you should know as a preservice teacher about the content of dance. The framework is meant to give you broad ways to organize your thinking about dance and to see how children can become skillful as creative and expressive dancers.

# UNDERSTANDING THE CONTENT FROM A TEACHING PERSPECTIVE

The core content for educational dance is rooted in the dance elements of locomotion, axial/nonlocomotor movement, and making shapes. It is through these elemental dance actions that the aesthetic dimension of children's lives can be explored through movement. As the exploration progresses, dance elements are refined and combined to build phrases and sequences, creating dance. Thus, choreographing dance becomes another content emphasis. Each of the core content ideas presented here as core content units has a teacher- or teacher-and-student-designed dance phrase or sequence as its culminating activity. For dance movement to become dance, it must go from just moving around in some creative way to moving in a coherent sequence with a choreographic intention. Children will lose interest if their dancing does not come to a sense of closure through the organization of the movements into dance sequences. Each individual dance unit within the framework needs to end with appropriate dance sequences of some type. The idea that children's work with dance content should culminate in a sequence is being used in this book to organize how the Core Content units for beginning teachers are presented. For each Core Content unit for the preservice teacher, there is a dance sequence that serves as the culminating activity for the development of that particular content idea. The Core Content within each unit could culminate in a limitless number of sequence possibilities. The individual sequences here are only one way of bringing together the unit Core Content ideas. The sequence designs were selected to collectively include all of the Core Content material for teaching educational dance and to collectively represent children's differing developmental levels in regard to their dance actions. We are not suggesting that these are the only sequences that illustrate each unit of Core Content for educational dance. We recognize that there are multiple solutions to the particular problem of content development. Different phrases and sequences could certainly cover the same dance components. The two general content categories—Dance Elements and Dance Choreography—are addressed but with some components being emphasized more than others. You will want to develop other sequences that are appropriate and exciting for the children that you are teaching when you address these particular content emphases.

The first three content units each focus on one of the three types of dance elements—locomotion, axial/nonlocomotor movement, and shapes. These elements are introduced and explored as expressive ways of moving through material from the different element and choreographic content components. The ending sequences are simple dance phrases meant to encourage expression of one's inner voice. Core Content 4 is centered on folk dance as a form of dance and selected as the ending sequence is the Philippine folk dance, Tinikling. Its inclusion provides an opportunity for children to understand the place dance can have in other cultures. The last three units focus on creating and performing dance sequences each with a different advanced emphasis. The emphases are props, the dynamic component of movement, and dancing as part of a group. While these ideas are sometimes parts of previous units, they are emphasized here aesthetically at more advanced levels. The core unit focus and content for each of the seven units are:

## CORE CONTENT 1. LOCOMOTION

Locomotor skills of walking, running, jumping, leaping, hopping, skipping, sliding, and galloping explored by using selected aspects of:

> *kinesphere*
> *size*
> *direction*
> *force/energy*
> *responding to a beat*

in relation to:

> *creating coherent phrases*
> *dancing individually*
> *personal meaning*

and including:

> *appreciating uniqueness of dance movement*

## CORE CONTENT 2. RISING AND SINKING

Axial/nonlocomotor skills of rising and sinking explored by using selected aspects of:

twisting

opening, closing

spinning

fall and recovery

kinesphere

size

initiation (lead) point

time

force/energy

space

responding to a beat

in relation to:

creating coherent phrases and sequences

dancing individually

focus

accompaniment influence

## CORE CONTENT 3. SHAPES

Shape-making in moments of stillness explored by using selected aspects of:

curling, stretching, twisting

kinesphere

level

symmetry

alignment

time

force/energy

responding to a beat

in relation to:

creating coherent phrases

dancing individually

kinesthetic awareness

focus

## CORE CONTENT 4. DANCE IN ANOTHER CULTURE

The locomotor skills of hopping, leaping, and jumping explored by using selected aspects of:

*dance from different cultures* (the Philippine folk dance, Tinikling)

## CORE CONTENT 5. DANCE PROPS

Creating dance sequences by combining locomotor and axial movements with the use of props explored by using selected aspects of:

pathway
level
direction
time
space
responding to a beat

in relation to:

creating coherent sequences
developing sequences from external sources
beginning, middle, and end structure
dancing individually
props

and including:

evaluating dance using aesthetic criteria
defining audience behavior

## CORE CONTENT 6. CONTRASTING THE DYNAMIC COMPONENT OF DANCE ELEMENTS

Creating dance sequences by combining locomotor skills, axial movement, and shape-making while contrasting dynamic components and explored by using selected aspects of:

time
force/energy
space

in relation to:

creating coherent sequences
developing sequences from personal sources
beginning, middle, and end structure
dancing with a partner
positioning
kinesthetic awareness
personal meaning

## CORE CONTENT 7. DANCING IN A GROUP

Creating group dance sequences by combining stepping, rising and sinking, and shape-making as the elements of choreography and explored by using selected aspects of:

kinesphere
time
responding to a beat

in relation to:

creating coherent sequences
improvising movement
beginning, middle, and end structure
order and reorder
dancing with small/large groups
personal meaning

and including:

observing and describing dance actions
evaluating dance using aesthetic criteria

The Core Content ideas are presented in a specific order. The order reflects what we believe is developmentally appropriate for introducing and emphasizing these content concepts. Within the dance elements framework category, locomotion is presented before rising and sinking. The expressiveness of the total body free to travel to other spots needs to come before the expressiveness of the total body restricted to moving on the spot. As children become competent and confident in expressing meaning in locomotor and axial movements, they are ready to use the stillness of shapes for expressive purposes. All three dance elements are further developed in later core units with the addition of new focuses in creating sequences.

## K–5 Progression

Figure 6–2 presents the organization and emphases of this content material for a K–5 physical education program. As with the suggested content emphases for educational games and educational gymnastics, the dark green segments represent when this material might be used as the major emphasis in designing lessons. The medium green segments suggest when the material might need to be revisited in order to make a task(s) less difficult for a class or individual children. The light green segments suggest when material could be used to design a task for an individual or small group of children to make it more challenging for them. It is suspected, however, that children will have had less experience with dance movement than they will have had with either games or gymnastics movement. Developing expressiveness will have to be encouraged constantly and consistently during the K–5 dance experience as children learn to move skillfully as dancers.

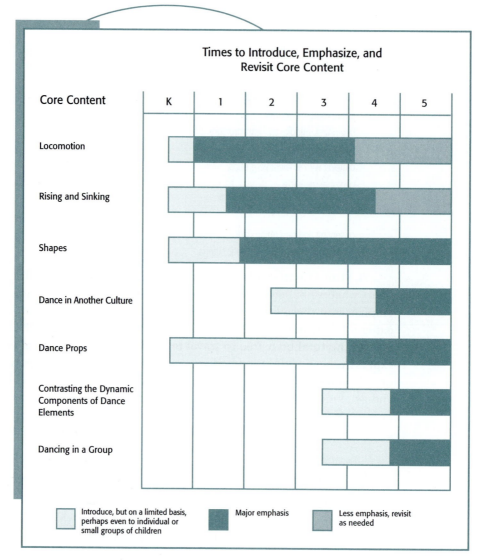

**FIGURE 6–2**
Suggested dance content emphasis by grade level.

## Remainder of the Chapter

After the seven Core Content units are presented, comments related to unique aspects of teaching dance content are provided to help you construct successful and meaningful dance experiences for children. The use of imagery in eliciting dance-like movement from children is discussed. Also discussed are the influence of accompaniment on dance movement and the teacher's need for a basic understanding of the characteristics of rhythm as they relate to teaching educational dance. Two resource lists follow the chapter references; one list is of companies or organizations that supply music useful for accompaniment in children's dance lessons and the other is a list of children's general book titles that have dance as a theme. These titles could be suggested to your school librarian for inclusion in the library inventory. Children should be encouraged to read about dance and the experience of dance to enhance their understanding of the contributions of dance to meaning-making. Connecting dance and reading also creates possibilities for integrating these two curricular content areas through the collaboration of the physical education teacher and the classroom teacher.

## *core content*

### Locomotion

FOCUS OF CONTENT

Locomotor skills of walking, running, jumping, leaping, hopping, skipping, sliding, and galloping explored by using selected aspects of:

    kinesphere
    size
    direction
    force/energy
    responding to a beat

in relation to:

    creating coherent phrases
    dancing individually
    personal meaning

and including:

    appreciating uniqueness of dance movement

ENDING PHRASE FOR CORE CONTENT 1—LOCOMOTION

Change from one locomotor pattern to another on a sound signal possibly combining changes of direction and changes of force/energy. For example:

- Run forward, on sound signal gallop forward or
- Skip forward, on sound signal walk backward or
- Run forward lightly, on sound signal leap forward vigorously or

- Skip forward strongly, on sound signal slide sideward lightly

**Accompaniment:** voice, drum, recorded music

## APPROPRIATENESS OF CONTENT

This content helps children in transforming ordinary locomotor actions into dance movement. Locomotion permits the dancer to travel about and change locations. It is a very prevalent dance action as locomotor skills are incorporated into virtually every dance danced. The ending phrase here is quite simple and most appropriately introduced as a culminating phrase in K and 1st grades. The emphasis is on both performing locomotor patterns with skillfulness and control, as well as with expression and meaning. Increasing the complexity of the ending phrase should be guided by the developmental levels of the particular group of children being taught.

### IDEAS FROM WHICH MOVEMENT TASKS ARE DESIGNED

- Traveling on feet using the five basic even-rhythm locomotor patterns and the three basic uneven-rhythm locomotor patterns

  vary the size of steps
  use different directions for travel
  vary the force/energy of steps

**PHOTO 6–1**
Traveling on feet in the even-rhythm locomotor patterns of jumping, leaping, and hopping emphasizing arms and legs.

PHOTO 6–2
Traveling on feet in the uneven-rhythm locomotor pattern of skipping.

travel without and with accompaniment

emphasize different body parts while traveling

- Combining traveling with an emphasis on stopping on balance
- Linking two ways of traveling by first traveling in one locomotor pattern then changing to a different one

change pattern on internal and external cues

vary the two-pattern combination

vary the direction of travel for each pattern

vary force/energy of the steps for each pattern

- Creating a dance phrase that shows changes in locomotor patterns possibly combined with changes of direction and changes of force/energy

### BIOMECHANICAL PRINCIPLES AFFECTING QUALITY OF PERFORMANCE

*Balance.* Center of gravity (COG) must be maintained over constantly changing bases of support as the body is transported through space. The child is in control of a locomotor movement through continuous adjustment of COG, allowing him to shift his focus to the expressive qualities of moving. When stopping, momentum must be slowed in relation again to retaining the COG over the base of support to keep from falling.

*Reception of force.* When landing from a locomotor action involving flight, the force of the body's weight should be absorbed through the sequential bending of ankles, knees, and hips. Giving with the weight through the lower body joints contributes to smoothness of the locomotor action, as well as to preparation for the next step. It is also a safety consideration.

## AESTHETIC PRINCIPLES AFFECTING QUALITY OF PERFORMANCE

The aesthetic focus on locomotion in this unit is to help students explore how it feels to travel in a dance-like way compared to ordinary locomotion. One way to help children make this comparison is to have them pay attention to the movement itself and not rely on habitual ways of accomplishing specified traveling actions. Asking children to vary the spatial, dynamic, and rhythmic components of locomotor patterns helps to release ordinary ideas about how to move and encourages children to explore different ways of traveling. Images such as "feeling magical as you run" and "walk as if you are sneaking up behind someone" may also help transform ordinary traveling into dance traveling.

## MOTOR DEVELOPMENT PRINCIPLES AFFECTING QUALITY OF PERFORMANCE

While the emphasis in dance is on meaning and expression and both of these can be present at all developmental levels of performance of locomotor patterns, there is information in the development literature related to the skills of hopping, running, skipping, and sliding (Roberton & Halverson, 1984). Developmental sequences for the skip are included here (see Table 6–2). The other three locomotor skills have been previously addressed.

This information can be used in observing where children are developmentally in performing these movements. Do not assume, however, that children who exhibit more mature forms of these or other locomotor patterns are doing so with meaning and expression in the aesthetic sense.

Generally speaking, locomotor patterns not involving flight are easier to perform than those that do involve flight. Children will only be able to do the three combination locomotor patterns (skip, gallop, slide) if they can do the individual skills involved in the combinations. A skip combines a step and hop on the same foot, alternating feet. A child, for example, cannot skip without first being able to hop and to hop successfully on each foot.

Additional developmental information related to locomotion and how it is presented in this unit includes the following hypothesized and research-supported ideas:

*Use of additional body parts.* In locomotion on the feet, other body parts emerge later as contributors to the action and to meaning and expression. In trying to step deliberately and carefully, for example, the arms may not be used at first to communicate expressiveness. They may hang down at the sides or be held out tentatively for balance. Later they may be deliberately held forward, slightly bent with outstretched hands, and palms facing forward to add to the expression of carefulness in stepping.

*Force/energy.* Sudden movement develops before sustained movement. Strong movement develops before light movement.

*Responding to a beat.* Moving to one's own internal rhythm or beat develops before moving to an external beat (e.g., drum beat, recorded music). A child will have no trouble traveling from one place to another in his own time frame but may arrive on the spot three counts early if he is given eight counts to get there. Also in responding to a beat, even-rhythm locomotor patterns generally are easier to do than uneven-rhythm patterns.

*Direction.* Development of directional movement is forward, backward, then sideward.

*Partnering component.* Dancing individually precedes dancing with partners and in groups.

## TABLE 6–2
### *Developmental Sequences for the Skip*

........................................................................................

**LEG ACTION COMPONENT**

*Step 1*    **One-footed skip.** One foot completes a step and hop before the weight is transferred to the other foot. The other foot just steps.

*Step 2*    **Two-footed skip; Flat-footed landing.** Each foot completes a step and a hop before the weight is transferred to the other foot. Landing from the hop is on the total foot, or on the ball of the foot, with the heel touching down before the weight is transferred (flat-footed landing).

*Step 3*    **Two-footed skip; Ball of the foot landing.** Landing from the hop is on the ball of the foot. The heel does not touch down before the weight is transferred to the other foot. Body lean increases over that found in Step 2.

........................................................................................

**ARM ACTION COMPONENT**

*Step 1*    **Bilateral assist.** The arms pump bilaterally up as the weight is shifted from the hopping to the stepping foot and down during the hop takeoff and flight.

*Step 2*    **Semi-oppositon.** The arms first swing up bilaterally. During the hop on the right foot, the right arm moves down and back only slightly while the left arm continues to move backward until the step on the left foot. Then, both arms again move forward and upward in a new bilateral pumping action. Now, however, the left arm moves back only slightly while the right arm moves backward until the step on the right foot. Although the arm action has the beginnings of opposition, at some time in the arm cycle both hands are in front of the body.

*Step 3*    **Opposition.** The arm opposite the stepping leg swings upward and forward in synchrony with that leg and reverses direction when the stepping leg touches the floor. The arm on the same side as the stepping leg moves backward and down in opposition to the stepping leg. At no time are both hands in front of the body.

........................................................................................

*Note:* These sequences, hypothesized by Halverson, have not been validated.

Reprinted by permission from Roberton & Halverson, 1984.

## PROGRESSION

There are instances in which one locomotor pattern naturally leads into another. A run with long, stretched out steps becomes a leap and a series of leaps that shifts to keep the same lead foot becomes a gallop. Other examples will suggest which patterns should come before others. As children begin to explore locomotion in a dance-like way, they can focus more clearly on the expressive component of the movement if they are comfortable doing the particular pattern. A child worried simply about how to gallop will be unable to gallop expressively as in galloping while emphasizing a high forward knee and swinging arms, for example.

There is also a progressive component to the complexity of the culminating dance phrase for this Core Content unit. The phrase has three possible parts—locomotor pattern (essential), direction, and force/energy.

The simplest sequence would be linking two different locomotor patterns done in the same direction and with the same force/energy. Complexity could be advanced by increasing the number of patterns, changing direction with locomotor pattern change, and/or changing force/energy with locomotor pattern change. At first, the teacher may want to designate which pattern, direction, and force/energy to use eventually having the children make those decisions for themselves.

### EXPERIENCES FOR REFLECTION

1. After creating your locomotor sequences in class, write them down showing which locomotor patterns, directions, and force/energy elements were selected. Note across the class the number of unique combinations used and discuss with your classmates the individual bases for your choices. Note the differences in complexity of sequences based on the pattern, direction, and force/energy changes that individuals selected.

2. Discuss with a dance instructor how he goes about observing for expressiveness in locomotor movement. Try then to identify a focus for your observational attention while teaching locomotor content and how you might go about interpreting a child's meaning from the movement that you see. Write a defining narrative on what makes locomotor movement expressive. What will you, as the teacher, look at when observing for expressiveness? Consider whether or not specific locomotor patterns, expressive qualities, or specific children would change your observational attention and, consequently, your interpretation.

*core content*

## Rising and Sinking

### FOCUS OF CONTENT

Axial/nonlocomotor skills of rising and sinking explored by using selected aspects of:

twisting
opening, closing
spinning
fall and recovery
kinesphere
size
initiation (lead) point
time
force/energy
space
responding to a beat

in relation to:

creating coherent phrases and sequences
dancing individually

focus

accompaniment influence

## ENDING PHRASE FOR CORE CONTENT 2 – RISING AND SINKING

- Begin in a low position close to the floor with feet as base of support
- Rise up in your favorite way taking four counts of accompaniment of a shaking tambourine (or similar continuous sound accompaniment)
- Travel in your favorite way taking eight counts with accompaniment and coming to a stop
- Sink down in your favorite way taking four counts with accompaniment
- End in a low position close to the floor with feet as base of support

    **Accompaniment:** voice, tambourine

## APPROPRIATENESS OF CONTENT

The content of rising and sinking is needed for children to expand their exploration of expressiveness through the use of axial movement. These two actions change the level of the body. Expressive possibilities increase when the body's level can be changed. As the body changes level, additional axial movements such as twisting, opening, closing, and spinning can be incorporated to further increase expressive quality. Rising and sinking are appropriately introduced early when children are ready for an additional focus beyond locomotion in exploring moving in dance-like ways.

### IDEAS FROM WHICH MOVEMENT TASKS ARE DESIGNED

- Using rising and sinking to teach fall and recovery as a safety concept
- Rising and sinking on the spot with feet as base of support

    vary the time, force/energy, and space components

    spin or twist while rising and sinking

    initiate the action with different body parts

    combine with opening and closing, varying the size of the movement

    without and with accompaniment

- Focusing on a leading body part to communicate expressiveness

    use different body parts

    switch focus during an action

- Rising followed by a locomotor action; a locomotor action followed by sinking

    vary the rising and sinking actions

    vary the locomotor actions

- Creating a short dance phrase beginning with a rising action, then traveling in a locomotor pattern, and ending with a sinking action

PHOTO 6–3
Linking rising and sinking with a twisting action.

### BIOMECHANICAL PRINCIPLES AFFECTING QUALITY OF PERFORMANCE

As the height of COG increases, stability over the base of support is harder to maintain. As children work on rising actions, they may find themselves a bit wobbly as they get underway. This is a result of trying to maintain control over their rising COGs. When they gain control and weight is centered over the base, they have a stable base from which to work. As children work on varying their rising actions, they may find themselves becoming wobbly again as they move around the axes of their bodies constantly needing to make adjustments in relation to COG.

### AESTHETIC PRINCIPLES AFFECTING QUALITY OF PERFORMANCE

The same aesthetic focus from the unit on locomotion continues in this unit on rising and sinking. Helping children explore changing body level as something other than merely standing up and stooping down is the content emphasis. Standing up is a habitual everyday action; rising up can be an expression of meaning. Stooping down is a habitual everyday action; sinking down can be an expression of meaning. Experiencing rising and sinking as the feeling of growing and shrinking, as well as of moving at different levels in relation to the floor, adds another dimension for children in using movement to express themselves.

Generally, rising and sinking are meant to be smooth, continuous movements all the way through to completion. Accompaniment for rising and sinking should also be smooth and continuous to elicit these qualities. Conversely, four individual drum beats for a four-count rising action might elicit four smaller, jerky rising actions instead of one smooth action that continues over four counts. The same is true for sinking. Keep in mind that the type of accompaniment used as a stimulus for action will affect the aesthetic qualities of the movement. (Accompaniment is addressed specifically later in the chapter.)

### MOTOR DEVELOPMENT PRINCIPLES AFFECTING QUALITY OF PERFORMANCE

Using rotation to vary rising and sinking actions involves twisting and turning. Turning is easier than twisting and some twists become turns when the nonrotating body part can no longer maintain resistance.

In sinking, the muscles must continually act against gravity pulling the body down quickly. Some young children have trouble sustaining the fight against gravity throughout an entire sinking action, especially if it is a very slow movement. You may see children giving in to the pull of gravity and flopping down toward the end of their sinking actions. Also in a slow rising action, you may find that children cannot sustain the movement all the way to completion and pop up toward the end to finish the move quickly.

Children do not explore rising and sinking in their extremes at first. Most children are skilled in the medium range for any particular element of focus. A rising action combined with an opening action, for example, often results in a kind of medium-stretched body position before a fully stretched position is shown for the dance element of opening. A fully stretched position and extremes of other dance elements should be emphasized and encouraged constantly during class to help children develop skillfulness in this aspect of dance movement. They need to experience dance elements at their extremes to enhance the communicative component of their movements.

### PROGRESSION

Locomotor movement permits the freedom of traveling from place to place with the focus on the body going somewhere. Nonlocomotor movement tends to focus the dancer's attention on himself, on the restrictive spot where he is moving. Thus, rising and sinking and other axial movements are appropriate to introduce after locomotion. Such movements can then be combined with locomotor movements to increase the choices for expression in creating short phrases or sequences.

The complexity of the ending dance phrase can be adjusted as part of the progression of this content. For example, a sinking and rising action with a different focus could be added after the first rising action. The locomotor pattern could be changed after four counts. The traveling action could begin as the rising action begins. Children who are ready for more choreographic elements in a dance phrase should have the phrase components adjusted appropriately.

This sequence also requires responding to a particular number of counts. If children are not ready to respond to an external beat or you do not wish for them to have to match each action to a specified number of counts, then have them link the actions together in their own time frame.

### EXPERIENCES FOR REFLECTION

1.  Videotape different classmates repeating a rising or sinking action—the first time without a focus on a particular body part and the second time with a focus. Discuss with the dancer how it felt contrasting the two. Review the videotape contrasting the movements with and without a focus. Does

the dancer's focus increase the aesthetic quality of the action? What meaning is being communicated with the absence of a focus? What meaning is being communicated with the presence of a focus?

2. Observe a child in an everyday movement situation, such as walking home from school, eating a meal, or taking out the garbage. Note how often and when any part of the movement was taken to the extreme. What part of the situation created the demand for an extreme action? Was a movement at the extreme needed at some point but for some reason not used? Or was there no demand at all for some type of extreme movement? What relationship might exist between expressiveness and use of movement extremes? Write a summary of your observation and reflection on these questions.

## *core content*

## Shapes

### FOCUS OF CONTENT

Shape-making in moments of stillness explored by using selected aspects of:

curling, stretching, twisting
kinesphere
level
symmetry
alignment
time
force/energy
responding to a beat

in relation to:

creating coherent phrases
dancing individually
kinesthetic awareness
focus

### ENDING PHRASE FOR CORE CONTENT 3—SHAPES

- Ready for travel on feet
- Take eight bouncy walking steps on the beat
- Make a shape on the next count and hold for three more counts
- Change to a different shape and hold for three more counts
- Repeat traveling and shape making (vary the component to be changed to create a different shape)

**Accompaniment:** recorded music ("Celebration" by Kool and the Gang)

## APPROPRIATENESS OF CONTENT

Shape-making as content is introduced generally in the early grades as children are beginning to be able to hold their bodies in moments of stillness. Shape-making is refined during dance work in later grades—3rd, 4th, and 5th—when they are able to focus beyond simply trying to be still. Like locomotion and axial movements, such as rising and sinking, making shapes is an expressive dance action from which dance sequences are constructed. The skillful use of shapes and their combination with other elements in sequences is grounded in children's exploratory work with this content and expanded in more sophisticated work with shapes that includes varying and clarifying them.

### IDEAS FROM WHICH MOVEMENT TASKS ARE DESIGNED

- Exploring one's kinesphere by molding the body in a variety of shapes
  - curl, stretch, twist into shapes
  - vary the level the shape is held
  - create symmetrical and asymmetrical shapes
  - vary the relationship of body parts to one another
  - vary the base of support
  - make shapes of different weights
  - vary the visual focus of the shape

PHOTO 6–4
Sophisticated shape work around the choreographic ideas of both dynamic shapes and shapes held in stillness, varying the level of the shapes, dancers' visual focus, and communicating the idea of individual/group separation.

- Changing shapes on signal

    vary the time to change (quickly, slowly) to new shapes

- Focusing on beginning and ending body shapes in connection with locomotor actions

    vary the locomotor patterns
    vary the beginning and ending shapes

- Dancing a short dance phrase including locomotion and making body shapes

### BIOMECHANICAL PRINCIPLES AFFECTING QUALITY OF PERFORMANCE

The content emphasis here is on the body in a moment of stillness, for this reason stability of the body over the base of support is important. A wide variety of shapes can be made on a wide variety of bases of support. The alignment of body parts in relation to the selected base must be such that the muscles can hold the body in a moment of clear stillness. A wide base of support on the feet makes it easier to maintain a still balance but will eventually limit the possibilities for shapes. As narrower and different bases are tried, children will need to explore where to place their body parts in making shapes to achieve balanced moments of stillness over stable bases.

### AESTHETIC PRINCIPLES AFFECTING QUALITY OF PERFORMANCE

Shapes that clearly communicate the desired expressive qualities are aesthetically pleasing. A strong shape in which muscle tension is firm throughout all body parts communicates clearly a sense of strength and powerfulness. A high wide shape in which the arms, fingers, and head are stretched and fully extended also communicates clearly a sense of openness or, perhaps, of reaching. Such clearly defined shapes enhance the aesthetic quality of the movement by increasing the power of its communicative quality.

Most often in dance, asymmetrical shapes are more interesting than symmetrical ones. Spaces created around asymmetrical lines capture the attention and invite a type of visual invasion by the viewer; they are different and interesting. Asymmetry also expands the positions in which the body can shape itself and, consequently, generates exciting new possibilities for meaning and expression.

### MOTOR DEVELOPMENT PRINCIPLES AFFECTING QUALITY OF PERFORMANCE

Moving and stopping are constants in daily life. Although we never absolutely stop moving, holding a shape in dance requires coming to a moment of perceived stillness. Children may think, however, that they are still when in fact they are slightly, but visibly, moving because their kinesthetic awareness is not fully developed. They may find it difficult to attain the muscle tension to keep their body parts as still as required. At first, they will also have trouble maintaining stillness once attained beyond very short periods of time. Using cue words such as "freeze" or "squeeze tight" and trying gently, but firmly, to physically move the children out of their shapes will help improve their kinesthetic awareness. Beginning with short periods and then gradually lengthening the time that a shape is to be held helps children maintain stillness beyond a few seconds.

### PROGRESSION

Before focusing on body shape in moments of stillness, children first need experience in moving freely using locomotor and axial movements. Then emphasis on body shape can be added and its expressive and communicative elements explored. Progression among the different components of shape-making that have been suggested to explore this Core Content is best determined by the individual teacher considering specific groups of children. The notion of a beginning shape for a dance sequence (position of the body before any movement begins) and an ending shape (position of the body when movement is completely finished) is part of the concept of shape. Emphasis on these two particular moments of stillness could come after shape-making has been explored as an individual dance element and as an element within a sequence.

### EXPERIENCES FOR REFLECTION

1. Discuss in small groups with your classmates what shapes you prefer to make. Share the reasons for your preferences. Relate how the shapes make you feel and what awareness they bring to you. Also, discuss shapes that you prefer not to make and the reasons for those preferences.

2. Draw pictures of three different shapes that you see your classmates making. Visualize the shape as you draw it, as if the seeing and drawing are one and the same. Do not worry about whether or not your drawing is good. Try to capture the shape's space as a picture on paper. Show your drawings to the people whose movement you drew and discuss with them what you saw. What prompted you to draw those three particular shapes? Is there a "type" of shape that seemed to attract your visual attention?

## Dance in Another Culture

### FOCUS OF CONTENT

The locomotor skills of hopping, leaping, and jumping explored by using selected aspects of:

dance from different cultures (the Philippine folk dance, Tinikling)

### WRITTEN DESCRIPTION OF TINIKLING

*Organizational Pattern.* Children are in groups of four, two tappers and two dancers. Each group has two eight-feet-long bamboo (or other appropriate material) poles and two wooden blocks approximately 18 x 3 x 2 inches. Groups are scattered throughout the room.

*Tapping the Poles.* Tappers sit or kneel at the ends of the poles holding one in each hand with a block in front of them and under the poles. Their seated positions and their hand positions should permit them to bring the poles together to strike them against each other and to take them apart without interference. The accompaniment is in 3/4 time with the accent on the first beat. (See Note on page 272.) The tappers begin with the poles on the outside of the wooden blocks. On count one the tappers lift the poles slightly and slide them together so they strike one another. For counts two and three, the poles slide apart and are tapped twice on the outside edge of the blocks. The cue for the tappers could be *together-apart-apart* or *in-out-out* for each of the three count measures.

*Dancing the Steps.* Jumpers step outside the poles when they are together (count one) and inside the poles when they are apart (counts two and three). There are a number of different step combinations that have been created to fit this arrangement. The basic Tinikling step is as follows:

PHOTO 6-5

PHOTO 6-6

Jumper is outside poles with left side toward poles.

Count 1: Hop on right foot in place outside the poles.

Count 2: Leap sideways onto left foot between the poles.

Count 3: Hop on left foot between the poles.

Count 4: Leap sideways onto right foot outside the poles in same place as count 1.

Count 5: Leap sideways onto left foot between the poles.

Count 6: Hop on left foot between the poles.

Counts 7–9: Repeat counts 4–6, continuing every three counts thereafter.

*Step Variations*
Side-to-Side

Count 1: Hop on right foot in place outside the poles.

Count 2: Leap sideways onto left foot between the poles.

Count 3: Leap onto right foot between poles.

Count 4: Leap sideways onto left foot outside poles on other side. Right side of body is toward poles.

Count 5: Leap sideways onto right foot between the poles.

Count 6: Leap onto left foot between the poles.

Counts 7–9: Leap sideways onto right foot outside poles on original side and continue as in counts 2 and 3.

*Note:* The hop on the first count of the phrase of music is to get the dance underway and as such is not repeated again in the sequence. A leap is done on the first beat of each succeeding three-count music phrase.

Straddle Jump

Count 1: Straddle jump outside poles.

Count 2: Jump inside the poles.

Count 3: Jump inside the poles.

Counts 4–6: Repeat counts 1–3.

Rocking Step: Same as side-to-side but done facing poles and moving forward and backward in a rocking motion.

Circling Step

Count 1: Beginning at one end and facing poles hop on right foot in place outside the poles.

Count 2: Leap onto left foot inside the poles.

Count 3: Leap onto right foot inside the poles.

Count 4: Leap onto left foot outside the poles.

Count 5: Take small running step with right foot outside the poles, circling toward the other end of the poles.

Count 6: Take small running step with left foot outside the poles, continuing to circle.

Count 7: Take small running step with right foot outside the poles, coming to face the poles.

Count 8: Leap onto left foot inside the poles.

Count 9: Leap onto right foot inside the poles.

Counts 10–12: Continue circling poles on other side to begin again.

*Organizational Pattern Variations*

Arrange four sets of poles in a square. Have children travel around the square from set to set using the circling step pattern done in a straight line between the sets and a half circle at each set.

Arrange sets of poles parallel to one another in a long line. Have children travel down the line using the circling step pattern done in a straight line between the sets of poles.

*Additional Variations*

Children turn while jumping.

Have jumpers work with partners or in groups of three.

Have partners dance on opposite sides from one another.

Have partners dance from same side.

Have partners dance side by side.

Have partners hold hands.

Have partners doing different steps.

Have students create their own variations.

**Accompaniment:** recorded music (Tinikling)

## APPROPRIATENESS OF CONTENT

Through its dance, a culture different from our own can be understood in a unique way. This Philippine folk dance suggests the movements of the long-legged tinikling bird found in the islands. Because the dance calls for vigorous, coordinated jumping over long poles moved along the floor by partners, it is most appropriately introduced at the fourth-grade level. Children enjoy dancing a sequence of defined steps and find the coordination of a jumping pattern with pole movement an exciting and fun challenge.

### IDEAS FROM WHICH MOVEMENT TASKS ARE DESIGNED

- Developing a feel for the three-count beat of the musical accompaniment

  clap repeatedly a three-count beat accenting count one

  hit rhythm sticks together with the beat of the music

  walk the rhythm, stepping forcefully on count one

- Practicing three of the five basic jumps—hopping, leaping, and jumping in three-count patterns

  hop on each foot in place three times

  leap sideways alternately

  hop continuously, frequently using a sideward leap to change the hopping foot

  jump alternately with feet close together and far apart

  try all three jumps over lines or ropes on the floor

  jump without and with the music

- Jumping in the specific combinations that make up the Tinikling dance

  hop, leap, hop/leap, leap, hop/leap, leap, hop/leap, leap, hop/ . . . . . . (this takes you in and out of the poles on the same side) hop, leap, leap/leap, leap, leap/leap, leap, leap/leap, leap, leap/ . . . . . (this takes you in and out of the poles alternating sides with each combination)

jump feet apart, jump feet together, jump feet together/ . . . . . (this takes you in and out of the poles on both sides at the same time; right foot on right side, left foot on left side)

- Practicing tapping the long poles

    clap hand once, hit floor twice while kneeling
    repeat action with poles
    tap without and with music

- Coordinating the actions of the dancers with those of the tappers in performing the dance

    dancers jump while tappers move hands in rhythm without the poles
    combine dancers jumping with tappers tapping with the poles
    dance without and with the music
    alternate the type of jump used
    increase the number of dancers per set of poles
    alter the spatial arrangement of the sets of poles on the floor
    alternate tappers and dancers

### BIOMECHANICAL PRINCIPLES AFFECTING QUALITY OF PERFORMANCE

*Application of force.* Sufficient force must be applied to the body both to lift it up over the poles, as well as sideward into and out of the poles. The poles should be lifted only high enough to permit them to be tapped together without scraping the blocks. Dancers should not have to exert additional force to clear unnecessarily high poles.

*Reception of Force.* When landing from a locomotor action involving flight, the force of the body's weight should be absorbed through the sequential bending of ankles, knees, and hips. This must be done rapidly because the body has to immediately apply force through the sequential extending of hips, knees, and ankles to make the next jumping action on the beat. In addition, sufficient space for the jumpers' feet to land on the floor between the poles, not on the poles, must be created by the pole tappers.

### AESTHETIC PRINCIPLES AFFECTING QUALITY OF PERFORMANCE

This folk dance is meant to be done with lively feet and bouncy steps to its very strong beat. The varied jumping patterns and different pole arrangements make the dance fun to do and interesting to watch. The precise rhythmic coordination of the dancers and the pole tappers, who are actually working in opposition to one another, and the clear underlying beat of the music punctuated by the sound of the poles coming together create a sense of unity that is pleasing to feel, to see, and to hear in doing this island dance.

### MOTOR DEVELOPMENT PRINCIPLES AFFECTING QUALITY OF PERFORMANCE

Jumpers and tappers must work in opposition to one another in two different ways—seeing each other and hearing each other being cued. While the jumpers see the tappers taking the poles apart, they have their feet close together inside the poles. While the poles are struck together, the jumpers have their feet outside the poles. As the tappers are getting the verbal cue, *in-out-out,* for the poles, the jumpers must jump *out-in-in.*

Moving in opposition to an external stimulus can be developmentally difficult for children and they may have trouble with the concept. You will need to help each group focus on the task at hand.

Another example of moving in opposition to another occurs when more than one jumper is jumping at a set of poles. Partners could do the side-to-side step facing one another but going in opposite directions. If children have trouble successfully doing the step, then have the partners work back-to-back or have one child work at a time.

### PROGRESSION

Working individually on jumping and pole-tapping skills is easier than practicing them together, because the jumpers must be able to jump in opposition to how the poles are being tapped together and vice versa. Practicing the rhythmic jumping pattern alone, so that it starts to become habitual, helps the jumpers keep their pattern in place when the pole tappers start working in opposition. Practicing the rhythmic timing of the poles without the music is easier than with the music at first. But the music defines the precise rhythm of the dance, as well as adding interest and challenge, and should be added relatively soon in both jumping and pole-tapping work.

### EXPERIENCES FOR REFLECTION

1. Study the Philippine culture in relation to the Tinikling dance. Connect the dance actions to their roots in this culture. Write a two-minute commentary highlighting the cultural connections within this folk dance that could be used by a fourth grader to introduce this dance as part of a demonstration program for parents.

2. Study folk dance texts and materials to note how a particular culture manifests itself through its national dances. Note, for example, how gender roles are reflected in the style of the dance or how occupational movements are represented in folk dance forms. Discuss with your classmates the contributions of folk dance in understanding other cultures and why such understanding has educational importance for children today.

3. If you had to choreograph an American (or other appropriate country) folk dance that is representative of your hometown area, what would it look like? What part of your culture would be the focus? What kind of steps would it have? What kind of accompaniment? What costumes would be appropriate for your folk dance? What overall style? Write out a movement description of the dance actions for your folk dance.

*Note:* Tinikling can also be danced in 4/4 time. Poles would be tapped outside twice and together twice with corresponding adaptations to the dancers' steps.

*core content*

## Dance Props

### FOCUS OF CONTENT

Creating dance sequences by combining locomotor and axial movements with the use of props explored by using selected aspects of:

pathway
level
direction
time
space
responding to a beat

in relation to:

creating coherent sequences
developing sequences from external sources
beginning, middle, and end structure
order and reorder
dancing individually
props

and including:

evaluating dance using aesthetic criteria
defining audience behavior

## ENDING SEQUENCE FOR CORE CONTENT 5–DANCE PROPS

Prop:  6" rubber ball

Thirty-two count sequence of student-selected dance actions that includes one each of the following five different types of movements:

- locomotor action
- ball release upward
- roll of the ball
- flexible use of space with ball held in hand
- ball bounce

**Accompaniment:**  recorded music ("Theme from Masterpiece Theater" or "Beauty and the Beast")

## APPROPRIATENESS OF CONTENT

Using a prop as an external source of choreography is appropriately introduced with third, fourth and fifth grade children. They must be able to see the prop differently than the way it is normally seen. A scarf is no longer for keeping hair dry or for decorating clothing. It is a kite tail in the wind. It is a gentle breeze from a lake. It is a flame rising from a fire. Children must be able to understand the dynamic properties of the selected prop and how they relate to the choreographic problem at hand.

When dancing, dancers must concentrate on their movements and on the accompaniment, and now with a prop, they have an additional element on which to focus. This requires the ability to attend to a number of different things at once. Prior to their use as choreographic focuses for sequences, props could be introduced to children in dance in less demanding ways such as holding a prop or looking at it while dancing. Whether they are being used as a source for choreography or not, props can be a motivating influence on children in dance. They represent a new addition to the dance environment and bring excitement to the dance.

## IDEAS FROM WHICH MOVEMENT TASKS ARE DESIGNED

- Exploring the properties of a ball as a dance prop by using it in as many ways as can be imagined
- Experimenting with each of the sequence parts and how the ball could be used to fulfill the specified requirements

    traveling in relation to the ball
    tossing the ball upwards
    rolling the ball
    holding the ball while using space in a flexible way
    bouncing the ball

- Creating a dance sequence

    link sequence parts coherently
    show a beginning, middle, and end
    order the five parts of the sequence
    match parts with musical phrasing

- Refining the prop dance sequence

    create beginning dance and ending dance body positions
    show smooth transitions between sequence parts
    reorder parts as necessary
    clarify individual sequence parts
    perfect the match with the musical accompaniment
    communicate expression and meaning

- Performing one's own prop dance sequence and observing others

## BIOMECHANICAL PRINCIPLES AFFECTING QUALITY OF PERFORMANCE

The sequence requirements of tossing, rolling, and bouncing a ball relate biomechanically to the concepts of force production and absorption and object rebound but not in critical ways. Maximum force is not needed for any of these actions and, if used, would probably detract from the expressive component of the dance as it relates to the selected musical accompaniment. In bouncing the ball, it is important to understand that the ball will rebound from the floor at an angle equal to and opposite from the angle that it struck the floor. If the ball is to bounce straight up, it must be bounced straight down. If the ball is to rebound to a different place, that could lead, for example, into a forward traveling action, then it must be bounced on the floor at the angle and in the direction needed to equal the traveled distance. Since the children are free to create their own movements within the constraints of the sequence requirements, other biomechanical principles that affect their performances may emerge and will need to be dealt with at that time.

## AESTHETIC PRINCIPLES AFFECTING QUALITY OF PERFORMANCE

The two important aesthetic emphases in this core unit relate to the use of a prop as a source for choreographic inspiration and to the experience of choreographing a dance sequence. A prop is the focal point of the movement and as such it is used as an object to communicate expression and meaning. A ball was deliberately

PHOTO 6–7
A prop, as the focal point of the movement, communicates expression and meaning. The hoops capture the observer's visual attention and focus the dancers' quality of expression.

selected as the prop for this Core Content unit because it is directly connected with games. Having to use an object that is strongly linked to functional-type movement, in an aesthetic manner, focuses the attention on the expressive use of a prop rather than using it in a sequence of movement for utilitarian purposes. In dance, a ball cannot merely be manipulated through the air or along the ground as it is in games. It must be integrated with selected dance elements to present an aesthetic whole, that is the body and the ball moving in harmony with one another are essential in the expression of meaning.

Core Content 5—Dance Props is the first unit to specifically emphasize the process and structure of sequence development. Creating sequences as content was discussed in Chapter 5 and will not be repeated here. The four steps of sequence design—define a focus; explore and improvise; select, organize, and refine; share and evaluate—are as pertinent to creating dance sequences as they are to creating gymnastics sequences. It is the principle of coherence that gives dance sequences their aesthetic quality. Sequences need to be designed so that they flow together as a conceptual entity with a sense of rhythmic completion so that the movements naturally and effortlessly look like they belong together. Understanding this essence of aesthetics will certainly enhance the expressive quality of children's dance work.

PHOTO 6–8

### MOTOR DEVELOPMENT PRINCIPLES AFFECTING QUALITY OF PERFORMANCE

Developmental information for sequence construction was presented in Chapter 5 and is also applicable for sequence construction in dance. Children will work similarly in dance as they move through the four steps of building sequences.

Introducing an object that is already known or used for a particular purpose, as an object or prop for dance means that children will have to adjust the usual or normal way that object is perceived. They may at first select dance movements that only mimic habitual, functional ways of using the object. They will need to be challenged to see the prop differently and to move using it in creative ways.

### PROGRESSION

In selecting props to use in dance sequences, begin with ones that are very familiar to your children and that can be used in a large variety of simple ways. A ball, for example, can easily be thrown, bounced, held, rolled, dribbled, kicked, spun and so on. An umbrella, on the other hand, offers fewer immediate movement possibilities and the movements may be harder to do once you thought of them. As children have additional opportunities to use props as a source of choreographic motivation, increase the complexity of the prop used. Increased exposure to props depends on the number and type of props that the children have already experienced.

In most instances, working alone with a prop should come before working with a partner or in groups with props. Working with one prop per person in partners/groups should come before working with an unequal number of props and dancers.

**EXPERIENCES FOR REFLECTION**

1. Consider the requirements for the ending dance sequence in this Core Content unit and, as a class, develop a list of criteria that would make this sequence performance aesthetically pleasing. Each of you perform your sequence while the others apply the criteria to your performance making notes to support their observations. Collect and compare all of the aesthetic evaluations of your sequence. Discuss as a group how each individual criterion was applied by the different members of the class.

2. Attend a public dance performance—preferably a children's performance. Note how the audience behaves during the performance. What did they do that enhanced or inhibited your experience of the performance? Did any of their behaviors positively or negatively affect the dancers? How might good audience behavior vary with the context, or type, of dance performance? Develop an "Audience Viewing Guide," appropriate for children, that provides guidelines for how to behave as a member of an audience at a dance performance.

# *core content*  6

## Contrasting the Dynamic Component of Dance Elements

### FOCUS OF CONTENT

Creating dance sequences by combining locomotor skills, axial movement, and shape-making while contrasting dynamic components, explored by using selected aspects of:

> time
> force/energy
> space

in relation to:

> creating coherent sequences
> developing sequences from personal sources
> beginning, middle, and end structure
> dancing with a partner
> positioning
> kinesthetic awareness
> personal meaning

### ENDING SEQUENCE FOR CORE CONTENT 6—CONTRASTING THE DYNAMIC COMPONENT OF DANCE ELEMENTS

- Take a strong beginning shape apart from and facing your partner
- Travel toward partner with steps that show a pressing quality

- End the traveling in a shape that is preparatory for the partners to do an axial pressing movement in opposition to one another
- One partner presses toward the other, without touching, by extending one or both arms as if pushing the other person out of the way
- Other one responds by "going with" the press in the opposite direction from partner as if being pushed out of the way
- Reverse the action by pressing back to the previously held shape
- Repeat presses with partner roles reversed (the partner who pushed out of the way first is now being pushed out of the way first in this phrase)
- Both partners simultaneously step backwards away from each other using three different thrusting actions
- End with a thrusting movement that reaches toward the partner but that does not travel

**Accompaniment:** none; let partners develop their own rhythmic flow for this sequence

## APPROPRIATENESS OF CONTENT

The content in this unit expands work done previously where time, force/energy, and space were introduced as ways to vary dance elements in exploring the material of dance. The children should have previously experienced these three dynamic qualities as individual components in relation to dance actions. In this core unit, two effort actions—pressing and thrusting—which combine all three dynamic qualities (press—sustained, strong, direct; thrust—sudden, strong, direct) are refined and clarified through their selection as the expressive focal point of the ending dance sequence for this core unit. This material is appropriately presented when children are ready to move from dancing alone to dancing with another person and to work in partners to create dance sequences. Because the ending dance sequence has limited structure, this material generally may not be successfully handled before the 4th grade.

### IDEAS FROM WHICH MOVEMENT TASKS ARE DESIGNED

- Exploring the combination of sustained, strong, and direct dynamic components of movement as a pressing action while working alone

    vary the body part(s) used
    work on the spot and while traveling
    vary the direction of the press

- Exploring the combination of sudden, strong, and direct dynamic components of movement as a thrusting action while working alone

    vary the body part(s) used
    work on the spot and while traveling
    vary the direction of the thrust

- Contrasting the time component by linking pressing actions with thrusting actions

    start the combination with a press
    start the combination with a thrust
    use the second action to reverse the first

**PHOTO 6–9**
Exploring responding to a partner's pressing action as a reverse movement.

- Exploring responding to a partner's pressing action as a reverse movement

    alternate who initiates the action
    vary the body parts used
    vary the direction of the presses
    start the pressing from different shapes

- Traveling toward a partner with sustained, strong, direct steps

    vary the distance to be traveled
    vary the size of the steps
    begin in different positional relationships to partner (e.g., facing, front to back)
    end the traveling in shapes that show different relationships (e.g., levels, symmetry)

- Creating a dance sequence

    make partnership decisions (sequence beginning and ending shapes, preparatory shapes for pressing
        after the traveling section, who initiates and who responds in the partner pressing actions)
    learn the sequence order

- Refining the pressing/thrusting dance sequence

    practice until the rhythm of the sequence parts can be *felt* between the partners without need for
        external cueing

PHOTO 6–10
Refining pressing actions to clarify movement and enhance expression.

....................................................................................

        clarify movement to enhance expression and meaning

        sharpen the time contrast between pressing and thrusting

- Performing the pressing/thrusting dance sequence

### BIOMECHANICAL PRINCIPLES AFFECTING QUALITY OF PERFORMANCE

Thrusting is a fast forceful action. If done with enough force or with a body part needed for support, like a leg, then a loss of balance becomes a possibility. Children could thrust themselves off balance. They will have to actively adjust their COGs over their bases to maintain stability to compensate for the forces they create by thrusting.

Traveling using pressing actions also relates to the need to adjust COGs as the body moves itself through locomotion. The speed of the pressing movement, however, gives gravity a longer time to work against the nonsupporting, stepping leg, pulling it back to the floor. This makes locomotion using pressing actions more difficult to sustain.

### AESTHETIC PRINCIPLES AFFECTING QUALITY OF PERFORMANCE

Contrast is a way to highlight the aesthetic qualities of dance movement. In this sequence the press and thrust are contrasted against one another. Both actions have the same dynamic component of force/energy (strong) and of space (direct), but the time element is different—sustained for the press, sudden for the thrust. The communication of meaning is heightened by contrasting strong, direct, slow movements with strong, direct, fast movements. In this particular ending sequence, contrast can also be seen in the relationship of the partners to each other as the partners first move toward one another, then retreat, then reach toward each other again.

There is no musical accompaniment to enhance the aesthetic quality of this sequence. But its quality is not diminished by the lack of accompaniment. Partners who are in rhythmic synchrony with their movements have an aesthetic quality that does not need musical accompaniment. Two children moving together using strong, powerful movements have an expressive harmony to which silence is a contributing factor. Thus, the silent synchrony with which the movements are done contributes to the aesthetic quality of the dance sequence. Synchrony, contrast, and silence demand heightened kinesthetic awareness which also adds to the aesthetic component.

### MOTOR DEVELOPMENT PRINCIPLES AFFECTING QUALITY OF PERFORMANCE

Moving to an external beat is harder than moving to one's own beat. For this sequence, the child has to move in sync with an external beat which is the internal beat of another person. This internal/external dilemma creates a challenge. It will take practice for partners to come to the point of moving with one another, to feel they are in rhythm together. They also have the added challenge of trying to move in synchrony with both sudden and sustained movements; with sustained movements, more often, coming together first. Children love challenges, however, and they will work hard to time their movements with one another to achieve the necessary synchrony.

### PROGRESSION

This ending sequence is meant to help children refine their use of the dynamic components of dance movement. Time, force/energy, and space are so critical in developing expressiveness and communicating meaning through dance that children need to constantly revisit this content within increasingly complex movement problems. Introductory work with dynamic components focuses on one, or perhaps two, components and in the context of exploring a particular dance element—locomotion, axial movements, and shapes. Here, the focus is on the qualities themselves and in the combination of all three components.

With this unit, children are moving from working alone to working with a partner. The sequence now has the added dimension of the partner relationship and the increased movement possibilities that relationship brings. Partner work increases the individual's responsibilities as well. In working with a partner, children not only must focus on their own movement but also on that of their partners'. Also, having to create their own time frame for the sequence demands a different level of interaction and cooperation between partners to create and perform the sequence skillfully.

### EXPERIENCES FOR REFLECTION

1. Observe two children in a movement or play context, preferably a dance context, but that may be difficult to find. Are they working as partners jointly toward some goal or are they moving in close proximity to one another but seemingly independent of the other? What kinds of behavior show a partnership exists? What kinds of behavior show it does not? Reflect on the ways in which partners might have to work together in dance and on the types of decisions they might have to make to be able to dance together meaningfully.

2. Think of your family, friends, or people whose movements you know well; those whom you could identify if you heard their footsteps coming down the hall before you saw them. Most likely your identification would be based on their particular combinations of the dynamic components of time, force/energy, and space when walking. Contrast how your acquaintances are different from one another in their typical use of these qualities. Do you have a friend who is constantly walking a step ahead because he has a faster time dynamic? Do you have a relative who gently angles you off the sidewalk when you are meant to be walking straight ahead because he prefers a flexible use of space? How would you characterize your own walking along the extremes of the three dynamic dimensions? Develop a personal movement profile of the ways that you prefer to use the dynamic qualities of time, force/energy, and space while moving in particular situations. Study your profile to better understand your personal dynamic preferences in moving.

## *core content*

### Dancing in a Group

#### FOCUS OF CONTENT

Creating group dance sequences by combining stepping, rising and sinking, and shape-making as the elements of choreography and explored by using selected aspects of:

> kinesphere
> time
> responding to a beat

in relation to:

> creating coherent sequences
> improvising movement
> beginning, middle, and end structure
> order and reorder
> dancing with small/large groups
> personal meaning

and including:

> observing and describing dance actions
> evaluating dance using aesthetic criteria

#### ENDING SEQUENCE FOR CORE CONTENT 7—DANCING IN A GROUP

- Begin in groups of three in line one behind the other
- 1s hesitantly step forward on each of seven counts and explode into a shape on count 8; 2s and 3s wait in their beginning positions

- On the next eight counts, 2s move toward their respective 1s with seven hesitant steps and explode into a shape that is over, under, in, through, behind, beside, supported by or in some other way related to 1s' shape; 1s hold their shapes while 3s are waiting to follow in succession
- On the next 8 counts, 3s move toward their group's shapes with seven hesitant steps and explode into a shape that is over, under, in, through, behind, beside, supported by or in some other way related to the shapes created by the 1s and 2s; 1s and 2s hold their shapes
- Repeat the twenty-four counts ending with all in a low group shape
- From the last group shape, rise hesitantly in unison over eight counts to a high, stretched group shape
- Hold the high group shape for four counts. Then sink explosively in unison on the next count and hold the ending group shape for the last three counts

**Accompaniment:** recorded music ("Pink Panther Theme")

## APPROPRIATENESS OF CONTENT

Dancing in a small group is appropriate content for children who have previously worked alone and with partners and who can work cooperatively with others in solving movement problems. Moving successively and in unison as a group also require cooperative efforts in performing skillfully. Working together as a group adds a new dimension to the expressive possibilities of dance movement and children who are ready for the group sequences will enjoy expanding their dance experience in this way.

### IDEAS FROM WHICH MOVEMENT TASKS ARE DESIGNED

- Exploring hesitancy in stepping

    discover ways to express hesitancy (e.g., careful steps, arms tentatively at sides, gesturing with hands
        raised lightly forward or turning the head side to side)
    without and with accompaniment

- Creating a shape in a moment of explosiveness

    vary the different spatial components of the shape
    vary particularly the level at which the shape is made
    without and with accompaniment

- Combining hesitant stepping with explosive shape-making

    change shapes each time
    contrast hesitancy and explosiveness
    without and with accompaniment

- Stepping and making shapes as a class moving in successive groups

    divide class into three large groups—1s, 2s, and 3s—intermingled throughout the space
    practice sequence order for the two actions (as individuals)

    - 1s step for seven, explode into shape for one, hold shape for eight, hold shape for eight
    - 2s hold shape for eight, step for seven, explode into shape for one, hold shape for eight
    - 3s hold shape for eight, hold shape for eight, step for seven, explode into shape for one

- Creating a group shape

  work in partners then groups of three
  improvise successive shapes from existing shape
  vary individual position in relation to one another's kinesphere
  vary the spatial components of the group shape
  without and with accompaniment

- Combining hesitant stepping with explosive shape-making in groups of three

  work from sequence beginning position–line, one behind the other
  work in the sequence count of eight
  repeat sequence phrase several times
  without and with accompaniment

- Rising and sinking in unison as a group

  improvise the hesitant rising actions among group
  practice beginning and ending together
  contrast the explosiveness of sinking actions
  without and with accompaniment

- Ordering the sequence parts
- Performing the group dance sequence with music

**PHOTO 6–11**
Combining hesitant stepping with explosive shape-making in small group sequences.

## BIOMECHANICAL PRINCIPLES AFFECTING QUALITY OF PERFORMANCE

The biomechanical principles related to the dance elements that compose this sequence have been addressed in previous core units.

## AESTHETIC PRINCIPLES AFFECTING QUALITY OF PERFORMANCE

Hesitancy and explosiveness as expressive qualities of movement help create the aesthetic dimension of this dance sequence. The movement is meant to portray qualities of cautious observing, followed by quick action. The Pink Panther Theme suggests these qualities with its cloak of careful apprehension and "sneaking around" and its calm-before-the-storm feelings. The expression of this feeling through movement highlights the communicative component of the dance.

Contrast as an aesthetic principle functions in this Core Content material as in the last unit. Hesitancy and explosiveness are contrasted against each other to sharpen their differences and create a visual surprise for the dance observer.

## MOTOR DEVELOPMENT PRINCIPLES AFFECTING QUALITY OF PERFORMANCE

Movement that has a functional purpose is different from movement that has an expressive purpose. Expression in moving, which is what makes dance dance, will not be more than a dim possibility if children cannot get beyond perceiving movement only for utilitarian intentions. As children's movement changes over time, the addition of the expressive, aesthetic dimension to their movement is crucial for their continuing development. Certainly they will have already learned to move in functional ways before they have had the opportunity to choose to move meaningfully in expressive and communicative ways. Their developmental experiences will be richer for having dance as a part of their ways of moving and being.

### PROGRESSION

This core material takes the progression of the partnering component of dance choreography to dancing in a group. With beginning group work, the group number should be kept small—three in this unit-ending sequence—to increase the complexity of the partnering context gradually. An ending dance sequence can be choreographed for larger groups when the children are ready for working with more people. Not all children will be ready for larger group work at the same time and ending sequences certainly can be choreographed for groups that have different numbers. When every group is using the same accompaniment and a sequence such as the one for this unit that requires successive movement by the individuals within the group, however, adjustments by the groups would have to be made to accommodate for the different number of counts required.

The progression of the partnering component interacts with the dance elements of the choreography as well. The children's skill in performing the dance elements that are part of the ending sequence should be considered in selecting the partnering options for the sequence.

### EXPERIENCES FOR REFLECTION

1. Videotape the ending group sequences for this core unit, one group at a time. For the group that was the most expressive in your estimation, describe what you saw in contrast to the other groups that led you to this judgment. Make a list of the descriptive words that you used to assess expressiveness. Group your descriptive words and phrases into categories that could serve as criteria for evaluating the dance movement that comprised this sequence. What other ways could you develop criteria for evaluating dance movement?

PHOTO 6–12

As the partnering component becomes more complex (individuals to partners to small groups), note the differences in the movement response possibilities for the dancers.

PHOTO 6–13

PHOTO 6–14

2. Give two groups of different sizes, for example a group of three and a group of eight, the same dance movement problem to solve. The problem itself should be one where group size is not a factor. (Create a dance sequence of four different locomotor patterns that suggests the idea of advancing and retreating as opposed to the sequence for this Core Content unit.) Observe the group's dynamics as they go about the choreographic problem. Did group size affect group dynamics? In what ways, if any? How might your answers to these questions guide your use of the partnering component in dance choreography when you are teaching dance to children?

3. How might you "costume" this ending dance sequence to enhance the hesitant quality of movement and emphasize the contrast between hesitancy and explosiveness? Put on your costumes and dance the sequence again. Did the costume change your feelings of expressiveness? Were you able to communicate the choreographic idea more clearly? What other influences did the costume have on your dancing?

# UNIQUE ASPECTS OF TEACHING DANCE CONTENT

## Imagery in Teaching Dance

Trying to elicit a particular dance movement (like stretching sideward as far as possible without moving the feet from their spot), or initial movement responses to a new dance idea (like exploring different ways of standing from a low position), or a particular dynamic characteristic (like hesitation) by using only technical movement terminology can be inhibiting to your students and frustrating to you when you do not see a dance-like quality in their movement. Creating mental pictures, or images, of what a dance movement could look like can be very helpful in freeing children's movement responses and also in reducing your frustration levels. For example, if you are working with the movement idea of advancing and retreating, creating the image of a wave rushing toward the beach and then quickly flowing back out again may help students "see the movement" in their minds and more clearly understand what you are asking them to do. Their advancing and retreating actions would become more dance-like because the wave image suggests how the movement could be done.

Imagery can be useful in teaching educational dance in four ways. First, an image can help define a particular type of dance action. For example, you are working with axial/nonlocomotor movement in a lesson and to help students get the notion of moving without losing their initial point of supporting contact, you use the image of a boat at anchor. They are helped to better understand that axial movement is movement (the boat bobbing on the water) that occurs around an axis (the anchor chain) while being rooted in one spot (the anchor itself).

Second, images can generate variety in response to a movement task and suggest unfamiliar ways of doing familiar actions. Images give students ideas about how to move, which helps them get started with a new dance task. Standing up from a low position can simply be the familiar way of standing up. The images of a jack-in-the-box, a hot air balloon takeoff, and a swirling Wonder Woman, or the movements of any cartoon adventure character of the day, however, suggest different ways of standing up from a low position. They permit students to explore the dance action of rising in its many and varied dimensions. Students come to know that moving from a low position to a high position does not always have to be the familiar act of simply standing up.

The third way in which images can be useful is in improving the dynamic qualities of dance movement. For example, you want to have a lesson content focus of contrasting the qualities of hesitation and explosiveness in movement. The image of being in a totally dark, unfamiliar room and trying to find a way out is used to elicit hesitant movement qualities. Reaching out slowly and tentatively with the hands all around one's kinesphere and taking small careful steps keeping the feet close to the floor are actions that express hesitancy and that could be prompted by the dark room image. Such an image is more powerful in eliciting this expressive quality from students than merely telling them to move carefully and cautiously.

Fourth, images can serve as the idea or theme around which sequences can be constructed. The theme becomes the central choreographic thread and dance actions are woven together to develop and support the thematic focus. The selected theme should be about something with which the children are familiar and should have meaning for them at this time in their lives. Popular movie characters and favorite television shows are always relevant theme possibilities. During the autumn season, dance lessons around a theme of falling leaves would be exciting and fun for children. The way leaves droop, drift, and fall, swirl and get blown about, then end up crinkly and crunchy on the ground suggests many movement possibilities that can be explored and combined into a sequence.

Selecting images is a part of the teaching process that must be planned for, like all other parts of the lesson. A well-chosen image may be just what is needed to help transform ordinary moving into dancing. An image could be used for an entire dance sequence, one specific dance action, or even a specific action by an individual body part. Make sure, however, that the selected image suggests the precise qualities desired. Floating on water and a bird soaring on the wind each would bring out the quality of lightness in movement, but they would elicit different kinds of lightness qualities.

It is not a good idea to use an image to highlight an element of movement that you do not want to see. The image may stick in students' minds causing them to concentrate on an undesired response. Also images can be overdone by having one for every part of a dance phrase or sequence. Overuse reduces the power an image has for eliciting the desired response.

Image is not everything. Images should not be used exclusively to present instructional tasks to children for two reasons. First, students need a technical movement vocabulary for their dance actions with an understanding of the meanings of different dance terminology. Imagery should not supplant a technical movement vocabulary. (The Dance Core Content Framework presented in this chapter and the Movement Framework presented in Chapter 3 provide this vocabulary.) Thoughtfully used in combination with a technical dance movement vocabulary, images can evoke and enrich the dance responses of children and should be an important consideration in planning and teaching educational dance lessons.

Second, images can be confining if they serve as the sole stimulus for dance making. The task "move like a rabbit" would most probably elicit an entire class of children, with shoulders hunched over, hands curved forward and held in front of the shoulders, doing little baby bunny hops around the gym. By contrast, shifting the task to focus on the qualities of movement that a rabbit exhibits—light, quick, small, flexible—instead of telling the children to act like one, would elicit movement responses that help children expand their awareness of such qualities.

## Accompaniment for Dance

Choosing the appropriate accompaniment for dance work is an extremely important task for the educational dance teacher. Moving to an accompanying beat is a natural way to respond to sound and children find it stimulating and challenging to match the beat and the feeling of different sounds. Accompaniment enhances movement by giving it a rhythmic structure and a focal point. It also sustains children's involvement in their dance work by amplifying expression and stimulating interest. Accompaniment can take the form of voice, simple percussion instruments, and recorded music.

*Voice.* The teacher can accompany children's movements with rhythmic vocal sounds. The most basic vocal accompaniment is syllables spoken in rhythm. A step, step, skip, step locomotor pattern is vocalized as *da, da, de-a-de, da.* Saying the syllables as the children are moving assists them in performing the pattern. Movement vocabulary words can also be spoken rhythmically with pitch, volume, and intonation of voice used to elicit desired movement qualities. The spoken phrase *jump* (with the voice increasing in pitch) and *freeze* (in a sharp, short tone) and *twiiiirrrrlll* (drawn out) and *sink* (with the voice going lower and softer) supports and enhances the dance phrase of a high jump, with landing and freezing in a shape, followed by a twirl that continues for a bit, and ending in a sinking action. Vocal accompaniment can also be more formal such as dancing to a narrated story or poem.

Using your voice instead of musical accompaniment has the advantage of permitting you, the teacher, to set the rhythm for the movement. Accompanying children with your voice, especially with information other than counting out the beat in rhythm, takes practice—a lot of practice. For example, you are having the children change direction while traveling on a particular beat of your vocal accompaniment. You want to give a vocal reminder, such as *ready, change,* just before the beat to change occurs. You would say *ready, change* on the last two beats before the beat they are to change on occurs, and say it in the rhythmic pattern of the movement. If you want children to change direction on count 8, you would need to say *ready* on count 6 and change on count 7. It is also a good idea to use the same vocal prompt for recurring actions, like getting ready to dance. A vocal phrase such as *ready and* said in the same rhythm as the upcoming dance phrase or sequence accompaniment alerts children to the impending beat. It prepares them to make the first move right on the first beat. Saying the same phrase every time they are to start is a consistent way to help cue them to begin.

*Simple percussion instruments.* Percussion instruments produce definite sounds when they are struck or shaken. Examples of instruments that can be struck are drums, tambourines, rhythm sticks, wooden blocks, castanets, coconut shells, and the human body. Objects such as rubber tubes, brooms, inflated balloons, metal garbage can lids, or whatever else your imagination comes up with can become simple percussion instruments. The sounds produced by objects being struck are particularly useful in working with metric rhythm (the first beat in a group of beats), locomotor dance elements, accent, and pulsating movement. Some percussion instruments that are struck also resonate. These include cymbals, finger cymbals, gongs, triangles, and water-filled metal containers. Resonating sound is useful for movement that continues with an increase or decrease in its dynamic qualities, for a sudden beginning or change, and for free flowing movements. Percussion instruments are also shaken to produce a vibrating sound. Examples are tambourines, maracas, rattles, and sleigh bells. Vibrating sound suggests light, lively, and sudden movement. Pitched instruments such as xylophones and chime scales can be used to expand dance to different levels, as well as adding a sense of rhythmic completion to a phrase or sequence.

*Recorded music.*    Select recorded musical accompaniment that is simple, brief, rhythmically strong, and that inspires the desired feelings, mood, and movement qualities for the focus of the dance work. This is not an easy task most times. It can be difficult to find recorded music that has a strong beat, is brief enough for children's short sequences, and captures the appropriate mood as well. There are resources of music recorded specifically for dance that provide different rhythmic structures in different tempos. The newer technology of players, such as some of the CD players, permit recorded music to be accelerated or slowed down without sound distortion, making it easier to adjust the recorded tempo to a tempo that more closely matches that needed by children as they work with particular content ideas. Popular music, past and present, not created specifically as music for dance is also another possible source of recorded music for educational dance accompaniment.

*Student-generated accompaniment.*    Not all accompaniment needs to be provided by the teacher, nor should it be. Children can provide their own accompaniment with voice and percussion instruments. They especially like vocalizing sounds while they move to enhance the expressiveness of their phrases and sequences. They can beat a rhythm on a drum for one another or they can accompany themselves with finger cymbals, for example, as they dance. Children will need time to explore their own rhythms as accompaniment to their dance work.

Voice and percussion types of accompaniment work well as children explore dance elements and begin to construct dance phrases and sequences. Such accompaniment can be thought of as a musical skeleton without a melody for expanding expressive and communicative emphases. Recorded music fills in the skeleton by providing a melody. It extends exploration of dance elements and gives structure to introductory sequence choreography. You will want to bring it into lessons fairly soon after voice and percussion instruments as an expanded dimension to help children develop the aesthetic qualities of their movement.

## Basic Understanding of Rhythm

The teacher of educational dance, must have a basic understanding of rhythm and must possess some sense of rhythm. As the teacher, you will be unable to help children move rhythmically if you yourself cannot discern the beginning and end of a musical phrase, feel the tempo of a piece of music, identify the time signature of the piece, or ascertain whether a child is moving on or off the beat. If necessary, review basic music theory and practice responding rhythmically to different music pieces to develop your understanding of and skill in using rhythm.

Rhythm is the study of time. Two of the elements of rhythm are duration and structure. Duration (long or short) is the length of a sound, or involvement without sound, and is indicated by notes of different *values*. A whole note lasts twice as long as a half note and four times as long as a quarter note. A half note lasts twice as long as a quarter note.

The notes for a piece of music are divided into equal parts called *measures*. The value of every measure in a piece of music is the same even though there are different numbers of notes in the measures. Value for the measure is determined by the time signature for the piece, for example 4/4 time. The top number shows the number of beats in each measure. In this example, there are four beats to the measure. The bottom number shows which note gets one beat. In the example, the quarter note gets one beat. In a 4/4 time signature, therefore, a quarter note lasts one beat, or count, a half note for two beats, and a whole note gets four beats. (In dance, the duration of one movement could be over one count, two counts, or four counts. The rhythmic duration of the movement, however, must be comparable to the rhythmic duration of the music.) *Accent*, which is an emphasis or stress, can be placed on any beat in the measure though usually it is the first beat. Accent draws attention to that beat.

Structure is the rhythmic pattern that is formed by combining sounds of long and short duration that fit the time signature in different ways. The rhythmic structure of movement is a similar notion. You combine movements of long and short duration that fit the time signature of the accompaniment. For example, the rhythmic structure of a thirty-two-count dance sequence with a 4/4 time signature (eight, four count music phrases) could be constructed as follows:

| one movement | lasting eight counts | (two, four-count music phrases) |
| two movements | lasting four counts each | (two, four-count music phrases) |
| four movements | lasting two counts each | (two, four-count music phrases) |
| eight movements | lasting one count each | (two, four-count music phrases) |

It also could be constructed in a different pattern.

| one movement | lasting eight counts | (two, four-count music phrases) |
| four movements | lasting four counts each | (four, four-count music phrases) |
| one movement | lasting eight counts | (two, four-count music phrases) |

Obviously, a large number of other types of variations could be constructed, each with its own unique pattern. Understanding the notion of rhythmic structure is essential if the dance teacher is to help children develop coherence in their phrases and sequences as they learn to move to accompaniment. Children are capable of and need to understand the concepts of duration and structure of rhythm in their dance. A theoretical music vocabulary, however, is not appropriate for their understanding. Notes can become apples—a whole apple is divided into four pieces where the pieces are rearranged to make the apple look different—and you have rhythmic duration and structure without a theoretical vocabulary. Actually, a couple of divided apples is not such a bad idea for the teacher's understanding of rhythm either!

## References and Reading List

Clements, R. (1991). Making the most of movement narratives. *Journal of Physical Education, Recreation and Dance, 62* (9), 57–61.

Consortium of National Arts Education Associations (1994). *National standards for arts education.* Reston, VA: Music Educators National Conference.

Davis, J. (1995). Laban Movement Analysis: A key to individualizing children's dance. *Journal of Physical Education, Recreation and Dance, 66* (2), 31–33.

Feldstein, S. (1982). *Practical theory: A combination textbook and workbook that teaches music theory in a concise practical manner* (Vol. 1). Van Nuys, CA: Alfred.

Franklin, E. (1996). *Dance imagery for technique and performance.* Champaign, IL: Human Kinetics.

Hanrahan, C. (1995). Creating dance images: Basic principles for teachers. *Journal of Physical Education, Recreation and Dance, 66* (1), 33–39.

Hawkins, A. M. (1991). *Moving from within: A new method for dance making.* Chicago, IL: a cappella books.

Laban, R. (1975). *Modern educational dance* (3rd ed.) (L. Ullmann, Rev.). London: MacDonald & Evans.

Leonard, H. (1993). *Pocket music dictionary.* Milwaukee, WI: Hal Leonard Publishing.

Preston-Dunlop, V. (1980). *A handbook for modern educational dance* (Rev. ed.). Estover, Plymouth: MacDonald & Evans.

Roberton, M. A., & Halverson, L. E. (1984). *Developing children—Their changing movement: A guide for teachers.* Philadelphia: Lea & Febiger.

Russell, J. (1975). *Creative movement and dance for children* (Rev. ed.). Boston: Plays.

Stinson, S. (1988). *Dance for young children: Finding the magic in movement.* Reston, VA: American Alliance for Health, Physical Education, Recreation, and Dance.

## Music Resources for Dance

Educational Activities, Inc.
PO Box 87
Baldwin , NY 11510
800 645–3739
e-mail: learn@edact.com

Smithsonian Institution (distributor of Folkways Records)
955 L'Enfant Plaza, Rm 2600
Washington, DC 20560

Hoctor Records
PO Box 38
Waldwick, NJ 07463
201 652–7767
800 462–8679
www.DanceCaravan.com
e-mail: CARAVAN.PDTA@WorldNet.ATT.Net

Kimbo Educational Records
Box 477
Long Branch, NJ 07740
800 631–2187
e-mail: KimboEd@aol.com

The Lloyd Shaw Foundation
2924 Hickory Ct.
Manhattan, KS 66503
913 539–6306

Music in Motion
PO Box 833814
Richardson, TX 75083–3814
800 445–0649
www.music-in-motion.com
e-mail: catalog@music-in-motion.com

New World Records
701 Seventh Avenue, 10th Flr
New York, NY 10036–1596
212 302–0460

Nonesuch Records
51 West 51 Street
New York, NY 10019
*(Does not sell directly to individual consumers; libraries can place orders)*

Orion Enterprises
614 Davis Street
Evanston, IL 60201
847 866–9443

## Children's Literature and Books with Dance Themes (list spans different reading levels)

Ackerman, Karen (1988). *Song and dance man*. New York: Knopf.
    *Plot Summary:* Grandpa demonstrates his vaudeville routine for his grandchildren.
Bang, Molly (1985). *The paper crane*. New York: Greenwillow Books.
    *Plot Summary:* A man pays for dinner with a paper crane that comes alive and dances; follows a traditional Japanese folk-tale.
Berenstain, Stan & Berenstain, Jan. (1993). *Gotta dance*. New York: Random House.
    *Plot Summary:* Brother bear overcomes his fear of dancing and goes to the school dance.
Boynton, Sandra (1993). *Barnyard dance*. New York: Workman Publishing.
    *Plot Summary:* Barnyard farm animals dance.
Esbensen, Barbara Suster (1995). *Dance with me*. New York: HarperCollins Publishers.
    *Plot Summary:* Poems depicting the dance of nature.
Getz, Arthur (1980). *Humphrey, the dancing pig*. New York: Dial Press.
    *Plot Summary:* Humphrey "dances" his way to losing weight.
Isadora, Rachel (1976). *Max*. New York: Macmillan.
    *Plot Summary:* Max discovers his sister's dance class is a great way to warm up for his Saturday baseball games.
Marshall, James (1990). *The cut-ups carry on*. New York: Viking.
    *Plot Summary:* Two boys are forced to take ballroom dancing lessons and plot to win the final class contest.
Martin, Bill Jr., & Archambault, John. (1986). *Barn dance*. New York: Henry Holt.
    *Plot Summary:* Unable to sleep, a young boy hears music and discovers an unusual barn dance in progress.
McCaughrean, G. (1994). *The Random House book of stories from the ballet*. New York: Random House.
    *Plot Summary:* Stories of ten classical ballets.
McGrath, James A. (1972). *Dance with Indian children: The shape of the drum beat, the rattle sound, the flute voice*. Washington, D. C.: Center for the Arts of Indian America.
    *Plot Summary:* Poems, essays, and photographs on various aspects of Indian movement and musical instruments.
McKissack, Patricia C. (1988). *Mirandy and brother wind*. New York: Alfred A. Knopf.
    *Plot Summary:* African-American central character, Mirandy, tries to win first prize in a cakewalk.
Patrick, Denise Lewis (1993). *Red dancing shoes*. New York: Tambourine Books.
    *Plot Summary:* African-American central character; shows off new shoes by dancing through town.
Shannon, George (1982). *Dance away*. New York: Greenwillow Books.
    *Plot Summary:* A rabbit's dancing saves his friends from becoming dinner for the fox.
Shannon, George (1991). *Dancing the breeze*. New York: Bradbury Press.
    *Plot Summary:* Father and daughter dance among the flowers in the front yard.
Simon, Carly (1989). *Amy the dancing bear*. New York: Doubleday.
    *Plot Summary:* Mother bear tries to persuade Amy to stop dancing and go to bed with unexpected results.

Wallace, Ian (1984). *Chin Chiang and the Dragon's Dance.* New York: Atheneum.

> *Plot Summary:* Chinese boy dreams of dancing the Dragon's Dance.

Warren, Lee (1972). *The dance of Africa: An introduction.* Englewood Cliffs, NJ: Prentice-Hall.

> *Plot Summary:* Describes origins and significance of many African dances.

Wilder, Laura Ingalls (1994). *Dance at grandpa's.* New York: HarperCollins.

> *Plot Summary:* Young pioneer girl attends winter party at grandparents' Wisconsin home.

# 3

# Preparing for Teaching and for Being a Teacher

*i*dentifying movement as the content of physical education and understanding movement conceptually, biomechanically, developmentally, and aesthetically clearly start you on a path toward excellence in beginning teaching. Having a rich knowledge base from different perspectives of movement enables you to teach in ways that help children become skillful movers in a variety of movement contexts. Without such a base, you will be limited or restricted in the ways that contribute to their development of competence and confidence as moving individuals. Your growing knowledge base has roots in your past and current experiences as a performer and in your professional preparation in physical education teacher education. The courses that you take within the discipline of kinesiology (e.g., motor development, movement aesthetics, motor learning, exercise physiology), in movement performance (e.g., volleyball, invasion games, educational dance), and on teaching, as well as field experiences and books on human movement expand your knowledge base as you work toward receiving initial licensure to teach.

Knowing movement as a performer yourself and also as a student in the discipline of kinesiology preparing to teach physical education, however, is not all there is to understanding movement in order to teach it. You must be able to transform your knowledge into meaningful lesson experiences for the students that you will be teaching. Transforming what you know about movement into educational experiences for children requires forethought and planning. Chapter 7, Planning for Student Learning, provides guidelines for one part of this process of transformation. The guidelines help you organize your knowledge base of movement, specifically for teaching movement to children. The importance of developing one's planning skills as an essential part of becoming a successful teacher is emphasized throughout the chapter.

The last chapter revisits the main points of the text. The revisitation serves two purposes. It is a way to bring physical closure to the book. More importantly though, it also serves to challenge you to expand your understanding of the content of physical education for teaching beyond the pages of this book as you continue to construct your concept of self-as-teacher.

## *outline*

### CHAPTER 7
### *Planning for Student Learning*

### CHAPTER 8
### *"Off You Go"*

# C H A P T E R 7

# *Planning for Student Learning*

*e*xcellence in teaching is strongly tied to the teacher's ability to plan for student learning. Teachers who are noted for their excellence in teaching physical education plan thoroughly. Children in excellent physical education programs come to know the physical education experience through the eyes of their teachers. What they gain from these experiences, in particular the meanings associated with them, plays a central role in the value they will come to place on physical activity as a part of their daily lives. Planning helps to highlight this role. It is a responsibility that successful teachers take seriously and work hard to fulfill. As you move toward excellence in your own teaching, you will need to become competent and confident in the planning aspect of teaching.

## *The Necessity of Planning*

As a beginning teacher, planning becomes one of the major vehicles through which you learn how to teach as well as learn about teaching. All teachers need some form of guidance to help direct their planning efforts for student learning whether it be for a single lesson or a series of lessons; a full year or six years. Although most teachers are nervous when they teach, novices are more prone to this feeling because of inexperience. Planning has a way of focusing nervous energy into productive directions for teaching. Nobody wants children's learning to be aimless and meaningless because the teacher did not plan. Thus, planning is a critical skill for all teachers to learn to do well.

As a beginning teacher you are developing a rich and exciting knowledge base upon which to help children learn in a physical education context. Although you have taken many courses in your teacher preparation program and explored many ideas in relation to teaching physical education, it is difficult to know just how to use what you have learned in your teaching efforts. The process of developing a plan helps you learn how to take your knowledge base, the theory, and apply it to the real world practice of teaching and learning.

## Planning as a Specialized Form of Reflection

Planning is a process that can lead toward continuous professional growth because it involves decision-making about all aspects of teaching for student learning. It can be a powerful form of reflective thinking as it encourages individuality and personal involvement (Kirk, 1993). Planning focuses on the relationships between and among the different aspects of lessons and how these relationships evolve and change to enhance student learning.

Planning has the potential to foster flexibility and creativity in that it requires the use of imagination. Imaginative planning has the power to enrich what children learn while at the same time giving depth of meaning to teaching actions and their results. But planning has a risk factor associated with it. Sometimes a plan simply does not work, no matter how much time you spent creating it. In such cases, you will have to spend even more time making changes to the current plan or simply starting all over again.

## A Journey, Not a Destination

The type of planning that we advocate takes time to learn and to do well. Do not expect instant success with your initial efforts at planning. View planning as a journey, rather than a destination. It is a journey that begins in your undergraduate program and is taken with peers, university teacher education faculty, and cooperating teachers. It is a journey that continues throughout your teaching career and may be taken with others or perhaps alone. The sooner that you recognize the important role planning plays in teaching for student learning, the sooner you will sense its powerful effect on your ability to teach successfully.

## What Research Says about Planning

In truth, there is little research to guide us in knowing what is the best model for planning (Clark & Peterson, 1986) or the best way to teach planning (Lee, 1996). In spite of the limited research, however, there are questions related specifically to the planning process that are important for us to discuss as we begin the planning journey.

- What role do objectives play in the planning process?
- How can beginning teachers plan to better prepare themselves for the unexpected when teaching?

- How do value orientations about education and physical education affect planning?

*The role of objectives.*  Objectives traditionally have been considered the driving force behind planning (Tyler, 1949). Generally, they are the first planning decision that is made, whether planning a program, a series of lessons, or one lesson by itself. It is believed by many that for objectives to be useful, they should be stated as behavioral outcomes. Although most teacher educators probably view objectives in this way, teachers in school settings typically do not take this approach (Lee, 1996). In a recent summary of research on planning, most teachers regardless of their levels of expertise, related their planning decisions to "activities and content of the lesson rather than the goals and objectives" (Lee, 1996, p. 21). Student teachers often write their objectives *after* they have completed other aspects of their lesson plans such as the activities that they are going to teach. In practice then, it is unclear how objectives drive the lesson to be taught. The impact of objectives on the process of planning and on our teaching is something upon which we all need to reflect.

*Preparation for the unexpected.*  From studies comparing inexperienced teachers with experienced teachers, results have shown that inexperienced teachers find it difficult to alter their teaching strategies if they find their lesson going in a direction they had not originally planned. On the other hand, experienced teachers can and do alter their actions in midstream (Lee, 1996). This finding is not a surprise. It makes complete sense that the less experienced teacher would have difficulty changing a lesson plan course in midstream. Teacher educators, along with their undergraduate students, need to discover ways that will help beginning teachers plan so that they can be more responsive while on their feet.

*Personal value orientation.*  Within the past several years, researchers in physical education have recognized the strong impact that values have on teachers' pedagogical decisions (Ennis, 1996). This is a particularly important concept to understand at the lesson level, for it is here that the effects of such influence are truly visible. Your lessons will reflect what you believe about education in general and physical education in particular. In discussing this concept, the five value orientations identified by Jewett, Bain, and Ennis (1995)—disciplinary mastery, learning process, self-actualization, social responsibility, and ecological integration—are useful. Recent explanations about these value orientations (Ennis, 1996) places knowledge about and skill in movement at the center of the disciplinary mastery orientation and knowledge about and skill in how to learn motor skills at the center of the learning process orientation. In the self-actualization orientation, the curriculum revolves around the needs and motivation of the learners. Movement is used as a means or tool for learners to develop positive self-esteem. The development of positive, interpersonal relationships among learners is the central focus of teachers who support the social responsibility orientation. The ecological orientation supports the view that movement knowledge, the learner, and the social group are equally important. We believe that no matter what value orientation(s) you hold, it should be supported by a commitment to a deep understanding of movement because knowledge of movement is a common denominator across all of these value orientations. Knowledge of movement is crucial to your development as a teacher of physical education. How you use this knowledge, however, will differ depending on the value orientation that supports your teaching.

## Planning as an Individualized Process

Planning is a highly individualized process and it is also unique to each educational context. Thus, as a beginning teacher, you will need to develop your own approach to planning within the frame of a strong commitment to the planning process. We see teacher educators as facilitators in this process. To meet this end, this chapter focuses on the types of decisions that have to be made when planning for student learning, specifically applied to the curricular areas of educational games, educational gymnastics, and educational dance. A review of the three content chapters and those preceding them will remind you that collectively they represent a constructivist orientation to children's physical education. Our approach to planning reflects this orientation.

Because planning is so individualized and the contexts in which you will teach are so varied, no single plan format is being proposed. There is no "perfect" way to plan that works for all. A range of different formats can be found among current physical education textbooks. Further, your particular teacher education faculty will have well-defined approaches to planning that have proved to be successful over the years. These can all be appropriate ways to write lesson plans. The important outcome in planning, however, is the quality and usefulness of the information that is included, not the format. As you develop and refine a format meaningful to you, remember two things:

- The purpose of planning is to guide you in enhancing student learning.
- The plan must work for you.

You may feel at times that you are writing plans for someone else (e.g., your professor, your supervisor, your cooperating teacher), but do not let that feeling distract you. You are really writing plans for the children that you are about to teach in your next lesson and will teach in future lessons.

## The Scope of Planning

Teachers have to plan a program, units, and lessons. Program planning focuses on what students should be able to do after, for example, they have completed a K–5 physical education program. The major purpose of this form of planning is to help teachers set priorities related to their programs of physical education, as well as to plan for integration across the rest of the schools' curriculums. This form of planning takes a long time and is best done in groups. Efforts usually result in the development of documents referred to as curriculum guides. These documents will most often include long range goals or objectives, the scope and sequence of content to be included, and suggested methods of assessment and evaluation. Documents of this nature are written at local, state, and national levels.

Unit and lesson planning are closely related to program planning, as both derive their focuses from it. They are also closely related to each other. The basic difference between them is the time element—unit plans focus on a series of lessons over a longer period of time whereas a lesson plan focuses on a single lesson within the time frame for the unit. Because of the time element, lesson plans are naturally more specific and handle less content than do unit plans. Another distinction between unit and lesson plans relates to progression. Content progression in a unit plan would be larger in scope than in a lesson plan as the unit represents a greater amount of content to be developed.

As you build a foundation in designing rich lessons, these subtle, but distinct differences, become clearer. We believe unit planning develops from a sound base in lesson planning, and thus we cannot stress enough the importance of learning how to plan lessons well. Acknowledging this belief, the rest of the chapter focuses on designing and evaluating lessons. Before we discuss lesson planning in detail, however, we need to address factors that impact our construction of the lesson planning process.

# FACTORS THAT INFLUENCE THE PLANNING PROCESS

As mentioned earlier, how you plan and what you put in your plan reflect what you believe about physical education. Beliefs are influenced by a number of factors. The factors that affect our beliefs about lesson planning are stated here. As you study the planning process, you may come to realize that these same factors influence your beliefs about lesson planning. You may also come to realize that different factors are part of your planning for teaching. To become a teacher is a very individualized process and to reflect on the factors that influence your planning for teaching is an important part of the process.

## Planning Factors Related to the Content of Children's Physical Education

- Educational games, educational gymnastics, and educational dance are basic program areas for physical education. Teachers' understanding of movement, that is movement specific to games, gymnastics, and dance, is central to the planning process and a key factor in learning how to teach these three areas. Knowledge of specific movement forms, however, must be flexible and fluid (McDiarmid, Ball, & Anderson, 1989) if it is to be used effectively in meeting individual needs of learners.
- The movement within each of the three forms can be understood and taught from different perspectives. We have drawn on four: conceptual, mechanical, aesthetic, and developmental (see the four preceding chapters).

## Planning Factors Related to Teaching Physical Education

- There are knowledge concepts about teaching specific to educational games, educational gymnastics, and educational dance. Some of these knowledge concepts cut across all three areas while others do not. The major function of this pedagogical knowledge is to help teachers elicit from learners the specific movement skill, cognitive understanding, or personal meaning being taught at a particular point in time. Simply knowing this knowledge, however, does not imply that you will know when and how to use it. That has to be learned. This knowledge is closely related to, but is not the same as, knowledge of movement.
- There are knowledge concepts general to the teaching of educational games, educational gymnastics, and educational dance. The major function of this knowledge base is to aid in the creation of education environments that are conducive to high levels of learning.

## Planning Factors Related to Constructing Learning in Physical Education

- For learning to occur, instructional tasks must be developmentally appropriate, that is, they must be designed to demonstrate the interplay among person-environment-task.
- For learning to occur, children's safety must be considered constantly.
- It takes time to become increasingly more advanced in movement performance. The type of practice experienced by learners is related to their levels of success. Individual success may differ across educational games, educational gymnastics, and educational dance.

## *Planning Factors Related to the Goals of Physical Education*

- The development of increasingly competent and confident movers serves to focus the teacher throughout each lesson and from lesson to lesson. Progression toward this goal directs the development of each lesson plan.
- Knowledge goals and goals for personal meaning are integral parts of every experience and must be planned for. We are specifically interested in the knowledge about and the meaning for increasingly skilled movement that can be promoted through educational games, educational gymnastics, and educational dance and the potential effects these goals can have on promoting active lifestyles.
- No goals are possible to reach without children being willing and able to share in the responsibility for their own learning. Children need assistance in adjusting to the different environments of educational games, educational gymnastics, and educational dance and in developing acceptable inner control for their movement behavior.
- Lessons in educational games, educational gymnastics, and educational dance are performance centered, thus high levels of focused activity are expected to occur throughout each lesson.
- Educational games, educational gymnastics, and educational dance are powerful avenues through which to learn about, accept, and respect individual differences among children in physical activity settings and to acquire problem-solving skills.

# LINKING PLANNING WITH STATE AND NATIONAL STANDARDS

Throughout your teacher education curriculum you will be introduced to different state and national curriculum documents. These documents, along with your own professional preparation curriculum, serve to guide the development of an entire program of physical education, as well as planning for specific units and lessons. There are no national curriculums to which you are held accountable, but that may not be true at the state level. Your teacher education program, if it is held to specific state standards, will reflect this, and you will become familiar with the documents that explain in some detail what these standards include.

In addition to your state standards, you will want to become familiar with two curriculum publications developed by the National Association for Sport and Physical Education (NASPE). The first one, *Outcomes of Quality Physical Education Programs* (1992), identifies performance outcomes for physical education that support NASPE's definition of a physically educated person. The outcomes were presented in Chapter 2 and, as we have previously indicated, if the program goals presented in this book are achieved, then students who have participated in such programs will be said to be physically educated. The second document, *Moving into the Future: National Standards for Physical Education,* establishes content standards for physical education programs, as well as assessment guidelines for those standards (NASPE, 1995). Both of these documents can be very helpful when learning how to plan because they give examples of content considered appropriate for different grade levels.

# LESSON PLANNING

Learning to plan lessons and learning to write them out are two different, yet obviously related, tasks. Planning lessons requires that you understand the important components needed to design a productive and cohesive lesson. Transforming this understanding into a useful written document requires the ability to know how much to write down and how to write it in a format that will be useful to you when you teach.

Teaching is a dynamic phenomenon and the lesson plan is a tool for increasing the probability that the interaction of teaching and learning is productive. The pieces of information on a lesson plan are interrelated and the interrelationships are fluid and dynamic. The amount of information included on a written lesson plan varies according to teachers' previous experience teaching the material and their understanding of how learners of different developmental levels may approach learning the material. When teachers have had experience with the material and are familiar with the range of responses often demonstrated by children, they usually do not have to write plans in much detail. On the other hand, when teachers are not familiar with the material and how children respond to it, they usually need to plan in more detail. There may also be lesson plan requirements from your principal, for example, that outline the amount of detail which you need to provide in your plan. The degree to which you will be asked to write out detailed lesson plans, therefore, is unique to each situation—a blending of other's expectations and your own beliefs about planning.

When you first begin learning how to plan, write partial lesson plans. Move toward writing full plans only when you are comfortable with all the components. As you attempt to teach your first lessons in educational games, educational gymnastics, and educational dance, we suggest that you "over plan" and include lots of detail. Keep the detail in your plans as long as you need it and come back to it whenever you need it again. When your need for detail diminishes due to your developing knowledge base about movement and children's range of response possibilities to movement tasks, develop shorter versions of your plans. If your need for detail increases, for example you are teaching content that you have never taught before, then return to the more detailed plan. If you do cut down on detail, however, be sure the plans still provide the minimum information that you need to teach a productive and effective lesson. For those plans that you need to write out in full detail, you might consider making a shortened version of it just prior to teaching. This can be considered a form of mental rehearsal which will most probably impact your teaching effectiveness. Rich detailed lesson plans are difficult to remember unless you focus on the key points just before using them. When to write out partial plans, full plans, or shortened versions can only be determined on an individual basis. Everyone will not handle this task in the same way.

Although most licensed teachers in schools do not write out full lesson plans, good teachers still plan for student learning to occur. Much of their planning is carried out in their heads and does not have to be written down. When asked if they used to write everything down, they will probably answer yes, especially when they first began teaching. Writing out plans is a great way to help you learn to teach because it forces you to think about teaching; to resolve important questions about what and how you want your students to learn. You also learn from a plan that does not work because you will have to rethink the plan all over again. You will be amazed at what you will learn about content and teaching from the act of planning lessons.

Excellence in teaching is strongly tied to the teacher's ability to plan for student learning. It is a responsibility that successful teachers take seriously and work hard to fulfill. As a beginning teacher, we challenge you to become competent and confident in this aspect of teaching.

## Steps in Creating a Lesson Plan

The following material outlines eight steps that we recommend you use in creating lesson plans. This recommended outline is generated from years of observing beginning teachers plan. We suggest that you complete steps 1–4 in the order presented. The order for steps 5–8 should be decided upon by each individual planner or in consultation with the person teaching you how to plan. It makes sense for individuals to decide to order the steps differently. In traditional planning, decisions are usually made in the order presented. This linear approach, however, may not be the most effective strategy to use all the time because the information needed to make these decisions is highly interactive, a point made earlier. Step 7 is the aspect of the plan that guides you through the implementation of the actual lesson. It is the step for describing what you want to do and how you "plan" to do it. Step 8, the lesson (plan) evaluation, occurs after you have taught the lesson. It is the single most important step to take before you finalize plans for any subsequent lessons.

### STEP 1: PRELIMINARY INFORMATION

*Specifics.*   State the date, grade level, number of students for whom the lesson is planned, the length of the lesson, where the lesson is to be taught, and the program area (educational games, educational gymnastics, or educational dance). This information is used primarily as a recordkeeping tactic; it is an accounting of what you taught, to whom, when, and where.

*Unit Content.*   If the lesson plan that you are planning is linked to a unit plan, then state the unit content from which the lesson is being created. This statement will be the same for every lesson within the unit. When included, it helps to keep you focused toward long range objectives instead of only the immediate objectives for that one lesson.

*Place of Lesson within Unit.*   If designing a lesson based on a unit plan, state the number of lessons within the unit (e.g., third lesson of eight). This information helps you to evaluate the progress you are making toward meeting your unit objectives and to make any necessary changes to keep you on target.

### STEP 2: LESSON CONTENT

Identify the content for which the lesson is being planned. If the lesson is linked directly to a unit, briefly describe the relationship of the lesson content to the content of the unit.

### STEP 3: LESSON PURPOSE

State the lesson purpose. If the lesson that you are planning is part of a unit plan, then describe how the lesson contributes toward meeting the unit objectives. This information helps you clarify for yourself where you are heading with the lesson that you are about to teach. Without a strong sense of the lesson purpose, lessons can sometimes drift aimlessly.

### STEP 4: IMPORTANT INFORMATION/SAFETY CONCERNS

Describe any special considerations that may affect your ability to teach the lesson or your students' ability to learn the material. These factors may come from observations from previous lessons or specific knowledge that you may have about the learners or the context in which the lesson is being taught (e.g., weather, special events in the school). Include a full description of how you are planning for the safety of the children throughout the lesson. Be very specific. This information forces you to think through what you will do to keep the children safe. Once you have identified the safety factors that you want to consider, you may want to jot down reminders related to them throughout the plan.

### STEP 5: STUDENT OBJECTIVES/OUTCOMES

Describe what the students should be able to do, to know, or to feel as a result of participating in your lesson. These statements, when appropriate, should include all aspects of the whole child. If the lesson is part of a unit, review the unit objectives/outcomes and know the place this lesson has in meeting them. This information should guide you in designing actual tasks and assessment techniques. As you write this portion of your lesson plan, be sure to indicate the quality, or level of skill, for which you are striving.

### STEP 6: RESOURCES NEEDED

List equipment, apparatus, props, music, and other teaching materials needed. Specify types and amounts. This information helps you realize the amount of time you need to prepare for your lesson and to make transitions within the lesson from one part to another. Transitions require effective organizational patterns as well as students who can move into and out of them efficiently.

### STEP 7: LESSON IN SEQUENCE

Following is a list of decisions that you will need to make as you plan what you will actually do in your lesson. As you reflect on them, you may find some overlap. Do not worry about this. Overlap is normal when so many decisions that you have to make in planning are interrelated.

*How you plan to introduce the lesson.* Make this brief and easy for children to grasp. If you choose to start your lesson with a verbal introduction of the lesson purpose or objectives, focus it tightly and try to create in the children an interest in what they are about to learn. Remember, children come to physical education expecting to be active. Get them productively active as quickly as possible.

*The tasks that you plan to use (i.e., your progression) along with points you wish to emphasize initially.* Write out each task that you anticipate asking the children to do. Include in each task where appropriate any points for emphasis that you think are essential as children *first* try to respond. These emphases are often safety related (e.g., move into empty spaces; only go as fast as you can control your ability to stop) but others are related to movement quality (e.g., be light on your feet, soft taps when contacting the ball).

For whatever reasons you include them, use them sparingly at this point in the planning process. Further on in the process you will plan in some detail what to look for as children respond to the tasks. This specific portion of the plan leads you directly to identifying additional points on which you may want the children to focus.

As you design tasks, think about the reason for the task, its purpose, and how it relates to the development of your content over the entire lesson. Answer the following questions (Barrett, 1984; Rink, 1998):

- Does the task serve to introduce the children to the content or idea being taught? If it does, it is called a basic task and its purpose is to establish a starting point for the idea being introduced. Often, a progression develops from this task.
- Does the task challenge the children to perform at a more advanced level? If it does, it is called an extending task and its purpose is to make the task more complex and challenging, thus making the children's responses more advanced.
- Does the task allow the children to perform at an easier level? If it does, it is called a simplifying task and its purpose is to make the task easier, thus making the task developmentally appropriate for those less advanced.
- Does the task enhance the children's quality of response? If it does, it is called a refining task and its purpose is to elicit from children a more advanced movement pattern. It is at this point when designing movements tasks that particular emphasis is placed on mechanical requirements, aesthetic principles, and developmental characteristics needed to perform the movement more skillfully.
- Does the task challenge the children to use their movements in a new context? If it does, it is called an applying task and its purpose is to shift the children's focus from how to do the task to how to use it in different contexts and under different conditions.

*The estimated length of time you plan to spend on each task or selected parts of the lesson.*    Somewhere in the margin of your plan, estimate the time that you will spend on each task, series of tasks, and shifts in the organizational pattern for the lesson. Regard these estimates as flexible, for you will most likely have to adjust them as you see the degree of progress your children are making in the lesson.

*How you want children organized for optimal participation and how you plan to get them into the organizational pattern(s).*    Begin this aspect of your plan by drawing a diagram of your pre-lesson set up. Include the space (e.g., gym, field) and where your equipment or apparatus will be placed when the children first arrive. Use symbols in the diagram and provide a key.

Throughout the plan describe the ways in which you want both children and resources to be organized for each task. Transitions between organizational patterns should be carefully planned and described. Explain how you plan to distribute and put away any equipment or apparatus. Think of the directions that you give children as another kind of task—an organizational task. Presenting this type of task and guiding children to respond with control and self direction is at times just as challenging for you and the children as are the more complex movement tasks.

*What you will look for and emphasize as the children work.* Now you are ready to plan in more detail what you will look for and what you will emphasize. You want to focus on specific aspects of the task and assess whether or not the children are reaching your goals or expectations. The actions of looking for and emphasizing are two sides of the same coin; what you plan to look for defines what you emphasize. For example, if you plan to look for resilient use of the feet and ankles when children are traveling and jumping, you will look at what their feet and ankles are doing. Based on what you see, you will make a teaching decision. This decision could be to emphasize or re-emphasize the same points, use a different cue or, perhaps, give them an entirely different task that gets at the same thing. What you plan to look for and emphasize is guided by your knowledge of movement, the purpose of the task, and how well you know your class. If you plan this part of Step 7 well, and are able to use what you planned, it leads directly to the next phase of planning.

*Potential tasks and other strategies to use if the behavior that you are trying to elicit from the children is or is not emerging.* This part of your planning is directly related to what you decided to look for and to emphasize and should be planned at the same time. If you do not see what you are looking for or emphasizing, for example cutting into a space to receive a pass or a clear distinction between a sudden and sustained movement, then you must figure out another way to elicit the desired response right on the spot. That could mean designing a new task with a different goal, giving a different cue, asking a question (e.g., "Are you remembering to look for a space into which you can cut?") changing the equipment, or altering the organizational pattern. Assuming the task is developmentally appropriate, the kinds of tasks that you will have to design quickly could be any of those previously mentioned except the first one, the basic task. No matter whether you have to design tasks that are more challenging or less challenging for the children, you have to know your options and think them through carefully. Two options include adapting or modifying the environment and adapting or modifying the task.

*Ways in which the learning environment or the movement task could be adapted or modified to accommodate for the learning needs of individual children.* It is at this point in your lesson plan that you need to identify different ways in which you could alter the environment or specific aspects of a task to accommodate the learning needs of the class or individual children. Learning needs can be of two types—needs of the developmentally less advanced and needs of the developmentally more advanced. Here is how we suggest that you think about this aspect of planning.

- Think through the different ways children might respond to your tasks; describe how they might look as they attempt to perform each task.
- Based on these descriptions write out one or two ways that you could alter the environment or the task.
- For example, to alter the environment, you could place markers closer together so balls would not travel so fast or you could lower a gymnastics box to the degree that children can push off with both feet as opposed to stepping down with one foot following the other.
- For another example, to modify the task, you could alter the goal of a task, alter the amount and type of decisions shared with the children, or alter the equipment used in the task. Ask the children to strike a ball between four and six feet above their heads as opposed to just above the head (changing the goal). Shift from rising and sinking leading with different body parts to leading with elbows only (changing the number of decision choices). Remove some of the air from an 8" playground ball so it does not rebound so smartly off the children's feet when they are dribbling (changing the equipment).

*What techniques and strategies you will use to assess children's progress or regression during the lesson.*    The primary technique that you will be using to assess progress during a lesson is your ability to observe against a developmental framework. This means that you compare your observations of the children's movement patterns against what you know about how these patterns develop over time. From these observations you can asses children's progress or regression. Most of the developmental information that we currently know is found in the validated developmental sequences of fundamental skills. Where there are no developmental sequences available for what you are teaching, and this will be the case for the majority of what you teach, information can come from practicing teachers and from your own experiences. To get you started thinking this way, we have included this type of information in all content chapters, particularly in the sections on biomechanical, motor development, and aesthetic principles affecting quality of performance. Additional information related to specific gymnastics skills is included in the gymnastics sections on Integration of Skills and Focused Teaching.

In some lessons, you may want to plan for additional types of assessment and record your observations. These strategies can be applied to both product and process assessments and can be teacher directed, peer directed, or self directed (Veal, 1995). For example, you could plan to videotape your children's performances and then have yourself or the children assess their progress. Include in your plan how to organize the videotaping procedures. You could also develop and include with your lesson plan, a predetermined list of criteria against which assessments should be made.

Another assessment example is the development of a strategy to record quantitative data over a period of time (e.g., the number of times a child can consecutively hit a ball against the wall with a paddle, the distance a child can throw a ball overarm, the number of times a child can jump a self-turned rope). Develop a method of recording these scores and include it with your lesson plan, for example, a card with a sample format for recording. Also describe in your plan how to carry out the assessment procedures.

*How to close the lesson.* Write out how you plan to end and bring closure to your lesson. Most often this is done by bringing the children in towards you. Then, using a discussion format, guide them through a review of the experiences from which they would have constructed their learning. This can be done through questions where individual children are asked to respond or where you ask the entire group to reflect in their minds what they have just experienced in their bodies.

Sometimes it might be appropriate to plan this portion of your lesson using a movement task rather than discussion. For example, in a dance lesson you might ask children to respond to a series of tasks, given fairly quickly one after the other. These tasks must be designed so that all children can easily respond to them. You would point out how each one was linked to the lesson they just experienced. In this way the tasks would serve as a review for the children. We recommend that the last task be designed specifically to quiet the children; this requires them to be still and quiet for at least 15–20 seconds.

### STEP 8: LESSON EVALUATION

Leave a space on your plan or have an additional page on which you will include your lesson evaluation. What focus you take in evaluating your lesson is in the end a personal decision. If the purpose of an evaluation is to guide your next lesson, however, you will need to focus on what occurred in relation to your objectives. If your objectives are not strong enough to give you this guidance, then you can compare the children's responses to your expectations for them task by task. As you write about what occurred, acknowledge both positive and negative, and reflect on why they occurred. If changes are implied, then you can present them here. The purpose of this evaluation is to help you prepare for the next lesson with this class as well as learn about teaching this particular material to these particular children in a particular context.

# USING THE CONTENT CHAPTERS TO HELP YOU PLAN

Learning to plan is a critical part of your preparation for becoming a teacher. When you first start planning, writing lesson plans can feel more like an exercise than a meaningful task. Planning good lessons is challenging. A sound plan requires you to integrate knowledge from many sources, and that is difficult for a beginning teacher to do. You have studied many important concepts related to teaching. Planning provides the chance to bring these concepts together to help you teach.

The three content chapters, Teaching Educational Games, Teaching Educational Gymnastics, and Teaching Educational Dance provide you with ideas related to appropriateness of content, content progression, and selected information linked to biomechanics, motor development, and aesthetics. It is natural to wonder how this information actually helps in making planning decisions. We have chosen to illustrate this idea with three narratives of possible conversations each between a mentor teacher and an intern teacher. Each conversation is linked directly to a section or sections in one of the content chapters to demonstrate how certain information can be used to make planning decisions.

## Conversation between Mrs. Ketching and Gail

(Topics relate to Core Content 1, 2, and 3 in Chapter 4, Teaching Educational Games)

GAIL: I can't believe how smoothly your lesson went! You must have spent hours planning it. How did you do it? Would you tell me some of the things that you thought about while you were planning?

MRS. KETCHING: I can try. I can't always remember everything I thought about, though.

GAIL: That's O.K. Just what you can remember would really be a big help to me.

MRS. KETCHING: All right. Based on what I had seen my third grade class do in their last games lesson, I knew I needed more challenging, game-like tasks or a specially designed small-sided game that depended on the players' abilities to catch while running, sidestepping, and jumping. All tasks would involve a ball tossed by a classmate or teammate, not self-tossed. I wanted to challenge these children to move faster and farther into space when catching more difficult tosses; closer to the tempo and the way space is used in actual game play. The children demonstrated in their last lesson that when tossing to themselves, they can consistently and effectively position their bodies and hands to catch a ball, both when stationary and traveling. They can also keep their balance when catching away from the center of their bodies. Very few, however, could jump and catch.

That's still tough for them. Both their tosses and timing of the jump are off. I have also noticed that when they do catch the ball, most of the children still wait for the ball to reach them, rather than moving their hands toward the ball. I thought that by putting them in a more challenging situation that I could bring these actions out. And you saw that I was right.

GAIL: Yes, that was what was so impressive! They really took off! I was surprised because I did not think these particular children were that capable.

MRS. KETCHING: I started with bean bags so that the children would be clear in what I wanted them to do. I also wanted to be sure they had some control over the object in this new situation before I made it more difficult by using a ball. And bean bags don't roll! Once I saw consistent and safe object control, I took the lesson further to include tennis balls and 6" playground balls and slowly increased the speed at which they worked and the way space was used.

GAIL: Yes, I couldn't get over how easily the children handled the change of equipment and more challenging tasks when asked to. I hope some day my classes will look like that! I also liked the way that you helped them toss more accurately; not too far ahead of their partners or too fast, but enough of both to be safe, game-like, and challenging. How did you plan for that?

MRS. KETCHING: You plan for it in a number of different ways. First, you are sure that the amount of space you give the children is right for what you are teaching and that they can handle it; it helps them, not hinders them. Because I want children eventually to move more aggressively into the space, I gradually increased how far they could travel as they demonstrated increased control over their tosses and catches. You have to look for and emphasize this consistently. You will remember, at one point I had half the class work, and then the other half. I would have used thirds if I thought this would have brought out the energy and skill levels that I was seeking. Giving them more space was done to encourage them to move faster and catch balls farther away from themselves without danger of bumping into someone. I also planned several demonstrations of how to pass to partners safely, while at the same time challenging them to perform at more advanced levels.

GAIL: Yes, and I thought those demo's worked very well. From watching this class I understand better how different factors influence children's performance and learning. I saw clearly what happened when the toss was placed too far away. At one point, I noticed that you had to change the lesson and actually work on tossing ahead of a moving partner. It was like that became the skill you were teaching. Did you plan for that or did you make it up then and there?

MRS. KETCHING: No, those tasks were not on-the-spot decisions. I anticipated the need for them, because I know how easily children's performance can be affected by outside factors such as ball size, speed of the ball, space, organizational pattern, and by their levels of development. In this case, ball placement dramatically affected what many of the children could do. I knew without the tosses being changed that I could never meet my objectives. I designed those tasks before the lesson began, in case I had to use them.

GAIL: Linking these tasks to actual game situations, like in one of your demonstrations, really seemed to help them understand the task and its purpose. I liked that part a lot. I also like the small-sided game you used toward the latter half of the lesson. The games seemed to show the children the role of passing ahead and why sometimes they have to run and jump to catch a ball. One last question, did you also plan for the discussion of key points, the one you held toward the middle of the lesson?

MRS. KETCHING: Yes. That discussion was planned to support objectives that were related to helping the children understand how force absorption is related to catching, no matter the type of catch. You will see me return to this discussion in other lessons that focus on catching and collecting no matter whether it is with hands, feet, or implements, such as hockey or lacrosse sticks.

GAIL: There certainly are a lot of things to think about when planning. What you told me helps me see a bit more how some of the things that I learned in some other courses can be useful in teaching.

MRS. KETCHING: Perhaps after one of your lessons tomorrow you would share with me how you made your decisions and we can compare our approaches?

GAIL: Sure, but I will be nervous.

MRS. KETCHING: I know. I was too!

## Conversation between Mr. Rollings and Sandy

(Topics relate to Core Content 2 and Integration of Skills and Focused Teaching 5 in Chapter 5, Teaching Educational Gymnastics)

MR. ROLLINGS: Sandy, since I will be away next week when my fourth-grade gymnastics class meets, the one that meets on Wednesday, would you be willing to take over for me under the supervision of the substitute teacher?

SANDY: Is that the class that is working on taking weight on different body parts? If I remember correctly, at the end of your last lesson you had just introduced the task of taking weight on their head and hands, keeping feet low. You were having them try this idea on their own. I remember something about keeping feet low.

MR. ROLLINGS: Yes, that's the class. I think you'll enjoy teaching them. Would you like to talk a little about the direction of this lesson now, or is there a better time?

SANDY: No, this is a good time.

MR. ROLLINGS: From what you remember of this lesson, is there any particular part of it that concerns you?

SANDY: Yes, I am nervous asking all of the children to take their weight on their heads and hands at the same time. I saw what you did, but that was you! I am afraid they will work too fast for me, not follow my directions, and all fall over. How do I plan for that not to happen? I just know it will.

MR. ROLLINGS: That's a good question. Let me help you think it through. First, from a mechanical point of view, what is critical here for the children to remember and do, and for you to know and look for all the time that you are teaching?

SANDY: Keeping a wide base; wide enough so they can't fall over. Theoretically, anyway!

MR. ROLLINGS: The base in this task being what?

SANDY: The head and hands.

MR. ROLLINGS: Right. If you are worried they might fall over, what body shape do you want them to use that would potentially protect them from this happening?

SANDY: Curled?

MR. ROLLINGS: Yes. This shape helps keep the body's center of gravity lower, thus making falling over more difficult, but still not impossible. Now, think back to what you remember seeing the children do during that lesson. What were some of their responses when I asked them to take their weight on their heads and hands and keep their feet low?

SANDY: I noticed that many of them, even though they began with their head and hands placed in a triangle, moved their hands in line with their heads, as they began to shift some of their weight on to their heads. Their bases became very narrow. In fact, some of them, even though you told them not to, began with their hands placed along side their heads. Also, I saw many of them take their weight on the top and back of their heads. I also saw feet poking upwards into the air instead of staying close to the floor.

MR. ROLLINGS: Good observations. Now that you have seen them, you have to respect and expect these responses, because they will occur. Many children, for example, even if they try not to poke their legs in the air, as you so cleverly described it, will do this. It's almost as if it were a stage in their development. Same with the head/hands position. I think it occurs when they unexpectedly begin to lose their balance. It's a reaction to the situation, not a planned movement. Placing their hands at the beginning as you described is also a very real response. It seems to occur when children think or feel that they may fall over. Again, perhaps a reaction to the situation. You can count on this response from over 50 percent of this class. I noticed it too.

SANDY: Even if I know these responses might occur, you're not saying that in one lesson I can fix them?

MR. ROLLINGS: Oh, no, but you can design specific tasks so the children begin to become more aware of what their bodies can and cannot do. In time they will be able to make the changes needed. Once they can establish a firm base with their bodies curled, it does not take long for them to keep this balanced position as they slowly raise their legs. Now that you know some of the responses that you will see, how will you plan to help the children get past them to more skillful ones?

SANDY: I have a few ideas. To get the lesson started, I would like to begin by having them balance on different body parts—a sort of review from your last lesson. But taken a little further by increasing the range of body parts used for balancing and stressing a fuller extension through the free body parts. During this time I shall stress the importance of a stable base or a still balance and no toppling over.

MR. ROLLINGS: These are good ideas. How will you hold them accountable?

SANDY: I hadn't thought of that yet. Let me think. In relation to falling over, I probably would do what I saw you do—stop the entire class as soon as I saw one child fall over and ask everyone why they thought I stopped the class. But not point out the child that I saw falling over. Depending on the answer, I would go from there being sure that when they went back to work they were clear on my expectations. I am not sure I can come up with anything else just now, but I will think about this and talk with you before next Wednesday. I would like to weave in a discussion about this but I have difficulty leading one in such a way that children have to think through the questions and that I don't give them the answers that I want to hear.

MR. ROLLINGS: The important thing is that you hold them to what you asked them to do. Your class could get away from you, if you don't do this. On that day, their classroom teacher will be with them and she is very helpful. You will have the substitute teacher too. The children will do fine. They are a class that listens well and knows how to learn in gymnastics. I think we better stop now, I hear the next class coming. Before our next discussion, I want you to think through how you will plan for the leg extension phase of this skill. This class will need to move onto this idea, but at their individual paces. In addition, what tasks might you have in readiness for those children who will be able to do this on the first try? As soon as they get the feel of a firm and steady base in a curled position, the leg extension is actually not that difficult. You think about this and we'll discuss this plan some more tomorrow during our break.

SANDY: All right. What we have discussed gives me a good start on planning and lots to mull over. I am constantly amazed at how many things you have to think through when planning. Are you absolutely sure that you have to be away on Wednesday?

## Conversation between Mr. Pressing and Chris

(Topics relate to Core Content 1, 2, 3, and 6 in Chapter Five, Teaching Educational Dance)

CHRIS: Mr. Pressing, you saw what just happened when I tried to have my second period fifth grade class explore pressing and thrusting actions. I had planned for my next lesson to begin with the creation of partner sequences using these two actions as focal points, but I don't see how I can do that now. I need help.

MR. PRESSING: Before we make any specific plans, let's review what you think the children should be able to do, or what you would like them to do, coming into a lesson focused on pressing and thrusting; a lesson that you want to structure in such a way that gives them responsibility for much of their own learning.

CHRIS: OK. One thing I know I would like them to do is to use rising and sinking and stepping as their major locomotor and nonlocomotor movements when we go back to exploring pressing and thrusting. In addition, I would hope they could lead the pressing and thrusting actions using different body parts and show clarity in the shape of their bodies. In terms of the space around them, I would hope that they could at some time move through all levels—high, medium, and deep. As for the specific qualities in both the pressing and thrusting actions—firm, direct, sustained or sudden—I would not expect these to be well developed. Oh, yes, I almost forgot. I had hoped that the children knew what it meant to explore movement and could do so.

MR. PRESSING: Good, you seem to have a clear picture of what the children should be able to do prior to working independently on pressing and thrusting. Now that you have clearly identified what you had hoped to see, but did not, what does this tell you?

CHRIS: Oh, I see what you are getting at. Because their movement backgrounds, as well as their problem-solving strategies, were not at the level that I had expected, asking them to explore pressing and thrusting actions was simply too difficult. It was beyond them. We could say that it was a "developmentally inappropriate" lesson.

MR. PRESSING: Right, but there is nothing wrong in making these errors in judgment. That's how we learn. Now let's think about your next lesson. Based on your assessment, with which I fully agree, what ideas do you have about how you might develop the next several lessons?

CHRIS: I still want to have a sequence as one of my major objectives. That I know. But perhaps I will have an individual one, or give the children an option: work alone or with a partner. I think some of these fifth graders, in spite of what I saw happen, are ready to work with a classmate. Their approach to learning suggests this. I know it is easier to work alone, but I still want to make this choice available to them. I don't know how I'll do this yet, but I will think about it. Before I do this, I need to go back, and help children expand their use of different body parts while rising and sinking. Also, the different shapes their bodies can make. I know teaching this material will help.

MR. PRESSING: These are good ideas. Anything else? Remember you want the children to be able to explore fully. Rising and sinking using different body parts and shapes can be quite limiting.

CHRIS: Oh, of course. Space! I nearly forgot about it. I need to help these children to use more fully all of the space in the gym. And personal space, the space close to them as well as the entire space. When appropriate, I will also help them learn how to use all levels of space. I guess I didn't realize how important all this material was and just how strong an influence it could have on the success of my pressing and thrusting lesson, and ultimately the creation of a sequence. It's as if I wanted them to make up a sequence with nothing to make it up with—baking a cake without the ingredients.

MR. PRESSING: A great way to look at it! When you focus on the actions of pressing and thrusting remember, these are really the movement actions you were interesting in originally.

CHRIS: I will wait to bring these actions in until I see how they handle the other material first. On the other hand, I might experiment with asking them to do a specific movement, one that looks easy for them, using the dynamics of pressing and thrusting. I will lead them through this idea quite directly, as I now realize they need more structure when they are in unfamiliar territory. Which reminds me, I will have to figure out how to help these children understand what "to explore" means in action, since they seem to be satisfied so quickly. There is a lot to think about, isn't there?

MR. PRESSING: Yes, but teaching is a complex task! And you have tried to teach a very complex lesson while misjudging the class' ability to handle it! You are on the right track now. What you need to do is develop a series of experiences for the children that will begin to expand their background with the dance material that you have just identified. Then, when they are ready for the pressing and thrusting sequence lesson, you can revise your original plan and build on the children's richer movement backgrounds.

CHRIS: You don't think that they will consider what I am now planning too easy for them and not work?

MR. PRESSING: No, not if you keep them challenged and focused. Your idea to bring in pressing and thrusting early, but in a more structured manner, is a good idea. I would try it. With the children's additional abilities in making different body shapes and using different body parts throughout space, the children just might meet the challenge. They would enjoy trying it, I am sure of that. Also, keep in mind, that while the material you plan to teach them is new, they are fifth graders, and they will handle it much quicker than, let's say second graders. You may be surprised just how well they can handle it. Remember, your best progressions are often based on what you see the children do, not what a textbook tells you to do. Text material is to guide you, not paralyze you!

These conversations illustrate the potential applications of one's knowledge base about movement and teaching in planning for students' learning. They highlight the dynamic nature of the content of physical education as it is considered in the process of planning meaningful, developmentally appropriate, and safe experiences for children in physical education.

## Chapter Summary

Planning is a major vehicle through which beginning teachers learn how to teach, as well as learn about teaching. The planning assignments that you will be completing during your teacher education program serve to communicate to your instructors the degree to which you are understanding the content the students are supposed to be learning. For your instructors, the plans that you write are important assessment tools; tools that document your growing understanding of the content and how it might best be taught. Well written plans also serve as evidence that the teacher has planned for a safe and nonhostile environment, an important idea in our increasingly litigious society. Planning is a necessity.

While the individual nature of the planning process is emphasized throughout the chapter, general factors that influence the process related to content, teaching, learning, curricular goals, and state and national standards are presented for consideration. Eight steps to use in creating a lesson plan are provided to give you direction in how and what to plan. The steps are followed by three mentor-teacher—intern-teacher conversations that connect the educational games, gymnastics, and dance content ideas presented in Chapters 4, 5, and 6 with the information on planning in this chapter. The conversations reinforce the idea that physical education teachers teaching within the constructivist approach need to be skillful at planning lessons.

## References and Reading List

Barrett, K. R. (1984). The teacher as observer, interpreter, and decision-maker. In B. J. Logsdon, K. R. Barrett, M. Ammons, M. Broer, L. E. Halverson, R. McGee, & M. A. Roberton, *Physical education for children: A focus on the teaching process* (2nd ed.) (pp. 295–355). Philadelphia, PA: Lea & Febiger.

Clark, C. M., & Peterson, P. L. (1986). Teachers' thought processes. In M. C. Wittrock (Ed.), *Handbook of research on teaching* (3rd ed.) (pp. 255–296). New York: Macmillan.

Ennis, C. D. (1996). A model describing the influence of values and context on student learning. In S. J. Silverman & C. D. Ennis (Eds.), *Student learning in physical education* (pp. 127–147). Champaign, IL: Human Kinetics.

Jewett, A. E., Bain, L. L., & Ennis, C. D. (1995). *The curriculum process in physical education.* Madison, WI: Brown and Benchmark.

Kirk, D. (1993). Curriculum work in physical education: Beyond the objectives approach? *Journal of Teaching in Physical Education, 12,* 244–265.

Lee, A. (1996). How the field evolved. In S. J. Silverman & C. D. Ennis (Eds.), *Student learning in physical education* (pp. 9–34). Champaign, IL: Human Kinetics.

McDiarmid, G. W., Ball, D. L., & Anderson, C. W. (1989). *Why staying one chapter ahead doesn't really work: Subject-specific pedagogy* (Issue Paper 88-6). East Lansing, MI: The National Center for Research on Teacher Education.

National Association for Sport and Physical Education (1992). *Outcomes of quality physical education programs.* Reston, VA: American Alliance for Health, Physical Education, Recreation and Dance.

National Association for Sport and Physical Education (1995). *Moving into the future: National standards for physical education.* St. Louis, MO: Mosby.

Rink, J. E. (1996). Effective instruction in physical education. In S. J. Silverman & C. D. Ennis (Eds.), *Student learning in physical education* (pp. 171–198). Champaign, IL: Human Kinetics.

Rink, J. E. (1998). *Teaching physical education for learning* (3rd ed.). Boston, MA: WCB/McGraw-Hill.

Tyler, R. W. (1949). *Basic principles of curriculum and instruction.* Chicago: University of Chicago Press.

Veal, M. L. (1995). Assessment as an instructional tool. *Strategies, 8* (6), 10–13.

# CHAPTER 8

# *"Off You Go"*

"Off you go" is one of those many phrases that are part of a teacher's repertoire of ways to get children moving after a task has been given. "Go ahead," "you may begin," "ready, go," or clapping your hands are like the phrase, "off you go" in that they all signal that activity is expected next; it is time to get moving; it is appropriate to start now; you've gotten your instructions, so get going.

The main task presented to you throughout this book has been one of understanding movement as the content of physical education framed in a constructivist approach to teaching. The goal of this "teacher education task" has been to help prepare you to teach children to move in skillful ways through helping them be responsible and involved learners. Our focus has been on the why, the who, and the what of teaching. Although how to teach has not been the focus, there are places in the book where how-to information was appropriate to include in order to present a clearer picture of the concepts being discussed. It is difficult to talk about teaching as being composed of separate pieces because the act of teaching is a complex, highly integrated human activity. The interaction and integration of teacher (who), students (who), and content (what) are a focus of the constructivist approach (why). Content is viewed as flexible, adaptable, and relevant to learners. It is within this constructivist view of content that the presentation of the content of physical education—movement—and how it needs to be understood by the teacher in relation to the student are connected. The why, who, and what of teaching are interwoven with one another to give meaning to the act of constructivist teaching.

You have been provided a constructivist philosophical frame from which to consider the educational contexts in which you will teach physical education to children. A philosophical basis for teaching is important because making decisions about what to teach without framing those decisions in a well-understood and firmly held set of philosophical beliefs is reckless decision-making. Nothing about teaching should be done recklessly.

As indicated previously, constructivist educational philosophy puts the learner at the center of the educational process. It recognizes that children must learn to act responsibly in the diverse, ever-changing worlds in which they live. It is important to help children become responsible for their own learning so that they can continually adapt to change and also to bring about change. A constructivist learning setting is viewed as a community of learners where students previous experiences are acknowledged as important in the meanings they make from their experiences in school. A constructivist learning setting is also one in which children will gain the competence and confidence they will need to be fully contributing members of society.

Constructivist teachers were described as reflecting a particular type of personal identity—trusting, risk-takers with low ego needs and patience. At this point it should be obvious why these characteristics are identified with constructivist philosophy. It would be extremely difficult to teach from this approach without displaying these characteristics.

Constructivist goals for physical education have been proposed as sound educational experiences that develop competent movers, develop knowledge of movement competence, assist learners in constructing personal meaning from movement, and develop optimal fitness levels. Programs that meet these goals achieve the outcome of physically educated persons.

A number of threads related to teaching have been woven throughout the book. These threads are children's safety, reflection, and observation. Children's safety has been emphasized and reemphasized as an unwavering concern within the physical education environment. It is difficult for children to learn when their physical safety and their psychological safety are threatened. Safety must be an utmost consideration at all times. The notion of reflecting on one's teaching actions has been emphasized due to the dynamic nature of movement content and of the physical education context. This dynamic nature of both content and context has highlighted the teacher's need for excellent skills of observing during teaching. Skillful observation coupled with thoughtful reflection create the potential for meaningful physical education experiences for students and teacher alike.

An additional thread has been prominent throughout this book. We see a rich knowledge base of movement as a necessary prerequisite for successful teaching of children in physical education. It is not enough, however, that you simply know movement; you must know movement for teaching. Knowing movement for teaching means that you can take factual knowledge about movement and translate it into meaningful educational games, educational gymnastics, and educational dance experiences for your students. Knowing movement for teaching also means that you can integrate your experiences with movement, your observations of movement, and your knowledge about movement in ways that will contribute to helping your students become effective, efficient, and versatile movers. This book provides you with information to add to your knowledge base about movement itself and it suggests means to help you understand and go about the processes of translating and integrating your movement content knowledge in preparation for teaching children physical education.

# CONSTRUCTING LEARNING IN PHYSICAL EDUCATION TEACHER EDUCATION

A constructivist philosophy is not just a philosophy that you hold for students in the schools. As a preservice teacher, you are a student of teaching yourself. As you construct meaning for the concepts of teacher and teaching while progressing through your teacher education program, you must be committed to the same learning goals for yourself that you support for your future students. You must recognize that the gymnasiums of tomorrow will be different from the ones in which you are learning to teach today. You must define what it means to act responsibly in educational environments. You must take advantage of the opportunities that you are being provided to develop confidence in your ability to teach. And you must learn to accept responsibility for your own learning as it relates to what it means to teach.

Your formal undergraduate teacher education will soon end. It is not unusual to feel that it ends too soon; especially when you have a class full of bright smiling faces in front of you at the moment eager to learn what you have to teach. But there is more to learn. In fact, there is quite a bit more to learn about good teaching in physical education. It is your responsibility to recognize that you need to continue to be a "student of teaching" throughout your career. Do not get trapped into the misconception that once you have learned the behaviors, there is nothing else to learn or no higher level of teaching effectiveness to be achieved. You will need to be able to adapt to the specific educational contexts in which you find yourself and to continue to move toward excellence in teaching. Advanced degrees in physical education (i.e., masters, doctorate) are one avenue to continue the study of teaching excellence. Indeed, some states require advanced education or a graduate degree to achieve permanent or continuing licensure. The dynamic nature of the teaching–learning context demands continued professional learning on your part. You must be committed to meeting those demands and act on your commitment.

You have been given your task. "Off you go."

# Index

Accompaniment, for dance, 290–292
Activities of the body, 50
    classification of, 51
    locomotor, 52–56
Adaptability, fostering of, 6
Aesthetics, in gymnastics, 163
Alamance End Ball, 134
Apparatus, in gymnastics, 164
    height of, 210–211
    arrangement of, 208–210
    optimizing use of, 210–211
    safety issues in, 208–209
    type and amount of, 206–208
Applying force actions, 51–52
Assessment, of games, 93, 95, 143–147
Asymmetry, 62

Backswing in throwing, developmental sequences for, 106, 107
Backward roll
    importance of, 223
    teaching of, 223–226
Balance, 58
    biomechanical principles of, 171–172
    in gymnastics, 160–161, 166
Base Ball, throwing, 128–130
Bases, teaching rules and strategies about, 150–151
Beliefs, changing, 18
Bending, 56–57, 87
Body
    activities of, 50, 51, 52–59
    movement of, 47–48

Body parts
    actions of, 50–52
    as game content, 58
    relationships among, 66, 69
Bound flow, 65
Boundaries, teaching about, 149

Carrying, 86, 109
Cartwheel, 67–68
    importance of, 227
    task and environmental factors in, 41
    teaching of, 227–228
Catching, 86, 88
    activities for, 97–98, 99
    biomechanical principles of, 98, 121
    developmental sequences for, 100
    motor development principles of, 98–99
Change, adapting to, 6
Choreography, 252, 277–278
    activities for, 278–280
    aesthetic principles of, 280–281
    biomechanical principles of, 280
    motor developments, principles of, 281
    progression in, 281
Collecting, 86
    activities for, 97–98, 99
    biomechanical principles of, 98, 121
    motor development principles of, 98–99
Communication, movement as, 19
Competence
    aspects of, 24
    striving for, 23–24

Competition, 82–83
Concepts, relationships with, 71
Confidence
    influences on, 25
    movement, 24–25, 27–28
Constraints, on motion, 40
Constructivist approach, 4
    classroom in, 8–11
    defined, 5
    focus of, 9
    goals of, 5–8
    misconceptions about, 12
    reflection in, 16–17
Constructivist teacher
    assessment by, 11
    characteristics of, 12–16
Content
    characteristics of, 10
    relevance of, 10–11
Conventional games, 138–141
    vs. original games, 143
Cooperative work, in gymnastics, 163

Dance
    accompaniment for, 290–292
    aesthetics of, 258, 262
    choreography, 252, 277–282
    communication in, 232–233
    core content of, 234–249
    cross-cultural aspects of, 251, 267–272
    dynamic components of, 252, 277–282
    in group, 252–253, 282–287
    imagery in, 287–289
    music resources for, 294–295
    progression in, 259–260, 263
    props for, 252, 272–277
    rhythm and, 292–293
    shape-making, 42
    task and environmental factors in, 41
    teaching of, 233–234
    timeline for teaching, 253–254
    understanding from teaching perspective,
        249–287
    uniqueness of, 231–232
Decision-making, 6
Deck tennis, modified, 125–127
Developmental issues
    appropriateness, 37–38
    factors affecting directional paths, 39–41

sequences, 38–39
    task analysis, 41–43
Direction, 60
    changing, 91
Diversity
    fostering of, 6
    and learning, 11
Dribbling, task and environmental factors in,
    41
DTA (Developmental Task Analysis), 41–43

Educational dance, 231–296. *See also* Games
Educational games, 81–152. *See also* Games
Educational gymnastics, 153–230. *See also*
    Gymnastics
Effort, of movement, 48, 62–64
Ego needs, 16
Environmental constraints, 40
Equipment
    as game content, 58
    in gymnastics, 164
    arrangement of, 208–210
    optimizing use of, 210–211
    safety issues in, 208–209
    type and amount of, 206–208
Evaluation
    constructivist approach to, 11
    of lesson, 313
Extending, 87

Feedback, importance of, 1
Fitness, importance of, 29
Flexing, 87
Flight, 53
    in gymnastics, 162
Flow, of movement, 64, 65
Foot action, developmental sequences for, 107
Force
    applying, 51–52
    in games, 90
    receiving, 52
Forearm action, developmental sequences for,
    106, 107
Forward roll
    developmental sequences for, 183, 184
    importance of, 222
    teaching of, 222–223
Free flow, 65

Gaining possession of an object, 58
Games
    assessing educational value of, 93, 95, 143–147
    biomechanical principles of, 135
    classification of, 92
    competition in, 82–83
    conventional, 138–141, 143
    core content of, 83–93
    forms of, 84–92, 95, 137–143
    motor development principles of, 135
    original, 141–143
    as part of life, 83
    progression of, 136, 143
    skills learning in, 87–90, 95–96
    strategy and tactics in, 92–93, 95, 123–137,
        148–152
    timeline for teaching, 95–96
    understanding from teaching perspective, 93–152
Gesturing, 52
Goal-oriented tag, 151–152
Group dancing, 252–253, 282–283, 286
    activities for, 283–284
    aesthetic principles of, 285
    biomechanical principles of, 285
    motor developments, principles of, 285
    progression in, 285, 287
Gymnastics
    core content of, 158–165
    equipment and apparatus for, 164, 206–230
    purpose of, 157–158
    quality and variety of moves, 165
    sequences in, 164–165
    skills required for, 153–155
    timeline for teaching, 156
    understanding from teaching perspective,
        165–205

Hand balance/body curled
    importance of, 215
    teaching of, 215–216
Hand balance/body extended
    importance of, 226
    teaching of, 226–227
Hand tagging, 86
Head/hand balance
    importance of, 217
    teaching of, 218–219
Hopping, developmental sequences for, 212
Humerus action in throwing, developmental se-
    quences for, 106, 107

Ideas, relationships with, 71
Imagery, in dance, 287–289
Initiation, 61
Invasion games, 130–132
    Alamance End Ball, 134
    Keep Away, 132–134
Inverted gymnastics sequences, task and
    environmental factors in, 41

Jump/land/roll basic sequence, 187–188
    importance of, 219–220
    teaching of, 220–221
Jumping, 53, 86, 87
    concerns regarding, 171–172
    developmental sequences for, 212
    importance of, 212
    teaching of, 212–213
Jumping for height
    importance of, 229
    teaching of, 229–230

Keep away, 132–134

Laban, Rudolph, 73
Learning
    constructing, 323–325
    and diversity, 11
    experience and, 8–9
    planning for, 299–322
    self-direction in, 7–8, 11
    student input into, 7–9
Lesson planning, 303
    importance of, 306–307
    steps in, 307–313
Level, of movement, 60–61, 91
Locomotion
    activities for, 256–257
    aesthetic principles of, 258
    biomechanical principles of, 171–172, 257–258
    in dance, 250, 255–256
    development of, 169
    in gymnastics, 159–160, 166
    introducing, 168–169
    motor development principles of, 172, 258
    progression in, 173, 259–260
Locomotor activities, 52–56
    in combination with manipulative skills,
        116–122
    in games, 86–87, 94–95
Long jump, developmental sequences for, 181, 182

Manipulative activities, 58–59
    in combination with locomotor skills, 116–122
    in games, 86, 94–95
Meaning
    aspects of, 3
    construction of, 34–36
    making of, 21
    in movement, 18–20, 23
Modified deck tennis, 125–127
Motivation, competence as, 23–24
Movement
    conceptual view of, 45–73
    constraints on, 40
    as language, 45–46
    learning through, 19
    meaning in, 18–20, 23
    skills involved in, 33
Movement confidence, 24–25
    achieving, 27–28
    understanding, 28–29
Movement Framework, 46
    categories of, 47–48
    expansion of, 49–72

Nonlocomotor activities, 56–58
    games, 87–88

Objectives, importance of, 301
Objects
    gaining possession of, 58
    relationships with, 71
    sending away, 58
Organismic constraints, 40
Original games
    vs. conventional games, 143
    guidelines for, 141–142
Others, relationships with, 69–70

Pathway, of movement, 61
Patience, importance of, 16
Personal space, 59–60, 91
Physical education
    constructivist, 25–26
    content of, 75–80
    developmental perspective on, 36–43
    cooperative nature of, 36
    goals for, 26–29
    outcomes of, 30

philosophy of, 31
setting for, 29, 31–36
Plane, of movement, 61
Planning
    aids to, 314–321
    importance of, 299–300
    individualization of, 302
    influences on, 303–304
    objectives in, 301
    as process, 300
    as reflection, 300
    research on, 300–302
    scope of, 303
    standards and, 305–306
    for the unexpected, 301
    values in, 301–302
Program planning, 303
Propelling, 86, 109
    biomechanical principles of, 121
Props for dance, 252, 272–274
    activities with, 274
    aesthetics principles of, 274–275
    biomechanical principles of, 274
    motor development principles of, 276
    progression for, 276–277
Pulling, 58
Punting, developmental sequences for, 108–109
Pushing, 58

Receiving force actions, 52
Reflection, 16–17
    planning as, 300
Relationship, movement in, 48, 64–71
Respect, importance of, 32–33
Responsibility, fostering of, 6
Rhythm, and dance, 292–293
Rising, 260–261
    activities for, 261
    aesthetic principles of, 262
    biomechanical principles of, 262
    in dance context, 251
    motor development principles of, 263
    progression in, 263
    task and environmental factors in, 41
Risk-taking, 15–16
Rocking, 54
    in gymnastics, 161
Rolling, 54, 86, 87, 114
    activities for, 114–116

developmental sequences for, 183, 184
in gymnastics, 161, 172
Rotating, 87
Round, defined, 61
Rules, teaching about, 149–150
Running, 86
activities for, 110–111
biomechanical principles of, 111–112
developmental sequences for, 113
motor development principles of, 112

Safety
of gymnastic apparatus, 208–210
paramount importance of, 15
Self-confidence, fostering of, 7
Self-direction, fostering of, 7–8, 11
Self-image, movement and, 23
Sending an object away, 58
Sequences
gymnastic, 164–165
defined, 192–193
designing, 193–203
motor development principles of, 204–206
Shape, of movement, 61, 264–265
activities for, 265–266
aesthetic principles of, 266
biomechanical principles of, 266
in dance context, 251
motor development principles of, 266
progression in, 266–267
Shoulder balance
importance of, 216
teaching of, 216–217
Sidestepping, 86, 87, 111
activities for, 110–111
biomechanical principles of, 111–112
motor development principles of, 112
Sideways (Safety) roll
importance of, 214
teaching of, 214–215
Sinking, 260–261
activities for, 261
aesthetic principles of, 262
biomechanical principles of, 262
in dance context, 251
motor development principles of, 263
progression in, 263
task and environmental factors in, 41
Size, of movement, 61
Skillfulness, 27

Skills, combining, 88
Skipping, developmental sequences for, 259
Sliding, 54, 55, 86, 87
activities for, 110–111
biomechanical principles of, 111–112
in gymnastics, 162
motor development principles of, 112
Space
in games, 90–92
movement in, 48, 59–62
of movement, 64
Space awareness, in gymnastics, 162–163
Speed, in gymnastics, 163
Spinning, 58
Standards, and planning, 305–306
Standing long jump, developmental sequences
for, 181, 182
Step-like actions, in gymnastics, 161–162
Stillness
biomechanical principles of, 171–172
development of, 169
in gymnastics, 159–160, 166
introducing, 168–169
Straight, defined, 61
Strategy, 123
activities to foster, 124–137
in games, 92–93, 95
teaching of, 148–152
Stretching, 57, 87
Striking, 86
activities for, 99–101, 105
biomechanical principles of, 101–102,
121
developmental sequences for, 107, 108
motor development principles of, 103
Striking/fielding games, 127–128
Throwing Base Ball, 128–130
Student
experiences of, 8–9
integralness of, 31–32
as part of community, 33–34
self-direction of, 7–8, 11
reflectiveness of, 17
Subject matter, characteristics of, 10
Swinging, 54
Symmetry, of movement, 61, 62

Tactics, 123
activities to foster, 124–137
in games, 92–93, 95

Tag games, 135
    goal-oriented, 151–152
Tagging, 86
Task constraints, 40
Teacher
    assessment by, 11
    constructivist, 12–16
    personal input of, 17–18
    reflectiveness of, 17
    values of, 301–302
Teaching
    content issues, 304
    goals and, 305
    issues in, 304
    issues in learning construction, 304
    planning for, 299–322
Throwing, 86, 89
    activities for, 99–101, 105
    biomechanical principles of, 101–102, 121
    developmental sequences for, 106, 107, 108
    motor development principles of, 103
    task and environmental factors in, 41
Throwing Base Ball, 128–130
Time
    in games, 90
    in gymnastics, 162
    of movement, 63
    rhythm and, 292–293
Tinikling, 267–270
    activities in, 270–271
    aesthetic principles of, 271

    biomechanical principles of, 271
    motor development principles of, 271–272
Traditionalist approach, 4
    defined, 5
Trunk action in throwing and striking, developmental sequences for, 108
Trust, in teaching, 15
Twisting, 57, 61, 87

Unit planning, 303

Walking, 53
    in gymnastics, 161–162
Wall/net games, 124–125
    modified deck tennis, 125–127
Weight, of movement, 63–64
Weight bearing, 51
    biomechanical principles of, 178–179
    development of, 176–178
    in gymnastics, 160–161, 166, 174
    introducing, 175–176
    motor development principles of, 180
    progression in, 180–185
Weight transference
    biomechanical principles of, 191
    development of, 188–191
    in gymnastics, 161–162, 166–167, 185–186
    introducing, 186–188
    motor development principles of, 191
    progression in, 191–192
Wide, defined, 61